Despite numerous sources suggesting that Islamophobia is becoming both increasingly prevalent and societally acceptable in the contemporary world, there remains a lack of textual sources that consider either the phenomenon itself, or its manifestations and consequences. There is no authoritative text that attempts to understand or contextualise what might be seen to be one of the most dangerous prejudices in the contemporary climate.

Chris Allen begins by looking at ways of defining and understanding Islamophobia. He traces its historical evolution to the present day, considering the impact of recent events and their aftermath especially in the wake of the events of September 11, before trying to understand and comprehend a wider conception of the phenomenon. A series of investigations thematically consider the role of the media, the contemporary positioning of Muslims throughout the world, and whether Islamophobia can be seen to be a continuum of historical anti-Muslimism or anti-Islamism, or whether Islamophobia is an entirely modern concept. The issue of Islamophobia is considered from the perspective of the local, regional, and global.

The incidence of Islamophobia, and the magnitude of the phenomenon and its consequences, is one that warrants a greater investigation in the world today. This book is both academically and socially relevant and necessary.

For Ernie and Ivy; Ivy and Ron; Emily, Maisie and Harry; Rachel

Islamophobia

CHRIS ALLEN
University of Birmingham, UK

ASHGATE

Published by
Ashgate Publishing Limited
Wey Court East
Union Road
Farnham
Surrey, GU9 7PT
England

Ashgate Publishing Company
Suite 420
101 Cherry Street
Burlington
VT 05401-4405
USA

www.ashgate.com

British Library Cataloguing in Publication Data
Allen, Christopher, Ph. D.
  Islamophobia.
  1. Islamophobia. 2. Islamophobia – History. 3. Muslims in popular culture.
  I. Title
  305.6'97–dc22

Library of Congress Cataloging-in-Publication Data
Allen, Christopher.
  Islamophobia / Chris.
      p. cm.
  Includes index.
  ISBN 978-0-7546-5139-0 (hardcover : alk. paper) – ISBN 978-1-4094-1757-6 (ebook) – ISBN 978-0-7546-5140-6 (pbk. : alk. paper) 1. Islam – Public opinion. 2. Muslims – Public opinion. 3. Islam and politics. 4. Muslims – Non-Muslim countries. 5. Islam – 21st century. I. Title.
  BP52.A38 2010
  305.6'97–dc22
                                                                    2010028981

ISBN 9780754651390 (hbk)
ISBN 9780754651406 (pbk)
ISBN 9781409417576 (ebk)

Reprinted 2012

MIX
Paper from
responsible sources
FSC
www.fsc.org
FSC® C018575

Printed and bound in Great Britain by the
MPG Books Group, UK.

Contents

Acknowledgements

This book is the result of almost a decade's worth of endeavour. Unsurprisingly, a good number of people deserve to be recognised for their part in making it happen. These are listed below in no particular order (and for those who I have forgotten or overlooked, please accept both my apologies and gratitude in equal measure):

To Jorgen Nielsen for his support and guidance as my doctoral supervisor at the University of Birmingham and for the experience and knowledge gained through collaborating with him on the EUMC Islamophobia project.

To Dilwar Hussain, Mohammed Siddique Seddon, Robin Richardson, Muhammad Abdul Aziz and Anas al Shaikh Ali for their support and encouragement over many years and in many different ways.

To Musab Bora for far too many conversations and lunches over which this book, its contents and numerous other issues were discussed at length.

To Deirdre Burke, George Chryssides, Ron Geaves and Steve Jacobs who, at the University of Wolverhampton, were the first people to set me on this book's journey.

To the Arts and Humanities Research Council for its recognition and financial support to undertake research into Islamophobia in the days when it wasn't fashionable to do so.

To Joy Warmington and everyone at BRAP (www.brap.org.uk).

To David Stephenson, Karen Rowlingson and everyone in the Institute of Applied Social Studies at the University of Birmingham for their ongoing support into research in this area.

To Sarah Lloyd and everyone at Ashgate for making this book happen.

And finally, to the ones I love:

To my parents Ivy and Ron and my grandparents, Ivy and Ernie, all of whom I hope are proud of what I have achieved.

To my children – Emily, Maisie and Harry – for always offering hope and for a long time, being the reason to carry on. Believe in yourselves and you'll achieve what you want.

And to Rachel, for restoring my confidence and self-belief.

PART 1
Introduction

Chapter 1
The First Decade of Islamophobia

The 'first decade of Islamophobia'[1] began with the landmark publication of the highly influential report entitled, *Islamophobia: a challenge for us all: report of the Runnymede Trust Commission on British Muslims and Islamophobia* ('the Runnymede Report'). Of course, this is not when the phenomenon of Islamophobia began: it was merely the year in which the first major report was published. Since then, Islamophobia has gained a far greater prevalence across both the public and political spaces. In the most vocal instances, claim and counter claim to Islamophobia typically emerges from bi-polar extremes, from those who decry and denounce any criticism whatsoever of Muslims or Islam as being 'Islamophobic' to those who actively and openly espouse a vitriolic hatred: both sides basing their views on a multitude of different causes and justifications. Between these poles a much broader and diverse range of far less obvious and explicit issues and incidents exist. On the one hand are the loosely veiled attacks on Muslims and Islam by those such as the personality-cum-politician Robert Kilroy-Silk[2] and 'Will Cummins'[3] through to the more weighted comments of those such as Melanie Phillips in the United Kingdom ('UK'). In Europe the same applies, from Geert Wilders' internet-based *Fitna* film through various dialogues and diatribes by those such as Ayaan Hirsi Ali and Oriana Fallaci[4] elsewhere. In the political spaces, high

---

[1]   I coined this phrase with the publication of a 'think-piece' entitled *The First Decade of Islamophobia* in October 2007. This piece continues to be available for download at http://www.chris-allen.co.uk.

[2]   In the *Express on Sunday*, 4 January 2004 'Kilroy' as he is commonly known, penned an article entitled 'We owe Arabs nothing'. Being one in a line of many controversial articles that Kilroy had written, following complaints from within Muslim and other communities, he lost his daily chat show of 17 years on BBC1. Robert Kilroy-Silk, 'We owe Arabs nothing', *Express on Sunday*, 4 January 2004.

[3]   Will Cummins, 'We must be allowed to criticise Islam', *Sunday Telegraph*, 4 July 2004; Will Cummins, 'The Tories must confront Islam instead of kowtowing to it', *Sunday Telegraph*, 11 July 2004; and Will Cummins, 'Muslims are a threat to our way of life', *Sunday Telegraph*, 18 July 2004. 'Will Cummins' was a pseudonym used by Harry Cummins, an employee of the British Council, to write four articles that were overtly anti-Muslim and anti-Islamic. Following the uncovering of his true identity, Cummins was fired from his post. A useful overview of the 'Cummins affair' can be found at http://bmcs.gotadsl.co.uk/modules.php?name=News&file=article&sid=60 (accessed 21 December 2004, updated 2 September 2004).

[4]   See Oriana Fallaci, *The Rage and the Pride* (New York: Rizzoli, 2002).

ranking voices describe Muslims as 'whining maniacs'[5] while others in France, the Netherlands and Switzerland initiate debates about the extent to which the *niqab* – face veil – and other visible aspects of Islam are barriers to integration and whether minarets should be allowed to punctuate European skylines. On the more extreme fringes of the political mainstream, there exist those who claim that Muslims intend to establish an Islamic republic in London by 2025 – citing the 'super-mosque' being built in East London as evidence of this – duly followed by the eventual overthrow of Christian Europe.[6] Elsewhere, those such as Silvio Berlusconi openly differentiate between the superiority of 'Western civilisations' over and above 'Islamic civilisations'.

At the same time, these have been countered by a somewhat reciprocal process that has initiated a range of different legislative measures and various social policies being implemented. In addition to a number of Europe-wide reports being commissioned that consider the phenomenon, in the UK the growth of a burgeoning cultural awareness – read 'Islam Awareness' – industry that seeks to challenge and potentially halt the perceived growing acceptance of negative attitudes and ideas towards Muslims is beginning to flourish. With the latter venture being largely undertaken by Muslim organisations and institutions, some critics cite this as merely being a front for *dawah* more so than to improve or promote better understanding and awareness. But so too have other initiatives been established including an awards ceremony that recognises the 'Islamophobe of the Year'[7] and the setting up of an organisation dedicated to combating Islamophobia, the UK's Forum against Islamophobia and Racism (FAIR).[8] Whichever way one reflects upon the outcomes and events of what was the first decade of Islamophobia, it cannot be argued that the language, discourse, notion and concept of Islamophobia failed to acquire a contemporary British, European and global relevance. What with this permeating across such a wide range of public and political spaces, the need to explore and further consider both the meanings and manifestations of Islamophobia is therefore somewhat overdue.

This book seeks to be both timely and relevant: to contribute to the better understanding of this ongoing and rapidly developing phenomenon as well as raise numerous other questions that will require further consideration and investigation. This latter point is both essential and necessary. What with the increasing recurrence of events and the increasingly globalised nature of our everyday world, there would appear to be a concurrent process being played out, where despite Islamophobia either discursively or conceptually being increasingly referred to or spoken about, there remains a distinct lack of clarity about what Islamophobia is – and is not – as

---

[5]   Chris Allen, *Fair Justice: The Bradford Disturbances, the Sentencing and the Impact* (London: FAIR, 2003), 36.

[6]   British National Party, *I.S.L.A.M.: The Truth about Islam* (Bexley: BNP, 2001).

[7]   The Annual Islamophobia Awards have been recently established by the Islamic Human Rights Commission.

[8]   For more information about FAIR see, http://www.fairuk.org/introduction.htm.

well as what can be done about it. The asking of these questions has so far brought about some consternation and confusion that in turn has resulted in contestation: contestation that incorporates issues of definition, usage, meaning and ownership. In acknowledging this, there is now a desperate need for further investigation and enquiry. One way of beginning this process might be to consider the evolution and development of Islamophobia both as a name – or neologism as some sources prefer – and as a concept. This introduction therefore sets out a historiography of contemporary Islamophobia, mapping its birth, evolution and development, before considering how the emergent theories and discourses have been subsequently shaped and determined. From here, some consideration can be made about what is known of Islamophobia. Where and how then did 'Islamophobia' originate?

Origins of the Word: 'accès de délire islamophobe'

It is widely believed that, Islamophobia both as a concept and neologism has its origins in Britain. This may not however be entirely true. Whilst the Oxford English Dictionary suggests that the term was first used in print in a 1991 American periodical, *Insight*, other sources and literature would suggest that it was first used in France by Etienne Dinet and Slima Ben Ibrahim, when in 1925 they wrote, 'accès de délire islamophobe'.[9] In writing about the Prophet Muhammad, it would appear that Dinet and Ibrahim were not employing the term in such ways that it reflects the contemporary concept or usage. Elsewhere, other competing claims also exist. Those such as Caroline Fourest and Fiammetta Venner claim that the term Islamophobia was used during the Iranian Revolution by the 'Mullahs' to describe Iranian women who refused to wear the *hijab* and less so, Muslim feminists and liberals: 'islamophobie' fut inventé – on ne le dit jamais – par des mollahs iraniens juste après la révolution islamique'.[10] In addition to Fourest and Venner, Chahdortt Djavann[11] and Carla Amina Baghajati[12] offer similar affirmations, but as with the

---

[9] Etienne Dinet and Sliman Ben Ibrahim, *L'Orient vu de l'Occident* (Paris: Piazza-Geuthner, 1925). Whilst having not been able to access this text directly, this reference has been substantiated by Professor Jocelyne Cesari of CNRS-Paris and Harvard University via electronic communication (2 October 2005). In addition, this early usage is referenced in a number of French and German based texts and websites including Alain Gresh, *A propos de l'Islamophobie*, 19 February 2004 (3 October 2005). <http://oumma.com/article.php3?id_article=964> and Alain Gresh, *L'utilisation du mot 'Islamophobie'*, 20 February 2004 (3 October 2005) http://toutesegaux.free.fr/article.php3?id_article=21&date=2004-02.

[10] Caroline Fourest and Fiammetta Venner, 'Islamophobie?: Islamophobes? Ou simplement laiques!' *Pro Choix* (Autumn/Winter 2003): 27–8.

[11] Chahdortt Djavann, 'From the Franz of Anja Nattefort' 2003 (3 October 2005).

[12] Carla Amina Baghajati, 'Islamophobie: Gedanken zu einem Phänomen', 24 November 2004 (3 October 2005) http://www.derislam.at/islam.php?name=Themen&pa=showpage&pid=60.

1925 usage, here the concept of Islamophobia and the context within which it is being employed is different to how it is now. And most importantly, the way in which it is being investigated here. So whilst Fourest and Venner argue that this particular type of usage – as a means of describing *Muslims* frightened of Islam – was the premise from which it was re-contextualised by those such as al-Muhajiroun and the Islamic Human Rights Commission ('IHRC') to name the fear of *non-Muslims* towards Islam and Muslims, there is – aside from this single reference – little other evidence to suggest any inter-linkage between the two. This book then is concerned with Islamophobia as a phenomenon that is directed at *Muslims* by *non-Muslims* even if at this stage an exact meaning remains unclear.

Somewhat unsurprisingly, the coinage and origins of Islamophobia are also openly disagreed upon where a number of competing stories are in current circulation. Recorded in 1997 by the Hyde Park Christian Fellowship, the first theory suggests that Islamophobia as a term was first coined by a Muslim researcher at the Policy Studies Institute ('PSI') in the late 1980s.[13] At the same time though, rather more authoritative sources at the Runnymede Trust were claiming something quite different. Given that the term had already been used by the Runnymede Trust and had achieved some socio-political discursive resonance, the Hyde Park Christian Fellowship's theory appears to have little credence. However, it is true that Tariq Modood worked for the PSI in the late 1980s. This is interesting because over half a decade later, a French source – via the European Monitoring Centre on Racism and Xenophobia ('EUMC') – made a similar claim to that of the Hyde Park Christian Fellowship, specifically citing Modood rather than a mere 'Muslim researcher'.[14] Whilst Modood has used the term and was very close to being the first to use it in print, no evidence can be found to suggest whether he ever claimed coinage of the term himself. Attributing him with authorship therefore remains questionable.

Another theory about authorship is documented in the oral hearings of the House of Lords Select Committee on Religious Offences from October 2003. Here it states that Fuad Nahdi, one time editor of *Q News*, claims in his Curriculum Vitae that it was he who coined the term Islamophobia.[15] It would appear that Nahdi allegedly passed the term onto the late Dr Zaki Badawi who, as a co-opted member of the Commission on British Muslims and Islamophobia ('the Commission'), subsequently suggested it to them thus culminating in the report of the same name. Somewhat contradictorily however, Badawi also claimed ownership in the same proceedings: 'I am guilty because I am the one who coined the phrase'.[16] From

---

[13]   Jenny James, 'When Fear is a Crime' *The Muslim-Christian Debate Website*, March 1997 (14 November 2004) http://debate.org.uk/topics/politics/jenny4.htm.

[14]   Unpublished document as part of the RAREN 3 research programme that sought universal definitions for racism, anti-Semitism, xenophobia and Islamophobia.

[15]   The United Kingdom Parliament, 'Examination of Witnesses', *Select Committee on Religious Offences in England and Wales*, 23 October 2003 (29 October 2004) http://www.parliament.the-stationery-office.co.uk/pa/ld200203/ldselect/ldrelof/95/2102307.htm.

[16]   Ibid.

interviews and information gained about the Commission, it would seem that not all were aware of either Nahdi's or Badawi's claims. From interviews with Robin Richardson who drafted the text for the Commission's report, he suggests that the term was much less individually conceived: 'it was the term preferred by the targets and victims of the phenomena themselves'.[17] In this way, Richardson implies that the term was both used by and derivative of a collective Muslim experience rather than any one individual, a point that he has reiterated numerous times since.

Emerging Identities: 'their offspring say that they have a Muslim or Islamic identity'

Possibly the most credible theory comes from Khaleda Khan and her observations of the grassroots situation of Muslims in the London Borough of Brent in the early 1980s.[18] Whilst claiming that it was here that a distinct anti-Muslim prejudice was first identified, she also notes a simultaneous trend emerging where a previously unprecedented and distinct 'British Muslim' identity was also beginning to emerge. Such events do not however occur in a vacuum and so the socio-political context provides some explanation as to why this might have been so. As Yasmin Ali observes:

> At the beginning of the 1980s 'communities originating in some of the countries of the old empire' would have been expressed unselfconsciously as 'black communities'... it was a usage predicated on the politics of anti-racism. As such 'black' became 'hegemonic' over other ethnic/racial identities in the late seventies and eighties.

Adding:

> The moment was not to last. From within marginalised communities and from without there was, in the 1980s, a steady assault upon this fragile hegemony.

Since their arrival as one constituency of the mass migration to Britain from the West Indies, India, Pakistan and other Commonwealth countries following the Second World War, Muslim communities were, up until the 1980s at least, largely both politically and socially invisible not least because the first generation primarily defined themselves in terms of their country of origin albeit with a religious component. Initially therefore, Muslim communities both defined and described

---

[17] A series of written and electronic interviews were undertaken with Robin Richardson over the period of January to February 2003. For the purpose of this research, these interviews have been understood as constituting one complete interview.

[18] Unpublished documents collected as part of a proposed edited collection in collaboration with Yahya Birt.

themselves largely in terms of their heritage, namely: Pakistani, Bangladeshi, Indian and so on, a process that was reciprocated by wider society. Consequently, early Muslim communities became a part of the hegemonic collective that was known as the 'Asian' community.

As Muslim communities grew in numbers and social and familial networks began to emerge, so a first generation of British-born Muslims duly emerged that grew up to identify themselves in quite different ways to their parents. For many, especially in the second and subsequent generations, the country of ancestral heritage was attributed much less emotional or cultural meaning. For many today, ancestral heritage constitutes little more than one facet of increasingly hybridised identity. But most relevant for the purposes of understanding the context within which Khan identifies, for these British-born Muslims the role and prominence of their religion – Islam – became increasingly important. Bhikhu Parekh voices this point with some clarity: 'While the parents would have said that they were Muslims, their offspring say that they have a Muslim or Islamic *identity* ...' adding, '... the difference is deep and striking'.[19] Socially therefore a transformation was occurring which saw a shift away from a homogenous 'Asian' identity to a newer and more prominent 'Muslim' equivalent.

In parallel, so similar political processes and occurrences were also underway. As John Solomos writes, much of the political discourse that was associated with immigration and the newly established migrant communities had already undergone some shifting: from 'colour' in the 1950s and 1960s, to 'race' and 'blackness' in the 1970s and 1980s.[20] From this backdrop, in the late 1960s and early 1970s an anti-racism movement began to develop that was largely based upon the markers of race and colour that had come to dominate the political discourse which is not surprising. As Miles and Phizacklea argue, the anti-racism movement was a response to the underlying racism that was evident in the increasing legislative and political labouring that surrounded the control of immigration and the role of immigrant communities.[21] Because of the emphasis upon colour, race and little else, so 'Asians' became politically overlooked and possibly even marginalised. As Modood has since written, it was the response to the enactment of the Race Relations Act 1976 ('RRA76') that created and indeed insisted upon the consensus around the term 'black', first within a very specialist lobby but then in the wider socio-political spaces.[22]

---

[19]   Bhikhu Parekh (2006) 'Europe, Liberalism and the "Muslim Question"', *Multiculturalism, Muslims and Citizenship*, eds Tariq Modood, Anna Triandafyllidou and Richard Zapata-Barrero (London: Routledge, 2006), 179–203:181.

[20]   John Solomos, *Race and Racism in Britain*, third edition (Basingstoke: Palgrave, 2003).

[21]   Annie Phizacklea and Robert Miles, *Labour and Racism* (London: Routledge & Kegan Paul, 1980).

[22]   Tariq Modood (1994) 'The End of a Hegemony: The Concept of "Black" and British Asians', *Ethnic Mobilisation in a Multi-cultural Europe*, ed. John Rex (Aldershot: Ashgate, 1994), 87–96:84–94.

Whilst this hegemonic term became integral to the discourse of race relations, for Modood it was a term that harmed and excluded Asians on the basis of what he describes as seven points of contention. First, that 'Asians' were sometimes black but also sometimes not; second, that the focus on 'colour' as equitable with 'blackness' meant that too narrow a conception of racial discrimination ensued that overlooked the cultural antipathy shown towards Asians and other 'non-black' ethnic communities. Thirdly, Modood argued that the term 'black' created a false essentialism where all non-whites are understood to have something in common. Robert Miles supports this by citing Paul Gilroy's *There ain't no black in the Union Jack* as a perfect example, where Asians were granted merely a 'walk-on' part.[23] Modood also suggested that the term 'black' overlooked and obscured Asian needs despite them becoming an ever-growing population, adding that 'black' was also far too politicised that for Asians was little more than a 'political colour' that appealed only to a very limited aspect of their individual or community being. The final two arguments were that 'black' was non-conducive to ethnic pride and that there was a coerciveness by anti-racist advocates where the consent of Asians and others who were not culturally black became taken for granted and so negated their status and distinctive identity. Resultantly, Modood put forward the argument that new identities were needed that broke the hegemonic grip of 'political blackness'. However, Modood did not suggest – at this time admittedly – the need for those included within the broad marker of 'Asian' to be further differentiated or indeed differentiable.

It is interesting that Modood identified how markers of 'Asian' – and much later 'Muslim' – became important at the same time that those communities began to identify themselves with their own political causes, something that Khan is referring to when she acknowledges the fledgling British Muslim identity that was beginning to emerge at the time. Indeed, the situation may have been further exacerbated by the aforementioned RRA76 and the protection that it afforded on the grounds of the statutory definition of 'racial group' which included race, colour, nationality and national or ethnic origin as markers of identification. However, neither religion nor belief was included as applicable markers and so those communities that were identified as or self identified as 'religious communities' were excluded. Case law under RRA76 did however extend the definition of 'racial group' in the early 1980s to include mono-ethnic religious groups but this only afforded protection to mono-ethnic religious groups, namely Jews and Sikhs.

Legislation therefore failed to afford protection to multi-ethnic religious groups such as Muslims and Christians, something that may have necessitated – legislatively at least – Muslims to begin to see themselves differently from 'black' and 'Asian' communities. It therefore became unlawful to discriminate against blacks, Asians, Pakistanis, Bangladeshis, and so on, as well as Jews and Sikhs, but perfectly within the law to discriminate against someone on the basis of their being

---

[23]   Robert Miles (1999) 'Racism as a Concept', *Racism*, eds Martin Bulmer and John Solomos (Oxford: Oxford University Press, 1999), 344–55.

Muslim: a loophole that was exploited by far-right political groups following the attacks of 9/11. Legislatively therefore, Muslims were being earmarked as separate even if the communities themselves had not yet come to think about or perceive themselves in such ways. This was again furthered in civil anti-discrimination legislation when the first criminal offence was introduced on racial hatred in the Public Order Act 1986. Here, mono-ethnic religious communities were also protected from incitement of hatred. Consequently in a setting where a significant shift in prejudice and discrimination as well as emerging identities was underway, so an anomaly existed that made it legal to incite hatred against multi-ethnic religious groups such as Muslims.

In an attempt to try and offer some theoretical underpinning, some explanation might be sought in terms of what Martin Barker has described as the emergence of 'new racism'.[24] Whilst Barker's theories are explored in more depth later, it is important to note that following the election of the Conservative government in the late 1970s, a shifting focus was identified in political discourse: one that moved away from more traditional markers of race to newer and less legislatively protected markers based on cultural and religious difference. Unlike older forms of racism, 'new racism' was seen to exaggerate difference and the identification of different in much less explicit ways, where the markers of difference were not seen to underpin explicit hatred and hostility but implicitly infer and establish direct challenges and threats: challenges and threats that were posed against 'our way of life'. Indeed, this demarcation of difference was firmly established on the basis that it had to be understood to be either unacceptable or incompatible with the 'norms' of society. That is, the norms relating to 'us' and definitely not 'them' and so reinforcing a somewhat necessary demarcation.

As such, in addition to the criticisms posited by Modood about Asians failing to be accommodated within the hegemonic concept of 'black', so too did the same anti-racism movement not only fail to recognise that a there was a shift in identities becoming apparent within Muslim communities but they also failed to recognise a growing antipathy and hostility towards those communities that were increasingly being identified by markers of religious and cultural difference. The reality of such a shift towards religion and culture was either put to one side or outright rejected. Not only would it appear that the anti-racism movement overlooked the growing presence and significance of the Muslim community, but it also overlooked the subsequent political need for those communities to begin to self-identify more distinctly in order to address and tackle their own political causes and problems. In the context of this setting, it was only a mere handful of Muslim activists that recognised that a distinct anti-Muslim, anti-Islamic phenomenon was gaining ground and, more importantly, were responding to it. Whilst acknowledging some overlap with traditional racism clearly existed, a clear shift in markers of

---

[24]   Martin Barker, *The New Racism: Conservatives and the Ideology of the Tribe* (London: Junction Books, 1981).

identification that exacerbated Muslim-ness was becoming increasingly apparent in the discrimination and hostility that was being identified at the grassroots level.

Mobilising Muslims: 'Muslims in Britain must define their collective goals and move towards a consensus'

Acting as a grassroots catalyst, organisations such as An-Nisa were duly established out of this process. Whilst Khan suggests how even the notion of a distinctive Islamophobia was rejected by many from within Muslim communities, she acknowledges Nahdi as one of the first to grasp both the climate change and subsequent need to raise awareness.[25] Primarily, this appears to have been undertaken through the grassroots Muslim publications that Nahdi worked on at the time, in particular *MuslimWise*. Whilst the idea was written about on a number of occasions, the neologism of Islamophobia was not committed to print despite some claims to the contrary.[26] At the same time, other groups such as the UK Action Committee on Islamic Affairs ('UKACIA'), that later spawned the Muslim Council of Britain ('MCB'), also began to discuss the phenomenon. Some commentators however suggest that organisations such as UKACIA and the MCB remained uncommitted to either openly acknowledge or refer to Islamophobia in the beginning for fear of any political implications both for themselves and Muslim communities. Following the Satanic Verses affair in 1989, more articles about anti-Muslim and anti-Islamic prejudice appeared in both *MuslimWise* and in Nahdi's subsequent publications, *The Muslim Update* and *Q News* also, many of which were penned by either Khan or Nahdi although still without the phenomenon being referred to as Islamophobia. As regards coinage therefore, it might be most appropriate to locate it somewhere between the claims of Nahdi and the observations of Khan, whilst at the same time bearing in mind the influence of Modood. Despite there being a less than categorical answer to where the concept and neologism originated, anecdotal evidence would seem to suggest that the setting and context of Brent and its primary actors in the mid to late 1980s was nonetheless extremely influential.

This recognition of a distinct anti-Muslim, anti-Islamic phenomenon and the growing identification around a Muslim identity may also have been a catalyst for others too including Kalim Siddiqui's *The Muslim Manifesto: A Strategy for Survival*.[27] Published in 1990, the document's argument for why such a manifesto was necessary was set out clearly from the outset:

---

[25] Ibid.

[26] Archived copies of *MuslimWise* held at the Islamic Foundation were checked for any references to Islamophobia between January and March 2004.

[27] Kalim Siddiqui, *The Muslim Manifesto: A Strategy for Survival* (London: The Muslim Institute, 1990).

It is a matter of deep regret that the Government, all political parties and the mass media in Britain are now engaged in a relentless campaign to reduce Muslim citizens of this country to the status of a disparaged and oppressed minority. We have no alternative but to resist this invidious campaign. To do so Muslims in Britain must define their collective goals and move towards a consensus on major issues. The established network of 1,000 mosques and a wide range of organisations already serving the community must develop greater cohesion and dynamism. This manifesto attempts to provide a common text defining the Muslim situation in Britain. It also seeks to provide a framework for the healthy growth of all parts of the community as well as a common Muslim identity and purpose.[28]

Acting as a precursor to the establishment of The Muslim Parliament a few years later, the manifesto was another measure against which the emergence of a distinct British Muslim identity – and voice – could be gauged. If the manifesto was correct, then because of the fact that Britain's Muslim communities were feeling increasingly marginalised and under pressure, it was vital that changes that were occurring were also subsequently responded to. Quite irrespective of whether the manifesto set out a convincing argument or not, both the document and the ensuing Muslim Parliament attracted extensive media coverage, the majority of which was overwhelmingly negative. Through this, the mediatised form of Muslim identity was one that from the outset was overtly represented in negative frames and one that was highly politicised. Because it was also seen to go against the British establishment and fabric upon which Britain's institutions and values were founded, so a Muslim identity in the public and political spaces not only acquired negative attributions from the start but so too did it appear to be against 'us'. Despite or indeed maybe because of the Parliament's controversial nature – seen by many to be mocking the laws and governance of the British state – its role and influence was limited, and by the time of the death of Siddiqui in 1996, its intrigue and novelty value had significantly waned. Nonetheless, the impact it had at a time when the first recognition of British Muslim identities were becoming evident should be neither overlooked nor underestimated.

In terms of the coinage of Islamophobia as a term, one final claim is worthy of note. The writer and broadcaster Akbar Ahmed claimed, over and above existing evidence and without any seemingly new evidence to substantiate his claims, that it was in fact he who coined the term Islamophobia.[29] Being that his claim is the most recent of all, despite there being little or no evidence to substantiate such claims, little credence can be attributed to it. However what makes this worthy of note is that many prominent British Muslim figures have claimed coinage or authorship of the term. What with Islamophobia becoming increasingly socially, politically and discursively relevant, it may indicate a need or expectation from

---

[28]   Ibid., 4.

[29]   Ahmed's claim was made in his speech at the *Daniel Pearl Dialogue for Muslim-Jewish Understanding Conference*, 23 June 2004 (London: Moses Room, House of Lords).

within some quarters at least, for due recognition or accreditation to be made about this contemporary phenomenon. It could be less specific however with some seeking recognition for their role and contribution in relation to a growing Muslim presence in contemporary Britain more widely. For whatever reason or purpose this may exist – if indeed one does – one can only speculate. It is interesting though to record that such claims have been regularly made.

The First Throes of Islamophobia: 'a cultural sickness'

In terms of the word Islamophobia being recorded in print, as mentioned previously, the Oxford English Dictionary suggests that it was first used in 1991 in the American periodical, *Insight*. Whilst this appears to be inaccurate by some 66 years, in its contemporary guise Modood also employed the term in 1991 despite having written about the issue of an anti-Muslim, anti-Islamic phenomenon a number of times in both 1990 and 1991. Unfortunately, he did not refer to it as Islamophobia on either occasion.[30] What is interesting though is that whilst Modood's usage referred to the socio-political British Muslim experience – 'a cultural sickness' as he put it[31] – for *Insight*, Islamophobia had a distinctly international context: 'Islamophobia … accounts for Moscow's reluctance to relinquish its position in Afghanistan, despite the estimated \$300 million a month it takes to keep the Kabul regime going'.[32] The journey from London grassroots Muslim experience to American publishing house internationalism remains a mysterious one, and no apparent explanations are available to explain any inter-linkage between the two. Not least because the original source – *Insight* – is very hard to locate and so no further information can be conferred. In the British setting however, it is somewhat unsurprising that the first accredited use of Islamophobia in print reflected its socio-political origins.

A few years later in 1994, the first British non-Muslim acknowledgement of Islamophobia was made in the Runnymede Trust report, *A Very Light Sleeper: the Persistence and Dangers of Anti-Semitism*.[33] Incorporated under the heading, 'Anti-Semitism and other forms of racism', the report somewhat bizarrely

---

[30] Modood wrote about the subject matter of hostility towards Muslims and Islam in a number of articles throughout 1990 and 1991 in particular, the *Independent*, 5 February 1990, *The Times Higher Education Supplement*, 30 March 1990, and the *Independent*, 19 June 1990. His first recorded use of the term 'Islamophobia' was in the *Independent*, 16 December 1991. For all articles, see: Tariq Modood, *Not Easy Being British* (Stoke on Trent: Runnymede Trust and Trentham Books, 1992), 69–78.

[31] Modood (1992), 69.

[32] Runnymede Trust: Commission on British Muslims and Islamophobia, *Islamophobia: a challenge for us all: report of the Runnymede Trust Commission on British Muslims and Islamophobia* (London: Runnymede Trust, 1997), 37.

[33] Runnymede Commission on Anti-Semitism, *A Very Light Sleeper: the Persistence and Dangers of Anti-Semitism* (London: Runnymede Trust, 1994).

preferred to overlook all 'other forms of racism' and focus solely on Islamophobia. Whilst explored in greater depth in following chapters, it is worth noting that this report was the catalyst to establishing the Commission on British Muslims and Islamophobia, a Commission that was integral in the shaping of the definition and conceptualisation of Islamophobia in the public space. Having acknowledged it as a form of racism however, shortly after the report's publication, Ziauddin Sardar posited the view that contemporary manifestations of Islamophobia were in fact a re-emergence of historical anti-Muslim, anti-Islamic phenomena.[34] For him, 'Islamophobia and prejudice against Muslims, has a long memory and still thrives ...' where it '... resides so deeply in [the Western] historical consciousness'.[35] Consequently, the term was both transitory and retrospective, functioning in much the same way as anti-Semitism: a descriptor that is able to be employed to refer to all historical and paradigmatic anti-Muslim, anti-Islamic phenomena. Whilst Sardar's Islamophobia was therefore historical, transitory and retrospective, others have suggested otherwise.

Similar to Sardar, Milton-Edwards suggested Islamophobia was historically constant and ever-present, seen today as it was at the time of the Crusades and at all other historical junctures. Most prominently, this can be evidenced through the ongoing dichotomous 'Islam' and 'the West' narratives.[36] Another interpretation put forward by Dilwar Hussain[37] has been that historical Islamophobia is better understood in terms of a plurality of Islamophobias, where contemporary characteristics become dependant upon the historical context of the manifestation, linked but neither totally dependent. Contrary to Hussain's plurality, others have put forward the theory that anti-Muslim, anti-Islamic phenomena are endemic in

---

[34]   Ziauddin Sardar, 'Racism, Identity and Muslims in the West', *Muslim Minorities in the West*, eds Syed Z. Abedin and Ziauddin Sardar (London: Grey Seal, 1995), 1–17.

[35]   Ibid., 7 and 15 respectively.

[36]   Beverley Milton-Edwards, 'Researching the Radical: The Quest for a New Perspective', *Interpreting Islam*, ed. Hastings Donnan (London: Sage, 2002), 32–50, 33. I use the term 'the West' reluctantly what with it being extremely homogenous, simplifying the myriad identities and differences that exist within such a homogenous entity. However, the term was used by the LBC and indeed maintains credence within popular discourse, sometimes to describe that which is not 'Islam'. Consequently, I use it from hereon in such ways that 'the West' is commonly seen to be largely equitable historically to Christendom; a post-reformation, post-Enlightenment Europe; or contemporarily, as Yemelianova puts it, where:

> the West refers to countries of Western Europe and North America, the societies that function on the principles of bourgeois liberal democracies and the market economies, historically generated in Europe. Therefore, it does not include Japan and the newly industrialised economies of South East Asia which, although they share with Western Europe and North America similarly high technological and living standards, arguably belong to different political and cultural traditions. Galina M. Yemelianova, *Russia and Islam* (Basingstoke: Palgrave, 2002), 193.

[37]   Dilwar Hussain, 'The Impact of 9/11 on British Muslim Identity', *Islam and the West: a Post September 11th Perspective*, eds Ron Geaves et al. (Aldershot: Ashgate, 2004), 115–29.

European and Western culture, where recognition and observance function in cyclical periods of dormancy and intensification that reach epidemical levels following certain events. Examples of these might include the periods immediately after the attacks of 11 September 2001 ('9/11') or in the UK, the events of the 7 July 2005 London tube train bombings ('7/7').[38] One final theory suggests that Islamophobia is an entirely new and contemporary phenomenon, relevant only to the here and now and quite independent of history. Some of these issues will be considered in more detail in following chapters. Within a decade therefore, Islamophobia has made the transition from a socio-economic and somewhat experiential phenomenon in North London, to a phenomenon attributed with global, historical and racial dimensions, reinterpreted and re-defined by Muslims and non-Muslims alike, as well as by academics, policymakers and community activists.[39]

Genesis of the Decade: 'to fear or dislike all or most Muslims'

With the publication of the Runnymede report in 1997, not only did the report significantly influence the way in which Islamophobia was understood but so too did it ensure that Islamophobia was afforded public and political recognition. Preceded by a consultation document in March 1997,[40] it was the first source to posit a firm definition of Islamophobia: the 'shorthand way of referring to dread or hatred of Islam – and, therefore, to fear or dislike all or most Muslims'.[41] Because of the impact and significance of the Runnymede Report, a full exposition is undertaken in following chapters. Nonetheless, its impact cannot be underestimated because for those who have written about the topic, the Runnymede influence has been great. For example, Steven Vertovec's exploration of Islamophobia is indebted to the Runnymede Report[42] as indeed is Malise Ruthven's analysis of Muslims in the media.[43] Elsewhere, Elizabeth Poole's research on the representation of Muslims, whilst rooted in critical discourse analysis rather than Islamophobia per se, utilises

---

[38] Chris Allen, 'Endemically European or a European Epidemic? Islamophobia in Contemporary Europe' *Islam and the West: a Post September 11th Perspective*, eds Ron Geaves et al. (Aldershot: Ashgate, 2004), 130–45.

[39] I employ markers of 'Muslim' and 'non-Muslim' here to indicate the extent to which the processes of ownership and conceptualisation moved and not that Muslims in preference to non-Muslims – or indeed vice-versa – are more capable or indeed better qualified to conceptualise and/or define at any given time.

[40] Runnymede Trust: Commission on British Muslims and Islamophobia (1997).

[41] Ibid., 1.

[42] Steven Vertovec, 'Islamophobia and Muslim Recognition in Britain', *Muslims in the West: from Sojourners to Citizens*, ed. Yvonne Y. Haddad (Oxford: Oxford University Press, 2002), 19–35:24.

[43] Malise Ruthven, 'Islam in the Media' *Muslims in the West: from Sojourners to Citizens*, ed. Yvonne Y. Haddad (Oxford: Oxford University Press, 2002), 51–75.

Islamophobia in a distinctly Runnymede way.[44] Others include Ashrif who suggests the report's typology as useful for 'describing the condition' of Islamophobia,[45] Sheridan and Malik who quote from the report for explanatory purposes,[46] and Davids who locates the Runnymede typology as a point of reference.[47] All are deeply indebted to the Runnymede Report and its definition and model of what constitutes Islamophobia. This is true in both the policy and political arenas too, where the Runnymede influence features in a number of reports that include Ansari's *Muslims in Britain*,[48] Choudhury's *The situation of Muslims in the UK*,[49] and Hepple and Choudhury's *Tackling religious discrimination*.[50] This influence has continued and the Runnymede Report's impact continues to be seen across the entire spectrum of Islamophobia-focused research, from Garner's analysis of 'racisms'[51] through to Githens-Mazier and Lambert's excellent report on anti-Muslim hate crimes in London.[52] Yet still, Islamophobia remains something of an ambiguous entity and becomes apparent in some sources more so than others, not least the Home Office report into religious discrimination[53] and the Parekh report[54] Whether focusing upon usage, definition or conceptualisation therefore, across a range of different reports so an uneasiness and contestation about Islamophobia emerges: about its lack of clarity; what Islamophobia is; its spread and voracity; its problematic nature; and notwithstanding, whether Islamophobia actually exists.

---

[44]   Elizabeth Poole, 'Framing Islam: An Analysis of Newspaper Coverage of Islam in the British Press', *Islam and the Mass Media: Fragmented Images in a Globalizing World*, ed. Kai Hafez (Cresskill: Hampton Press, 2000), 157–79:158. Also see Elizabeth Poole, *Reporting Islam: Media Representations of British Muslims* (London: IB Tauris, 2002).

[45]   Shahid Ashrif, 'Beyond Islamophobia', *Multi-cultural Teaching*, Spring (2001).

[46]   Lorraine Sheridan and Nadeem Malik, 'Religious Discrimination: Historical and Current Developments in the English Legal System', *Encounters*, 7 (2001): 57–78.

[47]   M. Fakhry Davids, 'There but for the grace of God, go you or I' *The Quest for Sanity: Reflections on September 11 and its Aftermath*, eds Abdul Wahid Hamid and Jamil Sharif (London: Muslim Council of Britain, 2002), 121–7.

[48]   Humayan Ansari, *Muslims in Britain* (London: Minority Rights Group International, 2003).

[49]   Tufyal Choudhury, *Monitoring Minority Protection in the EU: The Situation of Muslims in the UK* (London: Open Society Institute, 2003).

[50]   Bob Hepple and Tufyal Choudhury, *Tackling Religious Discrimination: Practical Implications for Policy-makers and Legislators*, Home Office Research Study 221 (London: Home Office, 2001).

[51]   Steve Garner, *Racisms* (London: Sage, 2010).

[52]   Jonathan Githens-Mazer and Robert Lambert, *Islamophobia and Anti-Muslim Hate Crime: A London Case Study* (Exeter: University of Exeter, 2010).

[53]   Paul Weller et al., *Religious Discrimination in England and Wales*, Home Office Research Study 220 (London: Home Office, 2001).

[54]   Bhikhu Parekh, *The Future of Multi-ethnic Britain: Report of the Commission on the Future of Multi-Ethnic Britain* (London: Profile Books, 2000).

In the wake of the Runnymede Report, Muslim organisations became more proactive with the MCB beginning to voice its concern, as did those others such as the IHRC. Indeed, Richardson suggests that since its formation, the MCB has been foremost in credibly and legitimately establishing Islamophobia on the British public and political agendas,[55] a claim that in some circles at least might be strongly contested. Potentially more relevant to mapping the history of Islamophobia however has been the establishment of FAIR in 2001 and its niche remit of specifically tackling Islamophobia. A first of its kind in the British and possibly European settings, FAIR was initially set up to reflect the Council on American-Islamic Relations ('CAIR') albeit with a greater emphasis on Islamophobia rather than relations.[56] Whilst the organisation had some initial success, many of its strategies were significantly disrupted following the events of 9/11 so soon after the organisation's launch. Because of this and a number of organisational factors, it must be said that the organisation has struggled to identify a coherent direction, failing to fulfil its high initial expectations. This is not to undermine or negate FAIR as an organisation but to identify what would appear to be something of a missed opportunity.

Yet days before 9/11, both FAIR and the IHRC joined numerous other groups and non-governmental organisations in Durban at an event that has since become somewhat 'lost' in recent history. This 'lost' event included the formal recognition accredited to Islamophobia by the United Nations ('UN'), acknowledging it as a global phenomenon alongside racism and anti-Semitism not least because of its rapid proliferation in different parts of the world.[57] As the conference proceedings noted, Islamophobia was becoming increasingly normal,[58] a point reaffirmed by the British Member of Parliament ('MP'), John Denham who denounced the cancer-like spread of 'normative' Islamophobia in British society days after.[59] In accrediting Islamophobia with international recognition, it might be expected that the UN would have afforded such an accreditation with some definition or meaning. Unfortunately, and like so many others before them, no definition or meaning of Islamophobia was put forward by the UN leaving Islamophobia once more open to interpretation and contestation.

---

[55] Personal interview, 2003.

[56] For more information about CAIR see, http:// www.cair-net.org.

[57] World conference against racism, racial discrimination, xenophobia and related intolerance, 31 August, Durban, South Africa (8 September 2001).

[58] United Nations, *World conference against racism, racial discrimination, xenophobia and related intolerance: declaration and programme of action* (New York: United Nations, 2002).

[59] John Denham, 'Keynote Address', *Exploring Islamophobia Conference*, 29 September 2001 (University of Westminster: London).

Beyond 9/11: 'tell me your Islam and I will tell you who you are'

Three other interesting developments necessitate further consideration as
regards the discourse and understanding of Islamophobia. The first, the research
undertaken by the EUMC; the second, the typology of views concerning Islam and
the Arab world established by Timothy Garton Ash; and the third, the Copenhagen
Declaration on Islamophobia.

In terms of the EUMC, its research into Islamophobia following the events
of 9/11 across all of the then fifteen European Union ('EU') member nations
remains the largest monitoring project into Islamophobia to have been undertaken.
Following on from this, the EUMC has shown a clear commitment to better
evidencing and understanding the phenomenon, not least through the publication
of: *The fight against Anti-Semitism and Islamophobia: a summary of three round
table meetings*,[60] *The impact of 7 July 2005 London bomb attacks on Muslim
communities across the EU*,[61] *Muslims in the European Union: Discrimination
and Islamophobia*[62] and *Perceptions of discrimination and Islamophobia: Voices
from members of Muslim communities in the European Union*,[63] Yet throughout,
rarely has the EUMC attempted to define Islamophobia. Instead, as it sets out in its
2007 *Manifestations report*, it prefers internationally agreed standards on racism. Is
Islamophobia therefore equivalent to racism or is it something different? In each of
the EUMC's publications, Islamophobia is used in an assumptive way, one where
the reader is presumed to fully understand and adequately know what Islamophobia
is and possibly more importantly, what Islamophobia is not. And all this despite
the fact that Islamophobia is apparently a new and increasingly problematic
phenomenon across Europe. The question then is why an organisation that is so
committed to addressing Islamophobia chooses not to adequately define it.

As regards Garton Ash, despite setting out what appear to be remarkably similar
views to those set out in the Runnymede Report, at no time does he refer to what
he is explaining and setting out as being Islamophobia. Instead, he argues that
his typology comprises 'six views of the West's problems with the Muslim world
[that] reveal as much about those who hold them'.[64] The fact though that these are
being identified as the six 'problems' that the West has with Islam and Muslims

---

[60]   Anna Diamantopoulou, *The Fight Against Anti-Semitism and Islamophobia: A
Summary of Three Round Table Meetings* (Brussels/Vienna: EUMC, 2003).

[61]   European Monitoring Centre on Racism and Xenophobia, *The Impact of 7 July 2005
London Bomb Attacks on Muslim Communities Across the EU* (Vienna: EUMC, 2005).

[62]   European Monitoring Centre on Racism and Xenophobia, *Muslims in the European
Union: Discrimination and Islamophobia* (Vienna: EUMC, 2007).

[63]   European Monitoring Centre on Racism and Xenophobia, *Perceptions of
Discrimination and Islamophobia: Voices From Members of Muslim Communities in the
European Union* (Vienna: EUMC, 2007).

[64]   Garton Ash, Timothy, 'What we call Islam is a mirror in which we see ourselves',
The Guardian (15 September 2005).

could and indeed do, seem to overlap with 'problems' of Islamophobia. It must be noted however that some do openly contradict themselves, a point highlighted by Garton Ash who suggests that some would have bigger 'ticks' against them than others. His 'views' are: that the West has a problem with religion per se and not specifically with Islam; that the West has a problem specifically with Islam because it is perceived to be stuck in the Middle Ages; that the West has a problem not with Islam but with Islamism and its 'political ideology of hate';[65] that the West has a problem not with religion, Islam or Islamism but with its historical relationship with the Arab world; that the problem is not with 'them' but with 'us' manifested through imperialism, colonialism and Christian and post-Christian hegemonies; and finally, that the problem arises on the edges of where 'Islam' and 'the West' meet, 'in particular, from the direct, personal encounter of young, first- or second-generation Muslim immigrants with Western, and especially European, secular modernity'.[66]

It is interesting that Garton Ash never mentions Islamophobia yet in line with earlier pieces of research and enquiry, he too hints at a growing incidence, one where perceptions suggest that Muslims 'threaten to make Europe a less civilised, comfortable place to live over the next 10 years'. Likewise, he notes a growing receptivity to misconceptions about Islam and Muslims. As he puts it, 'Tell me your Islam and I will tell you who you are'. In doing so, he reciprocates the contestation with Islamophobia. And whilst appearing to acknowledge an identifiable phenomenon affecting the landscape of Europe and the attitudes of its inhabitants, he also appears to diminish its importance by failing to clarify what exactly this phenomenon is. Is a growing receptivity to Islamophobia becoming increasingly apparent? Maybe for Garton Ash the evidence was unconvincing even though he seemed to be reinforcing the point that a clear and growing anti-Muslim, anti-Islam phenomenon was becoming increasingly identifiable.

Finally, the Copenhagen Declaration was a statement that emerged from the proceedings of a conference organised by the *Islam Channel* in 2006. Largely as a response to the furore following the publication of a series of cartoons of the Prophet Muhammad printed in the Danish *Jyllands-Posten* newspaper on 30 September 2005 followed by numerous other news outlets across Europe and elsewhere, the conference brought together 150 participants, a live audience of around 1,000 people, and a broadcast audience of thousands more across Europe and north and west Africa. Arguing that all the participants were united by 'a deep concern about the growing phenomenon of Islamophobia – the demonization of human beings for no other reason than their Muslim faith'[67] – the Declaration set out the following seven recommendations:

---

[65]   Ibid.

[66]   Ibid.

[67]   Details of the Copenhagen Declaration can be found at http://www.theislamophobia. com.

- that freedom of expression was far from absolute and that legal recourse was necessary against incitement to violence, discrimination or the spread of hatred towards any group in society on the basis of religion, race or sex;
- that dialogue aimed at both opening and building bridges of understanding between the various different faiths and communities was to be encouraged;
- that inter-faith committees were to be established to review curricula and activities in educational institutions;
- that governments monitored discriminatory or other activities inciting hatred, including Islamophobia or at least financially supported those organisations that did;
- that the US should take the lead in undertaking a massive injection of capital and technology to establish a viable economy and education system for the people and State of Palestine;
- that the Islam Channel should follow up the recommendations of the conference and monitor any new developments regarding Islamophobia;
- and finally, to hold an annual conference to promote the aims of the Copenhagen Declaration.

Contested Concept: 'different forms of discourse, speech and acts'

The Copenhagen Declaration clearly continued the tradition of anti-Islamophobia measures that had preceded it. Despite making recommendations and talking about Islamophobia's unwanted consequences, it simultaneously failed to define or even set out what Islamophobia was, whether as a legitimate and tangible entity or as a series of different or overlapping conceptual or otherwise phenomena. It was assumptive in its remit in that Islamophobia was something that was known and to some extent, quite obvious. Any such assumption is of course flawed and problematic, a point highlighted by Maussen not least because:

> 'Islamophobia' groups together all kinds of different forms of discourse, speech and acts, by suggesting that they all emanate from an identical ideological core, which is a 'fear' or a 'phobia' of Islam. However, we should distinguish between different kinds of discourse, for instance between academic discussions on the relations between Islam and modernity, public discussions on whether Islam recognises the principle of separation of state and church, public outcries about Islam as 'a backward religion' or as a 'violent religion', and the forms of hate speech one can find on internet forums and in newspapers, such the speech of the late Dutch filmmaker Theo van Gogh, who systematically called Muslims 'goat-fuckers'. It may well be that these different kinds of discourse and speech are

related and feed into one another, but we cannot simply equate them all and treat them as comparable illustrations of a core ideology named 'Islamophobia'.[68]

As he notes, because Islamophobia is so multifarious and wide-ranging, it is not only difficult to incorporate it under a single neologism but it is also unclear where the boundaries between 'what is' and 'what is not' might be clearly – and rightly – drawn. Without some better grounding of meaning, this will continue to be a problem where the process of claim and counter-claim about Islamophobia – referred to at the outset of this chapter – will continue to rage and even possibly deepen the rift that exists between these bi-polar extremes, a point reiterated by Millward and the recognition that positions adopted in relation to Islamophobia are either too narrow or too broad.[69]

This recurring problem makes it extremely difficult to answer the question 'what is Islamophobia?' The intention of this book is to therefore try and seek some redress to this situation, attempting to explore and consider the necessary factors relevant to Islamophobia in the here and now at the same time as looking towards putting forward a better definition and conceptualisation of the phenomenon. In doing so, a number of key questions will need to be answered which include: does 'Islamophobia' exist? If it does, then what might 'Islamophobia' be? Are new or better terminologies required to assist the naming, defining or conceptualising of 'Islamophobia'? And finally, if existing definitions and conceptualisations are shown to be lacking in any way and subsequently contributing to the sense of contestation that exists, how might 'Islamophobia' be better defined and conceptualised? To achieve this, it will be necessary to consider the historical and the contemporary, as well as the settings and contexts within which phenomena become manifested. This historiography will therefore be an integral backdrop of reference against which this will be undertaken.

It is necessary then to look back at history to begin asking whether today's Islamophobia is little more than a return to the old fears about Islam and Muslims or whether indeed, it is something entirely new and contemporary. The next two chapters start by doing this. From these, a detailed analysis and unpacking of the Runnymede Report – in particular its model and definition of Islamophobia – is considered in two further chapters: the first explores the origins, publication and subsequent response to the report; the second, an exposition of the Runnymede model alongside an evaluation of the ongoing relevance and validity of its model and definition and model of Islamophobia. From here, this book considers Islamophobia in the context of a post-9/11 landscape: first, in the setting of the UK and second, across Europe. Both chapters explore the various manifestations of

---

[68]   Marcel Maussen, *Anti-Muslim Sentiments and Mobilization in the Netherlands. Discourse, Policies and Violence* (Paris: Challenge, 2006), 100.

[69]   P. Millward, 'Rivalries and Racisms: "Closed" and "Open" Islamophobic Dispositions Amongst Football Supporters', *Sociological Research Online* 13:6, www. socresonline.org.uk/13/6/5.html, 2008.

Islamophobia that are apparent as well as consider some of the underlying factors and causes that are apparent. The final section of this book explores the critical and timely questions that are now necessary, beginning with an exploration of whether Islamophobia exists, the final chapters look at how Islamophobia compares with other models and theories of discrimination such as racism, before concluding with the positing of a new definition of Islamophobia as well as a new means by which to understand exactly what the phenomenon might be. In doing so, some of the contestation that surrounds and is attributed to Islamophobia may itself, begin to be contested.

PART 2
History in Context

Chapter 2
Revelation to Reformation, Orientalism and Colonialism

As with many of the theories set out in the opening chapter, it has been repeatedly voiced that Islamophobia has a historical aspect to it. As Weller puts it, Islamophobia is undeniably 'rooted in the historical inheritance of a conflictual relationship that has developed over many centuries involving the overlap of religion, politics and warfare'.[1] Given this recurrent emphasis, a brief consideration of the role of history and certain key events might provide a better understanding of the relationship – if indeed one exists – of the role and function of history and contemporary Islamophobia. The purpose of this chapter is not to present a historical analysis of either Islam or the Islamic encounter, but an opportunity to consider key historical events and junctures that may have acted or had some significant influence on current thinking and Islamophobia in the present day. Before doing so however, it is necessary to set out a few key distinctions. The first is that throughout this chapter 'the West' is used reluctantly, with it simplifying the myriad identities and differences that clearly exist within such a marker. However, the term is and has been widely employed by a range of different writers and commentators: one that at times describes and defines a place, a people and in some ways, an ideology. At times, it might also be somewhat simplistically argued that 'the West' is little more than a term used to describe all that is not 'Islam'. As such, 'the West' is used from hereon in such ways that its weaknesses are clearly acknowledged but nonetheless maintains some relevance. To clarify this it is as Yemelianova puts it, where the West is:

> countries of Western Europe and North America, the societies that function on the principles of bourgeois liberal democracies and the market economies, historically generated in Europe. Therefore, it does not include Japan and the newly industrialised economies of South East Asia which, although they share with Western Europe and North America similarly high technological and living standards, arguably belong to different political and cultural traditions.[2]

In doing so, 'the West' takes in everything from Huntington and his 'Clash of Civilisations' thesis[3] to the many junctures, in Esposito's observation, when 'the

---

[1]   Weller (2001), 8.

[2]   Yemelianova (2002), 193.

[3]   Samuel P. Huntington, *The Clash of Civilisations and the Remaking of World Order* (London: Touchstone, 1997).

history of Christendom and Islam [that] has more often than not been marked by confrontation rather than peaceful co-existence and dialogue'.[4] This is not to suggest that each of these junctures or different paradigmatic settings are part of a continuum or are immediately relevant, but instead that they can be considered in terms of a linear history that have some interdependence. It is therefore from the beginning of this linear history that this chapter begins.

The Start of History: From the Birth of a Prophet to 'Militaristic Pilgrimage'

Tracing history to the birth of the Islamic tradition, the three decades that followed the death of the Prophet Muhammad witnessed a spread of the religion that was dramatic and explosive. From the Qur'anic doctrine of transforming the world through direct action in it, Islam's spread was religious and social and political, successfully interweaving religious orthodoxy with social policy from the outset. From its spread into Spain, France and the Balkans, Europe's first encounter with Islam was perceived by some as a threat: informed by the experience of Eastern Christendom in particular the loss of the holy city of Jerusalem as well as other important centres that included Damascus and Egypt. Largely united behind the Vatican and the Roman Christian tradition, Europe saw Islam as presenting a three-prong challenge to its stronghold and wellbeing. First, Islam was both a religious and social ideology, one perceived to be able to challenge Europe's relative stability. Second, it was a proselytic religion, one that had the ability to challenge the ascendancy of the Roman Church as well as the expansion of Christianity. And third, if Islam was to be understood as a new dispensation from Heaven – one that was claiming to have completed the Abrahamic revelation – not only might it be argued theologically that it had superseded Christianity, but through conversion and any social foothold gained within Europe's borders, so it might have had the potential to confine Christianity to the spiritual, theological and social wildernesses.

Despite Christianity having lost out to Muslim rule, both Damascus and Baghdad were two of the earliest seats of dialogue between Muslims and Christians. As well as theology, ideas were exchanged in the fields of philosophy, logic, and society also. An important figure in this period was St. John of Damascus, also known as Yahya Al-Dimashqi and Johannes Damascenus depending upon the sources and cultures preferred. John was renowned not only for his role in the formation of Christian orthodoxy – rather than 'Orthodox Christianity' – but also in developing and giving a voice to Christian polemics against the heretical 'Saracen': a name synonymous with Muslim at the time and one that has since been attributed with some of the most virulent anti-Islamic, anti-Muslim meanings. Somewhat contrary to what might be presumed, the first anti-Islamic, anti-Muslim discourses therefore

---

⁴   John Esposito, *The Islamic Threat: Myth or Reality?* (Oxford: Oxford University Press, 1994), 59.

emerged from a setting where both the language of Islam and the people of Islam – Muslims – were known. At the outset therefore, Islam and Muslims were far from the distant and unknown 'Other' that later historical periods would suggest may have become the norm. It was in Europe however where the overriding notion of the threat of Islam was widespread and where these discourses became coupled and embellished by the absence of direct contact. Consequently, Europe's Christian elite began the long history of codifying what might be described as its subjectively informed scholarship about Islam and Muhammad. This period and setting was therefore vitally important in recognising and understanding the meanings and perceptions that have permeated much of the thinking throughout Europe, Roman Christendom, and beyond, both in terms of the interaction between Europe and the Muslim world as well as establishing the concept of Muslims as Other. One way of describing this might be to suggest that Europe begun to know Islam and Muslims in absentia.

As Islam continued to encroach on the peripheries of Europe's borders, so European powers felt the need to respond. With this, Pope Urban II backed the Reconquista or the re-conquering of Spain (c.1000 CE) as well as sanctioning the liberation of Italy and Sicily in 1061. Ten years later, the Byzantine Empire's Alexus I called on the Vatican and the entire Roman Christendom to unite and mobilise against the advancing Abbasid armies. The Vatican agreed and called upon Christians to undertake a 'militaristic pilgrimage' – popularly known as the Crusades – to defeat the burgeoning Muslim armies and free the holy city of Jerusalem.[5] For the Pope, this was an opportunity to reassert the supremacy of the Roman Church both in Europe as well as in the countries of the Eastern Mediterranean. The Crusades were enthusiastically received and the Vatican duly consolidated its strength when in 1099 the Crusaders re-conquered Jerusalem. But as Esposito suggests, history perpetuates two great myths about the Crusades: the first that Jerusalem was liberated; the second that Christendom triumphed. As he goes on, if success equated the liberation of Jerusalem, then success was short lived as control of the city returned to Muslim rule in 1187 CE. Likewise, the Crusades were not solely undertaken against the ensuing Muslim armies that Alexus I had called for. In the march towards Jerusalem, many on the Crusades co-operated in massacring not only vast numbers of Muslims but so too Jews as well as those Christians that the Vatican deemed heretical. The threat and encroachment of Muslim armies therefore provided a convenient scapegoat, a much-needed and necessary enemy against which the Vatican and its supporters could wage war. Doing this to such good effect has meant that the Crusades are reflected upon as something that brought about the unity of Europe. In reality however, this may be far from the truth.

Despite spending many years in the Middle East, the Crusades brought about little improved knowledge or understanding about Islam and Muslims. Instead, folk stories and myths returned from the Holy Lands with the Crusaders, many

---

[5]   Ibid.

of which did little more than reinforce the misconceptions and misunderstandings already in existence about Muslims and Islam. Lurid tales of pagan and idolatrous practices mixed with legends about great warriors such as Saladin (Salah al-Din al-Ayyubi), supplemented by fantastically inspired stories about the promiscuity, wealth and luxury of Muslims were all given credibility as they were retold by those who seen such things with their own eyes. Compliment this with the treasures brought back from the Middle East and the process of constructing a far-off fantasy world that was immersed in the luxuries of temporality and worldliness merely reinforced the wicked and un-godly nature of the heretical infidels that the Crusaders had been divinely inspired to defeat. In many ways, Islam and Muslims became overly fantastical and to some degree, the romanticised opposite of Europe at a time when the vast majority of its people were living in inherent bleakness.[6] Yet at the same time – not least because all of this fantasy was perceived through conflict, murder, atrocity and war – Muslims were also undeniably barbaric and without any doubt whatsoever, the enemy of Europe and Christianity.

As the Roman Church's influence begun to wane across Europe in the centuries that followed, so too did theological criticisms of Islam also wane. Replacing this however emerged a greater emphasis on how Islamic or Muslim culture – Islamic civilisation? – was inherently different and obtuse to its European or Western equivalent. Despite the lessening of theological criticisms, the Church still commissioned translations of the Qur'an. Starting during the Crusades, the first translations into Latin were overseen by Peter the Venerable. The primary reason for doing so was not for Europe or Roman Christendom to acquire a deeper understanding of Islam or its theology, but to better understand this growing and equally proselytic religion. Nonetheless, the perception of Islam as opposite and even enemy was once significant in this. Christians and their institutions wanted to better understand their 'enemy'. Although the number of people in Europe who were able to engage with and learn from the translations was extremely low, these same translations formed the start point from which the European study of Islam was begun and indeed continued throughout Middle Ages and beyond. With a premise of Islam as enemy, it is not surprising that they provided those looking to criticise or even denigrate Islam with what they perceived to be tangible evidence.

Folk Lore and Fantastical Myths: 'Mahomet le prophete'

In addition to the myths and stories that returned with the Crusaders about Muslims, so too did stories about the Prophet Muhammad or 'Mahomet' to use his Latin equivalent. Prior to the twelfth century, little evidence exists to suggest that any substantive writing about Muhammad from a European context was in evidence. Yet following the Crusades, a newly emergent and greater eschatological

---

[6]   Norman Daniel, *Islam and the West: the Making of an Image* (Oxford: Oneworld, 2000).

focus was placed upon him, one that supported many of the notions about Islam being heretical. One significant aspect of this was the belief that Muhammad was the anti-Christ and, via Christian theological interpretation at least, heralded the impending end of the world. The apocalyptic framework within which Muhammad and the spread of Islam was therefore understood seemed to theologically fulfil the New Testament's promise and so became somewhat self-perpetuating. As with the differences that were seen to exist between European culture and Islamic culture, so the same was evident in the way in which Muhammad's temporal qualities became increasingly compared with the spiritual qualities of Jesus as the Christ. Consequently, Muhammad became imbued with qualities that included licentiousness, promiscuity, sexual depravity and political power. This latter point was used as evidence to reinforce European views that Islam – as a Satanic force – was planning to destroy Christianity. Aside from Christian theological interpretations, the figure of Muhammad also emerged from the Crusader myths in similar ways, violent, barbaric and merciless and the epitome of all that Islam was seen to be. Recurrent in many of these myths was the way in which Muhammad was believed to have dealt with his enemies – especially Jews and Christians – taking gratuitous pleasure in torturing and then eventually killing them.

Such stories and myths, as well as the meanings and understandings that underpinned them, remained evident across the centuries. Even in a post-Reformation Europe, one where the continent was struggling to establish a new era founded upon the separation of the state from the church, so these same meanings and understandings remained apparent. The context though had of course changed. Bolstered by an unprecedented surge in European interest in the cultural aspects of Islam and the Muslim world, Islamic civilisation was now being observed and encountered by the West from what was perceived to be a more superior intellectual premise: one that was far removed from the inherent backwardness of its Islamic counterpart. Consequently, Europeans began to re-write, re-interpret and re-present Islam from an entirely Westernised, and increasingly secularised perspective. Whilst being deeply influenced and derivative of the preceeding centuries' meanings and understandings, contemporarily a far greater emphasis was being placed on what Europe perceived to be its superior sense of rationalism in comparison to Muslims and Islam: a rationalism that included an increasingly overt disdain for religion. Examples of this can be seen in the work of those such as the French Enlightenment writer and essayist, Voltaire. Whilst writing hundreds of years after the Crusades, he maintains many of those earlier understandings about Islam and Muhammad. In *Fanatisme ou Mahomet le prophete* for example, the figure of Muhammad is presented as a model of fanaticism and barbarism that at the same time is also highly sensual.

With this surge in interest about Islamic civilisation, many of Europe's aristocracy and wealthy elite began to travel to the Middle East to experience Muslim culture first hand. Travelogues detailing their experience became increasingly popular and formed a sizeable body of literature at the time. In many ways, these travelogues were similar to the way in which stories and myths returned to Europe following the Crusades: first hand accounts that were rooted within fantastical and mythological frames but were eagerly consumed by a willing public audience. Edward Said suggested that these processes – the processes through which meaning became known and embedded into the European understanding – were the first buds of the 'Orientalist' tradition.[7] For Said, whilst Islam had already been firmly established and rationalised as Europe's Other – in Said's lexicon, 'the Orient' – so Islam was now taking on a much broader and protean form, one where it was far more romanticised and even fetishlike. Through these stories, the Orient was also becoming all that its European counterpart – 'the Occident' – was not. More importantly, the Orient was becoming all that Europe or the Occident *did not* want to be: a very important distinction. The Orient therefore became embedded and made known through exotic and fantastical means, imbued with characteristics and attributes that were increasingly violent, barbaric, depraved and inferior: characteristics and attributes that those such as Shaheen have suggested continue to inform and shape the constructions of Islam, Muslims and indeed Arabs by the Hollywood film industry today.[8] As Murden put it, 'the Orientalist tradition was based on myth, misunderstanding and what was left unsaid about the Orient…'.[9] To some, this also opened the way for the Occident to begin to identify what was seen as the need to begin 'civilising' the Orient: something that many have suggested found credence and gained fruition through colonial expansion in the following few hundred years.[10]

Orientalism: 'myth, misunderstanding and what was left unsaid'

Unsurprisingly, alongside the growing populist interest, so too was there a similar rise in the academic enquiry into Islam and Muslims across Europe. Largely driven by political, economic and militaristic concerns, the eighteenth century simultaneously also witnessed a number of European countries expanding their empires across the globe. With imperial growth and academic enquiry functioning in close collaboration, so new understandings about Islam and the Muslim world began to emerge that were not only premised and established as being rationalised and scholarly, but endorsed by power too. Emerging out of understandings that had for centuries considered Islam and Muslims as an enemy and rival, so newly emergent meanings began to be perceived from a more dominant position, one

---

[7]   Edward Said, *Orientalism* (London: Penguin, 1979).

[8]   Jack Shaheen, *Reel Bad Arabs: how Hollywood Vilifies a People* (Roundhouse Publishing: London, 2001).

[9]   S. Murden, 'Cultural Conflict in International Relations: The West and Islam' Baylis, J. and Smith, S. eds, *The Globalization of World Politics an Introduction to International Relation* (Oxford: Oxford University Press, 1997), 381.

[10]   R. Zakaria, *The Struggle Within Islam: The Conflict Between Religion and Politics* (London: Penguin Books, 1988).

where Europe was becoming increasingly powerful: a power that was inextricably linked to the processes of colonisation and all that this afforded. The vast amount of knowledge and information about Islam and the Muslim world that was being disseminated across Europe at the time was not only interested in feeding the appetite of those intrigued with the Orient, but so too did it feed the new power relations that Europe's expansion was allowing. As Said suggested, much of this continues to inform and shape understandings about Islam and Muslims in the contemporary setting, as much the images, ideas, meanings and understandings as indeed the categories, typologies, classifications and terminologies themselves. And through the substantive body of work that emerged from these scholars – whom Said describes as the 'Orientalists' – so an enduring legacy begun that has continued to shape many of the parameters within which the modern study of Islam and the Muslim world has been undertaken. As Hussain states, this process established 'an absolute and systematic difference between the West ... and the Orient, which is aberrant, undeveloped and inferior'.[11] More worrying for him though, and in offering some explanation of what was to follow, Hussain explains that what emerged was a notion and preconception of the Orient that was 'uniform and incapable of defining itself ... either to be feared ... or to be controlled'.[12]

With the blossoming of the Orient as the inevitable Other to the normative Occident, so today's Islam and the West dichotomous relationship would seem to have found its first legitimised manifestation. Despite the significant and dramatic interest shown in Islam, the Orientalist tradition did little to challenge the position that Islam and Muslims had held in previous centuries. In many instances, the inherently negative meanings and understandings that were widespread, many relating to the attributed threat and danger presented by the heretical Saracens some thousand years beforehand, were merely regurgitated in newer more relevant and resonant frames: frames that were backward and retrogressive to Europe's rationally perceived forwardness and progression. Orientalism therefore oversaw the embellishment of a much fuller and informed process, seeing Islam and Muslims as an inferior civilisation that was inherently backward, irrational and inferior populated by violent and barbaric people who, quite paradoxically, were also highly sensual, exotic and romanticised. Despite this, it is difficult to conclude that the meanings and understandings that were evident in Orientalist discourses were part of a continuum that linked the medieval John of Damascus with the Will Cummins of the contemporary. Instead, Orientalist discourse was a juncture in the evolution of those discourses that are evident in the here and now as indeed they were in the distant past.

---

[11] A. Hussain, *Western Conflict with Islam: Survey of the Anti-Islamic Tradition* (Leicester: Volcano Books, 1990), 30–31.

[12] Ibid.

Europe's Colonial Quest: 'reforming Islam'

Without doubt, the processes of Orientalism that were quasi-intellectually codified
were also reflected in the military objectives and capabilities that afforded Europe
the might to control the Orient as indeed it did other swathes of land throughout
the world. However, it is worth reiterating Hussain's observation about the West's
need to either fear or control the Orient, something that may have been particularly
relevant to the development of colonialism across the Muslim world. It is worth
noting though that there is little evidence to suggest that European colonial powers
intended at any time to eradicate Islam not least because religion – including
Islam – was largely seen to be dying anyway. Instead, evidence would seem to
suggest that colonialism's intention was to control. As Murden put it, because of
the position that the Orient found itself in, 'its subordinate position meant that
[Europe] could'.[13] Europe's nations, in particular Britain and France, shifted the
balance of power severely against the traditional rulers in the Orient and imposed
themselves as both heirs and successors, making it the first period in history since
the birth of Islam that parts of the Muslim world had been ruled by non-Muslims.
Because of European perceptions of Islam as a dying civilisation, colonialism was
also deeply embellished with the notion of imposing its own forms of control and
governance. So whilst Islam was not being sought to be eradicated, one underlying
aspect of colonialism was the aim to remove what it saw to be the final throes of a
religious or theological power that was soon to be replaced with a European model
of secularised nationalism. As Zakaria noted, the intention of the colonialists was
of 'reforming Islam ...' where 'reform' meant 'to secularise it'.[14] In essence, the
colonialists sought to assist what was seen as the looming natural death of Islam.

Unsurprisingly, colonialism was far from welcomed by most of the countries
that came under its jurisdiction. Many Muslim countries saw the numerous
impositions that were part and parcel of the colonised experience as being
derogative and destructive not only to the spirit of Islam but also the indigenous
identities of the people it subordinated. It was also seen to be divisive of the
ideological *ummah* – the Islamic belief in a universal brotherhood of Muslims
united in faith – by seeking to undermine its doctrinal significance and influence
through the imposition of man-made legal and political structures which included
the sharply drawn man-made borders that sought to divide, conquer and ultimately
rule. Tellingly, by the 1920s, European colonial powers controlled more than three
quarters of the Muslim world, a situation that was further exacerbated following
the two World Wars when the US reinforced, expanded, and in some instances,
even replaced European colonial powers. This further destroyed and fragmented
Muslim countries in both the Middle East and Africa, where imposed rulers and a
heavy military presence not only ensured the subservience of the population but
also the traditional means of governance that large swathes of those regions had

---

[13]   Murden (1997), 381.
[14]   Zakaria (1988), 164.

traditionally employed. Beyond the Second World War, of the 42 Muslim countries that were recognised, only four existed without a colonial power governing it. Slowly, traditional Islamic structures and identities were being differentially and, in many places, systematically subsumed by pseudo-European ones. At its worst, the Muslim world and the position of Islam was left humiliated and defeated.

Despite this, colonialism occurred outside of and somewhat arbitrarily to the existence and presence of Islam. Indeed, colonialism was far from being an Islamo-specific process and so extensive areas that were non-Islamic including South and Central America were also colonised. Colonisation was not then unique to Islam or to the Muslim world although it is worth suggesting that because of Orientalism, it might have been that the colonisation of the Muslim world took on a different form and expression. Embodying and endorsing many of the meanings and understandings that had evolved historically, given further legitimacy through the discourses of Orientalism, the period of colonialism saw Islam and Muslims as part of a retrogressive and backward tradition, one that was immensely inferior, impossibly subordinate, and unable to engender the European values of truth through its inherent manipulative nature and its lack of civility. To complete the picture, Muslims were seen to be the antipathy of progress or development, something that Europe saw itself as being at the forefront of. Colonialism was therefore consolidated upon the long held belief that Islam was 'a civilisation doomed to barbarism and backwardness for ever'[15] thus justifying its subjugation, denigration and domination. Islam and the Muslim world became 'caught up in processes of social and cultural construction ... invented, reinvented, produced and reproduced ...' which helped shape European actions, responses, attitudes and behaviours that were 'determined primarily by security concerns, political and economic interests, and the drive for power and prestige, not by some value and belief related factors'.[16] And as Esposito has since noted, it is this same legacy that has occupied forever the 'psyche of Muslims'.[17]

History's Legacy: 'invented, reinvented, produced and reproduced'

It is interesting then to revisit the theories relating to the influence and determinative power of history. For Sardar, contemporary Islamophobia is a mere 're-emergence' of a historical anti-Muslim, anti-Islamic phenomenon: a continuum that stretches from before the Crusades to the present day and no doubt into the future.[18] For him, anti-Muslim, anti-Islamic phenomena have resided deeply in the memories of Europe and its partners, historically rooted and informed, likewise Milton-Edwards. Yet as shown by this brief historical exposition, this is not the case and

---

[15] Ahmed (1999), 60.
[16] Hunter (1998), 17–23.
[17] Esposito (1999), 44.
[18] Sardar (1995), 1–17.

whilst the consideration of such phenomena has been albeit brief, more detailed studies and the comparative narratives that exist highlight a significant disparity. Take for example the narratives of Daniel and Said.[19] Whilst similarities exist between what Daniel suggests were prevalent meanings and understandings during the Medieval and Middle Ages, Said's conclusions about the understandings that emerged from Orientalist discourses were different and far more substantiated in terms of what might have been described as evidence: formed and constructed on selective learning rather than on mere analogy, fiction or myth.

Maybe such an understanding would appear to suggest that Dilwar Hussain's notion of a plurality of 'Islamophobias' be more appropriate, where characteristics become dependant upon the historical context: linked but neither necessarily dependent nor evolutionary of each other.[20] Given this historical consideration and the observation that similar reference points and images continue to crop up in the present day, such a theory would appear to have some substantiation. Given that ideas and themes were recurrent in the different historical paradigms that were explored, so Hussain's plurality approach would seem to have some legitimacy. One way of better understanding this might be to suggest that anti-Muslim, anti-Islamic phenomena are endemic in European culture, referencing the point made by Esposito previously about how deeply embedded in the Muslim psyche history is. Maybe the same is true for Europeans also, where such phenomena go through periods of dormancy and intensification that reach epidemical levels at different junctures.[21] As Yaqub Zaki suggested, the phenomena's 'intensity varies according to time and place ... yet [it remains] endemic in the European psyche; endemic even if at times it becomes epidemic'.[22] It is important to clarify that by suggesting that a phenomenon lingers or resides dormant, does not necessarily mean that the same phenomenon remains unchanging and constant or indeed that the people that might draw upon this are normatively anti-Muslim, anti-Islamic. On the contrary, by endemic it is meant that such views and understandings are a condition of a particular setting or people: something that can be drawn upon and expressed in different ways and at different times as well as being rejected and replaced also.

A final theory suggests that Islamophobia is entirely contemporary and independent of the past's historical manifestations and contexts. However, history clearly informs, shapes and provides a frame of reference for understanding without necessarily insisting that all such manifestations of anti-Muslim, anti-Islamic phenomena are constant and unchanging and so rendering this theory seemingly invalid. As set out in *Islam and the Myth of Confrontation: Religion and Politics in the Middle East*, Halliday seeks to explain this process:

---

[19]   See both Daniel (2000) and Said (1995).

[20]   Hussain (2004), 115–29.

[21]   Allen (2004), 130–45.

[22]   Y. Zaki, 'The Politics of Islamophobia', *Re-present* (Winter/Spring 2002), 8–18.

> to identify these relics and revivals [of anti-Muslim expression or belief] is not to prove a continuity of culture or politics[23]

but instead, one where:

> the past provides a reserve of reference and symbol for the present: it does not explain it ...

as the

> ... significant differences of emphasis, prejudice and engagement depending on the colonial histories, the geographical location and the composition of the immigrant community

that need to be taken into account and considered.[24]

History therefore is neither to be rejected nor repudiated, and most definitely not to be seen to be a constant and unchanging backdrop against which simplistic and somewhat superficial understandings about Muslims and Islam can be easily contextualised. Instead, history and its paradigms must instead be used as a framework of reference to contemporarily assist and explain contemporary understanding. The power of history is therefore quite different to that which Sardar et al suggests. History and the informing and framing influence that this has should be utilised to promote greater understanding but it should also be remembered that it is not necessarily any more reliably informed of that which is happening, occurring and being made known now. It is deeply important therefore to consider and explore those changes that have occurred, in particular those that distinguish the modern from the historical, and how this might have influenced the situation today. It is necessary therefore to consider the context and events that linked colonialism to the contemporary emergence of today's Islamophobia.

---

[23] Fred Halliday, *Islam and the Myth of Confrontation: Religion and Politics in the Middle East* (London: IB Tauris, 1999), 179.

[24] Fred Halliday, *Two Hours That Shook the World: September 11, 2001 – Causes and Consequences* (London: Saqi, 2002), 125.

Chapter 3
From Revolution to Revival, Rushdie and the Clash of Civilisations

In the latter part of the twentieth century, that which was understood and made known about Islam and Muslims was more salient than that in circulation in earlier historical paradigmatic contexts, particularly those ideas that encapsulated the Orient as sensual, despotic, backward, promiscuous, aberrant, irrational and mysterious. In fact in many ways, even the term 'the Orient' had become somewhat redundant and misplaced. This is not to say that a complete break with the past had occurred. Some of the more historically resonant meanings and understandings about Islam and Muslims continued to persist, irregularly cropping up in some of the most unpredictable representations. Whilst Orientalism and its discourses therefore remain vitally important in the broader contextual landscapes, the latter half of the twentieth century's modes of approaching, interacting, understanding and explaining Islam and Muslims were played out through arenas that were far more politicised and militarised and maybe less Orientalised. This transition has fed into and transformed many of the historical givens about Islam and Muslims, bringing about a greater sense of mistrust and doubt, and sometimes even outright hatred.

As a consequence – or possibly consequential of this – something of an exclusive focus has been placed on what has come to be known and labelled as political, militant and initially 'fundamentalist' Islam. The use of these and other appellations – Islamist, radical, extremist and so on – has sought to reduce much of the wider discourse and understanding to that which culminates solely in terms of political and military confrontation. Increasingly, this is sub-categorised and played out through events such as the ongoing situation in the Middle East or the 'War on Terror' for example. For many in the West, Islam became a way of understanding the causes of various 'problems' around the world, with each of Palestine, Iraq and Afghanistan offering a specific case in point. In doing so, notions of Islam as Other have continued but with a much greater emphasis on the violent and militaristic. And possibly more recently, as a monolith that is hostile and resistant to progress and development manifested in terms of a distinctly anti-Western ideology. But it is the threat of Islam – something that Islam has been perceived as embodying ever since its earliest historical establishment in the West – that has become increasingly understood as being one that is against the West as a 'civilization', a 'people' and in terms of its 'values'. Note again Berlusconi's comments about Islam in comparison to Western or European civilisation earlier this century.

The Iranian Revolution: the 'Great Satan' and the 'Westoxification' of Islam

In 1921, British colonial powers endorsed the overthrow of the Iran's theocratic rulers and their replacement by Reza Khan who later crowned himself Shah, a title derived from Persian for king. British influence was integral to his reign and was privy to the abolition of the *hijab* and the compulsory wearing of European attire. Following his alliance with Germany in the Second World War however, his relationship with the British deteriorated to the extent that the Allies forced him to abdicate in order that his son – Muhammad Reza Shah Pahlavi who supported the Allies – could be duly installed and crowned. Through his son, Western interests continued to be protected not only during the War but so too throughout the Cold War as well. As Buckley notes, 'Iran was regarded as a solid bulwark against communism'.[1] The strategic and economic value of Iran became increasingly significant and following the sharp rise in oil prices instigated by the Organisation of Petroleum Exporting Countries in the early 1970s, a great deal of Western investment was made in Iran to ensure continued it maintained access to one of the world's major energy sources. Investment brought about a large influx of wealth, although not all Iranians saw their standards of living increase and the class divide in the country widened. Nonetheless, for the West its military stronghold remained intact, its continued availability of oil remained economically viable, and Iran remained a necessary ally in the Middle East. For Iranians however, it was a breeding ground for social and political unrest especially following the implementation of the Shah's 'White Revolution' that many saw as diminishing the role of Islam further.

Expelled from Iran in 1963, it was the Ayatollah Khomeini who was at the forefront of the political, albeit initially rhetorical resistance against the Shah during this time. For him, continued Western influence was increasing Iran's subjugation to commercialism and secularism. As a response, the Ayatollah believed it was necessary to ideologically fight for the brotherhood of all Muslims – strongly echoing Marxist concepts of the proletariat and bourgeoisie – which he believed to be the only means by which to defeat the 'Great Satan' that was America and its influence.[2] To oppose what was deemed the 'Westoxification' of Islam,[3] Khomeini called for a return to the fundamentals of the religion: something that turned out to be the first successful Islamically motivated resistance to Western domination for many centuries. Commanding the theological, social, economic, and political spheres of influence, Khomeini employed an ideological Islam – derived from Shi'a Islam – that would not only

---

[1]   Richard Buckley, 'Iran and the West: A Failure to Communicate', *Understanding Global Issues* (London: Bantam, 1997), 1.

[2]   Richard Tanter, *Rogue Regimes Terrorism and Proliferation* (London: Macmillan, 1999).

[3]   Leo Kurtz, *God's in the Global Village – The World's Religion in Sociological Perspective* (London: Pine Forge Press, 1995).

resist the West, but more importantly, defeat it also. Following an intense period of social unrest, the Shah fled Iran for the US on the 16 January 1979 and on 1 February that year, Khomeini made a successful return to Iran. Ten days later, Tehran radio announced, 'this is the voice of Tehran, the voice of true Iran, the voice of revolution. The dictatorship has come to an end'.[4] On the 1 April, Khomeini took control of the country with an overwhelming majority.

The Islamic Revolution in Iran was a hugely significant event and undeniably integral to the way in which Islam and Muslims have since been attributed with understanding in the West. Possibly less to do with the actual revolution itself, its impact was as Buckley writes, one where 'the sudden collapse of the Shah's regime took most Western observers by surprise'.[5] Significantly adding to this surprise were the previously unheralded global television news networks and their dissemination of pictures showing more than 3,000 Iranian students storming the American Embassy in Tehran. These televised images were the first time that the 'conceptual' threat of a newly resurgent Islam had been brought into the very epicentre of the West. Not only did it bring this conceptual threat – one that evoked and reinvigorated many of the historical meanings and understandings about Islam and Muslims that many believed had been subjugated under colonial rule – but it did so through the medium of television: a medium that existed inside the previously safe confines of Western homes. Despite the physical distance that existed between Iran and the West, the dissemination of images into the very heart of Western living seemed to conceptually eradicate that same distance and the safety this afforded simultaneously. In what Said described as 'news overkill', television networks repeatedly broadcast some of the most extreme forms of Shi'a Islam including self-flagellation, black clad women, the burning of American flags, and screaming mobs chanting for America's death.[6] Likewise, recurrent images of the black-robed Khomeini were so often broadcast that in many ways his persona – as constructed reality and identity – became the epitome of evil: personifying a rampant and uncontrollable anti-Americanism, the antipathy of Western values, morals and beliefs. Spending more than one million pounds per day to get the images and stories they wanted,[7] Western – primarily American – news agencies had inadvertently stumbled upon what became a vital propaganda weapon in responding to the unfolding events in Iran. Through Khomeini and his association with what was increasingly being reported as the most extreme and untenable form of Islam, so a new discourse relating to 'Islamic fundamentalism' or just 'fundamentalism' was conceived and born: a discourse entirely derivative of a media driven agenda that was conceptually closer, more urgent, more damning

---

[4]   Riaz Nima, *The Wrath of Allah, Islamic Revolution and Reaction in Iran* (London: Pluto Press Ltd, 1983), 83.

[5]   Buckley (1997), 3.

[6]   Edward Said, *Covering Islam: How the Media and the Experts Determine How we See the Rest of the World* (London: Vintage, 1997), 104.

[7]   Ibid.

and far more real than anything that had proceeded it in terms of the threat posed by Islam and Muslims.

A number of important issues are worthy of further consideration at this point. First, as with the initial interpretations of Islam and the role of Muhammad, so recurrent views throughout the coverage of the Iranian Revolution was such that Muslims remained as violent and barbaric as they always had been perceived to be. It was again being reiterated that a resurgent Islam was being spread by the sword, a spread that was also undeniably threatening. Islam was also being represented as a religion that was irrational, backward, static, dogmatic, regressive and manipulative. Such justifications were also posited by various commentators as being significant in being the root causes of why – and even how – the situation in Iran had developed in the way that it had, both of which were reductive and dismissive of any actual or real factors. It was though the identification and association of Islam with violence and militancy that had the greatest impact. Drawing upon the vast historical frame of reference – both actual and mythological – that Halliday suggested was vital for understanding, so the Islamic Revolution became seen to be something of a direct challenge to the West: one that saw Islam as a menacing power irrefutably focused on bringing down and subsequently overthrowing the West and everything that it stood for. Similar to more recent suggestions that London will be a *shariah* state by 2025 or that Christian Europe will soon be overthrown by Islam.

The discourse to emerge from the Revolution and the growing spectre of 'fundamentalism' – the name attributed to this resurgent anti-Western Islam at the time – was such that whilst there was no doubt whatsoever that violent and militaristic factions and groups were in existence throughout the Muslim world, the discourse that accompanied it became far more indiscriminately embedded and loaded. As part of a coded lexicon that incorporated not only the language of fundamentalism but so too words relating to militancy, extremism, Islamism, radicalism, Saddamism, and so on, a mere mention of them immediately conjured damning and dangerous connotations. More worryingly, it began to permeate the discourse of Islam and Muslims per se, essentialising and reducing everything about Islam and Muslims to a very clear and easily deducible set of statements and understandings. And as media interest and further coverage continued to become more widely disseminated, increasingly emphasising the menace presented by the spectre of fundamentalism, so this discourse became increasingly non-differentiable. As Said wrote:

> since the events in Iran caught European and American attention so strongly ... they have portrayed [Islam], characterised it, analysed it ... licensing not only patent inaccuracy but also expressions of unrestrained ethnocentrism, cultural and even racial hatred.[8]

---

[8]   Said (1997), XI.

The Revolution therefore became both the source and the benchmark against which contemporary negative and stereotypical representations of Islam and Muslims developed. It was a contemporary watershed in the West's understanding of Islam and Muslims, seen through the historical lens of what the West knew and more importantly, thought it knew about Islam as Other. Indeed this same discourse can be seen underpinning such contemporary events such as the 'War on Terror' and through the construction of such groups as al-Qaeda amongst others.

The *Satanic Verses* Affair: 'I call on courageous Muslims to execute them'

The Iranian Revolution was a critical juncture in the process of defining and understanding the contemporary relationship between Islam and the West, despite the fact that the Revolution was no more a real event than the Crusades were centuries earlier. Yet in spite of this, throughout the 1980s the spectre and menace of fundamentalism and the resurgence of a revitalised Islam remained prevalent in the global political discourse, albeit at times hidden behind the Russian Communist behemoth. With the re-emergence of this fear of Islam globally, it is important to remember the context in the UK, where an anti-Muslim prejudice was first being identified and where a distinct 'British Muslim' identity was also emerging. And it was events that took place in the UK in 1989 that first brought the global and the local together in dangerous ways at the local setting. It was in 1989 that both the conceptual and physical distance between Islam and the West was removed. No longer were 'Islam' and 'Muslims' out-there and external: beginning with 1989, so the proximity – the previously critical distance necessary – was removed to the extent that Islam and Muslims were acknowledged as being here and more troublingly, within. The prime events associated with this change was the unfolding of the *Satanic Verses* affair in the UK and Khomeini's fatwa; the emergence of the *hijab* debates emerging in France at the regional level; and the fall of communism.

As the Commission on British Muslims and Islamophobia reflected years later, 'the Satanic Verses affair was one of the formative, defining events' in shaping how Muslims and Islam have since been known and understood.[9] Being his fourth novel, Salman Rushdie's the *Satanic Verses* was first published in 1988 and was understood by many to be constructed around stories from the life of Muhammad, the title itself referencing Ibn Ishaq's biography of the prophet. Causing some controversy at the time of its publication, the book was interpreted by many Muslims as being blasphemous due to its analogous storylines denigrating Muhammad, his prophet-hood and wives. Similar accusations were also made against the theological tenets and beliefs of Islam. Following India's lead in being the first to ban the book, Khomeini however took the matter to a new and unprecedented level by issuing a fatwa that called for the death of Rushdie. The fatwa was not merely for the people

---

[9]   Runnymede report (1997), 27.

of Iran though. Khomeini declared that the fatwa insisted that it was the duty of every Muslim around the world to obey his pronouncement. Somewhat amazingly, Khomeini confessed to having never read the book and confirmed that those who were to uphold the fatwa were not to read the book either. In a broadcast on Iranian radio on the 14 February 1989, Khomeini he stated:

> I inform all Muslims in the world that the author of the book, The Satanic Verses, which is against Islam, the Prophet and the Qur'an, and all those who have published it knowingly are condemned to death. I call on courageous Muslims to execute them as soon as possible wherever they may be.[10]

In the immediate aftermath, some outbreaks of pandemonium ensued: Hitoshi Igarashi, the Japanese language translator of the book, was stabbed to death in July 1991; Ettore Capriolo, the Italian language translator, was seriously injured in a stabbing in the same month; and William Nygaard, the Norwegian publisher, survived an attempted assassination in October 1993. More recently and in spite of Khomeini's death in the interim, on 14 February 2006 Iranian state news reiterated the fatwa, again calling for the death of Rushdie which was to remain in place indefinitely.

In the UK, the response to the publication of the book was overwhelming. On the 14 January 1989 a large number of Muslims took to the streets of Bradford and publicly burnt copies of the book. Whilst the local and national press initially showed little interest, a small group of protesters videotaped the proceedings to later distribute it to news agencies in an attempt to increase exposure and highlight their displeasure. Despite being poorly produced, within hours images of Muslims burning books on the streets of England were broadcast all around the world. Evoking comparisons to the Reconquista, the Inquisition and the Reformation, the most damning comparisons were those that recalled Hitler's Nazis a half century beforehand. In what was an attempt to gain publicity, the footage was a catastrophe that inadvertently signalled the beginning of a much wider process: not just in terms of widespread condemnation but the indiscriminate vilification of all Muslims without differentiation.

Irrespective of the outcomes however, an alternative explanation exists about the inadvert nature of the footage. As one source said years after the event, 'the Bradford incident was staged by certain sections of the media and a London solicitor was behind the "management", in order to spread a negative image of Islam'.[11] Little evidence exists to clarify which version of events was accurate. Nonetheless, the result was that the presence of Islam in Britain and the role of Muslims were brought sharply under the public and political spotlight. Given that British Muslims and the presence of Islam in Britain had previously been unacknowledged – collectively defined within the homogenous marker of 'Asian'

---

[10]   Kepel (1997), 139.
[11]   Kepel (1997), 138–9.

as identified by Modood previously – so the first formal recognition of British Muslims and Islam in Britain was such that it became indistinguishable from fundamentalist forms of Islam that were seen to exist elsewhere in the world. In maintaining the homogeneity that was already present, so British Muslims became incorporated in the same perceptions, understandings and representations to those attributed to Khomeini and the resurgent forms of Islam witnessed during the Revolution. No clear demarcation was duly made.

Almost immediately, the protests took on even greater global consequences and within a month of the events in Bradford similar protests had taken place in Bombay, Kashmir, Dacca and Islamabad, the latter seeing five protesters being killed and hundreds more injured. Unsurprisingly, these protests were broadcast around the world by news agencies, similar to the coverage and images associated with the protests that followed the second publication of the cartoons of Muhammad in the *Jyllands-Posten* in early 2006. Both were highly mediatised and became almost hyper-real. For the media, the call for Rushdie's murder by the epitome of evil and fanaticism merely reinforced those perceptions and stereotypes that were already in circulation, embellished by the notion that this resurgent fundamentalist Islam could no longer even be contained or halted by national borders. And as with the debates that emerged following the Danish cartoons furore, so the Satanic Verses affair was one that was seen to present a direct challenge to many of the deeply held values of the West: freedom of expression, equality, democracy and tolerance amongst many others. In fact, this legacy continues to shape the responses and reactions of both Muslims and non-Muslims alike. Included in this might be the response by some Muslims to the showing of Geert Wilders' *Fitna*, the proposed publication of *The Jewel of Medina*, the art of Sarah Maples or more recently, the 'dog Muhammad' drawings of Lar Vilks and the response of some non-Muslims who subsequently espouse the need for freedom of expression, equality, democracy, tolerance and so on. Whilst specifically referring to the Satanic Verses affair, Poole's observations have wider resonance when she notes how the media cover such events in ways that are seen to pose a serious threat to liberal and progressive British and Western values from archaic, retrogressive and irrational Muslims: adherents to an outdated and outmoded religious belief system that has historically been shown to be violent, barbaric and intolerant.[12] What was unique about this unfolding crisis however was that at no time previously in history had Muslims been seen to be challenging or threatening the West simultaneously from both inside and outside its real or perceived borders. 1989 was the year this dramatically changed.

Throughout – and in line with practices that continue to punctuate the representation of Muslim communities in the UK – the media focused on a small number of outspoken British Muslims who, through their inflammatory rhetoric and declarations, became inappropriately employed as representative voices. Not only were Muslims – all Muslims – being characterised and attributed without

---

[12]   Poole (2000), 165.

differentiation, but given the global dimensions of the events, so too were Muslims becoming increasingly homogenised: essentialised and reduced to the lowest of common denominators. So when those such as Muhammad Siddiq argued that 'if [Muslims] could get away with killing [Rushdie] without getting caught, anybody would go out and do it', so the media accepted without question that this was the view of all Muslims, despite the fact that other vastly different responses were also being aired.[13] Similar processes can be seen contemporarily where the views and opinions of those such as Anjem Choudary and his Islam4UK organisation are presented as being representative of all Muslims without differentiation. Increasingly seen as being the voice from *within* British society, the alleged threat to British society and its core values from Muslims in relation to the Satanic Verses affair became increasingly important and prominent in the public and political spaces. In many ways, what had been playing out ten years previous to the Satanic Verses affair on the global stage was now being played out on the local stage here in the UK. The main and immensely significant difference however was that whilst on the global stage the perceived threat remained conceptually remote, in the British setting that conceptual – and critical – distance had been eradicated. Because of this, that same threat was now perceived to be much closer and far more real and by consequence, far more dangerous. Critical distance had been eradicated and Muslims – and all that this meant whether perceived or actual – were now closer than they had ever been throughout history.

The worldwide Muslim threat that had already gained significant resonance in the West had now infested the body of Britain and its values, indeterminably and increasingly framing the lens through which Muslims and Islam were being seen. At a time when Muslim communities in Britain were first beginning to negotiate the borders that existed between themselves and other new minority communities this had a tremendously significant – and negative – impact. The need for greater social and political engagement was such that it is no surprise that Muslim activists began to form organisations such as An-Nisa and UKACIA. For British Muslims, a growing political need was evident that not only required them to be more active but to also begin to identify themselves in such ways that they might address and tackle the very specific issues and problems that were relevant to them. For wider British society, who continued to contextualise events against the backdrop of 1979 and Halliday's notions of a shared history, so these borders were perceived as being infringed, destroyed and at worst, invaded. Whereas history had continually juxtaposed mythological Muslim Others alongside equally mythological Western and European norms, the contemporary location and positioning of Muslim communities in 1989 was unique and unparalleled. For whilst parts of Europe had historically been under Muslim rule and indigenous Muslim communities had existed in Eastern Europe for a number of centuries, never before had the proximity of Muslims – or maybe more precisely, the recognition of that proximity – been as close: whether that be conceptual or physical.

---

[13]   Ruthven (1990), 121.

Virtual Geography: 'from reds under the beds to fanatics in the attics'

There is little doubt that since the Satanic Verses affair, news and media networks have located an undeniably disproportionate newsworthiness to Muslims and Islam. The effect of this has been that the perceived threat presented by Muslims and Islam has been overblown and exaggerated, an observation resonant with the rhetoric and discourse of the 'War on Terror'. This ever increasing focus of newsworthiness, the exaggerated threat, and the mistrust that emerges from such a combination are of course highly influential and determinative of how Muslims and Islam are made known and given meaning. And with every time that another news story appears about Muslims or Islam, or the threat of Muslims or Islam is seen to be getting closer, so those processes of fear and mistrust become further reified. Conceptually at least, since the events of the Satanic Verses affair, the imagined Muslims and Islam of old that were once remote and distant now have the ability, irrespective of geographical location, to infiltrate the lives, homes and relative security of each and every front room in the West. The spatial mapping of the Western media no longer infers that either imagined or real Muslims are a separate externality but more so that the two are largely equated: both simultaneous and synonymous. As such, the undoing of proximities becomes that through which the local and global become infused and indistinguishable.

At the European and global levels, similarly significant events were unfolding also. In October of the same year, the French national press were reporting how three Muslim schoolgirls had been refused entry to their classes at the Gabriel Havez school in Creil for wearing the *hijab*. Despite attempts to try and re-focus debates away from particularising Islam and Muslims, the ensuing debates in the media and political spaces developed two particular strands themes. The first was that the girls should be allowed to wear the *hijab* in school as their attendance and participation at state schools would help them avoid being drawn into the first throes of Islamic fundamentalism. Here the argument suggested that if they were to be excluded from the state and its secular educational system, the girls' only alternative was to be taught at an Islamic educational institution. Quite openly, the assumption was that traditional Islamic educational institutes were places that fermented fundamentalist ideologies in their pupils, something that many in French society were particularly fearful of what with having already overseen what they believed to have been the shift from the 'Arabisation' of many of its large minority communities to a more worrying and threatening 'Islamisation'.[14]

The second response came from those that focused on the notion that excluding these Muslim students would be a rallying cry to all those who felt marginalised and excluded from French society, something that had the potential to initiate a process that would see many more youngsters drift towards Islamic fundamentalism as a viable alternative to liberal French society and its secular ideology. Without doubt, the debates focused around the perceived threat of Islamic fundamentalism rather

---

[14]   Kepel (1997), 184–5.

more so than the right of the girls to wear the *hijab* in the school environment. Consequently, many French Muslims believed that the girls were being used as a smokescreen to obfuscate the real worries and concerns that many in positions of power had about France's Muslim communities. As Kepel notes, French public and political discourses at the time were openly racist and highly xenophobic towards Muslims, a term that was widely synonymous with the term and notions of 'fanatic'.[15] It is interesting to note how the synonymy of Muslim with fanatic was far from new, identifiable in the writing of Voltaire centuries earlier. And as with the UK, the underlying issues surrounding the debates highlighted the fear of a revived and resurgent Islam, and the consequences – potential or otherwise – that this might have given that it was now seen to be *within* French society rather than existing in isolation outside it. Similar sentiments and ideas would seem to underpin the recent announcements by the now French President, Nicolas Sarkozy that the full face veil – the *niqab* – would soon be banned in France.

A month after the first *hijab* debate began in France, a more significant and symbolic event was being played out on a much broader global canvas in neighbouring Germany: the demolition of the Berlin Wall. Materially, the Wall brought about the reunification of East and West, of both Germany and Europe. Metaphorically, its demolition was the beginning of the end of the Cold War and the ending of the global political and military models that had dominated international relations for the past forty or so years. If simplistic arguments and theses can be in any way useful, what was occurring at the global level was, as Huntington put it, that both the West and Islam were being forced to shift their global perception and relationship: 'the collapse of communism removed a common enemy of the West and Islam and left each the perceived threat of each other'.[16] Whether conclusions can be so easily drawn remains open to debate, but given the historical context that had shaped and informed the relationship between the West and Islam, then it is at least reasonable to suggest that if nothing more, the climate was one that was conducive for a greater mistrust, suspicion and fear to ensue. Rather more anecdotally, it was a time when the fear of 'reds under the beds' was replaced by the fear of 'fanatics in the attics'.

Huntington and Beyond: beginning the 'clash of civilisations'

Undoubtedly these events informed the debates that underpinned Huntington's influential and oft-cited article, *The Clash of Civilizations*, and later book, *The Clash of Civilisations and the Remaking of World Order.*[17] Both expounded Huntington's thesis that in a post-Cold War setting, geo-political conflict would increasingly occur along 'civilisational' and religious lines rather more so than

---

[15] Ibid., 185–6.
[16] Huntington (1997), 211.
[17] Ibid.

any ideological or political equivalent, as had been the case for the greater part of the twentieth century. In its most simple guise, Huntington suggested that the West would be most at threat from Islamic, Sinic (Chinese) and Hindu civilisations. However Huntington's thesis was also interpreted by some as a warning that the greatest conflicts would be between Muslims and non-Muslims, reinforcing the already established Islam and the West dichotomy that had been gaining credence since the Iranian Revolution. In a post-9/11 setting, Huntington's thesis was once again being widely cited, the attacks on the twin towers interpreted by some to be the necessary evidence to substantiate the thesis. Because of this, Huntington's work has recently been accredited with greater credence and legitimacy in wider, previously dismissive circles. Despite his highly subjective standpoint, Huntington's original thesis largely relied on anecdotal evidence and despite seepage of his ideas into various different geo-political and intellectual spaces contemporarily, especially the neo-con political movement in the US, it might be suggested that there remains little empirical evidence to back up his claims. Nonetheless, its impact was – and indeed continues to be – highly significant.

Bookended between the events of 1989 and the publication of Huntington's thesis, an embryonic Islamophobia – or at least an embryonic anti-Muslim, anti-Islamic phenomenon – began to be recognised. This embryonic shift was the impetus for the Oxford English Dictionary to record the first use of the word 'Islamophobia' in print, notable for it being the first time in which Islamophobia was referred to as a specifically anti-Muslim, anti-Islamic phenomenon emanating from non-Muslims and directed at Muslims. In referring back to the opening historiography, as events were unfolding at the British grassroots level, so too were situations and events occurring at the global level that simultaneously fed into and bolstered attitudes both about and indeed by Muslims. Maybe then it is fair to conclude that Islamophobia should be recognised as having the ability to incorporate both the macro and micro aspects of any given event or situation at any given time. Maybe, Islamophobia was given impetus by the processes of 'glocalisation'. And so throughout the early 1990s, global events occur continued to reinforce and reify the emergent phenomenon. In similarity with the way in which the archetypal figure of Khomeni and the Iranian revolution became known and manifested previously, so too in the 1990s did the first Gulf War, the war in Bosnia and to a lesser degree, the war in Chechnya enter the same everyday spaces. And on every occasion, the events were increasingly played out on small screen as events that were against or involving 'Muslims': more importantly, 'Islam'. As Poole identified in her study of the media at this time, 'the news media's selection of pictures and words, the omission of information, the possible consequences of media concentration and the preconceptions of policy makers combine to create grave distortions of the facts'.[18] Unquestionably, an unwanted homogeneity, an essentialisation of Muslims, and the processes of reduction duly ensued. And in the context of the news media, reporting and representation reinforced and indeed

---

[18]   Poole (2000), 228.

reinvigorated the stereotypical and chimerical archetypes associated with Muslims and Islam.

The impact of the media in this period cannot be underestimated. At the outbreak of the Gulf War in 1991, CNN provided a live account of the start of the war from inside the 'enemy capital' of Baghdad with estimates suggesting audiences of more than 58.9 million worldwide.[19] Throughout the war, CNN's audience increased five-fold and with those images of Islam and Muslims that were being presented and re-presented – by this time, Saddam Hussain had begun to undergo the same personification of evil process Khomeini had previously[20] – so they became disseminated to a much wider and more indiscriminate audience. Oft repeated reports included stories about Saddam's nuclear capability targeting Europe with his 'supergun', his preparations for biological warfare against Israel, his personal shield of human hostages, and his army being the fourth largest in the world. Alongside these, comparisons were made about how Iraqi bombs were indiscriminately landing on Tel Aviv at the same time that coalition force's cruise missiles were pinpointing their targets with accuracy and without causing any apparent harm to Iraqi civilians. For CNN and others, Ahmed suggests that the war soon became a dualistic one that was being waged between 'Islam' and 'the West': between civility and barbarism.[21] Likewise with the wars in Bosnia and Chechnya, albeit with wholly different contexts, causes and consequences, so the amplification of the role of Muslims and Islam and their differentiation from the West became increasingly paramount not only in the ensuing coverage associated with the crises but also in the debates and discourses that ensued.

It is interesting and maybe also somewhat unsurprising to note that the Runnymede Report recognised this period as being one in which British people's attitudes towards Muslims changed. So much so, that it added that the period underpinned the emergence of what it saw as being a new reality that needed naming: a contemporary Islamophobia. In the next two chapters therefore, the ground-breaking 1997 report by the Commission on British Muslims and Islamophobia will be fully considered.

---

[19]   Zelizer (1999), 345.
[20]   Morley and Robins (1995), 135.
[21]   Ahmed (1999), 222

PART 3
A Decade of the
Runnymede Report

Chapter 4
Recognition: A New Reality that Needed Naming

Formed in 1968 as a think tank, the Runnymede Trust was set up to deal with issues of ethnicity and cultural diversity: 'to challenge racial discrimination, to influence anti-racist legislation and to promote a successful multi-ethnic Britain. [To] advise on ... how best to promote the value of diversity in our communities'.[1] Its first acknowledgement of a phenomenon identified as Islamophobia evolved out of its 1994 report entitled, *A Very Light Sleeper: The Persistence and Dangers of Anti-Semitism.*[2] In noting that, 'In the Jewish community, as in other minority communities in modern Britain, there is an increasing sense of threat and fear',[3] the report went on to suggest that anti-Semitism could be sub-divided into four key distinctions: historical developments and paradigmatic manifestations; contemporary British manifestations, including the far-right, extreme left and Christian churches; manifestations in Europe; and finally, its relationship and interaction with forms of racism. The report concluded with a series of recommendations for media, education, legislation, religious bodies, organisations and policy-makers. The report also set out three forms of anti-Semitism – anti-Judaism, anti-Semitic racism and anti-Zionism – before broadly defining anti-Semitism as a term that 'subsumes a wide spectrum of attitudes from unconscious and implicit prejudice through to open hostility, and to individual and organised acts of violence'.[4]

The inclusion of Islamophobia is to some extent puzzling because whilst identified as a form of racism, the report overlooked all other forms of racism including those based upon markers of 'race' or skin colour. Interestingly, Islamophobia was neither defined as a form of racism in the report nor was it in the *Islamophobia Report* that followed a couple of years later. Nonetheless, the report did acknowledge similarities between anti-Semitism and Islamophobia in that there was 'a strong religious component in both kinds of hostility'.[5] In comparing both phenomena under the heading of racism, the report sought to highlight likenesses between religious and race-based discriminations. And as

---

[1]   Runnymede Trust, 'Who We Are', *The Runnymede Trust Website* (26 February 2003) http://www.runnymedetrust.org/who.html.

[2]   Runnymede Commission on Anti-Semitism (1994).

[3]   Ibid., 11.

[4]   Ibid., 33.

[5]   Ibid., 55.

with the observations made by Khan in the 1980s, it also identified how both anti-Semitism and Islamophobia was apparently marginalised by the more socially accepted and mainstream anti-racism movements that had emerged in the previous two or so decades.

The Commission on British Muslims and Islamophobia: 'much needed objectivity and credibility'

The rationale for the Commission on British Muslims and Islamophobia evolved out of the *Anti-Semitism Report* and was established in 1996. Undertaking various consultative visits to Bradford, Tower Hamlets and Waltham Forest, it also collected and collated data from a number of other local authorities including Birmingham, Bradford, Camden, Haringey, Kirklees, Manchester, Newham, Rochdale and Sheffield. The Commission was made up of 18 members plus the Chair – Professor Gordon Conway – who the late Zaki Badawi said was chosen by the members because they felt that a non-Muslim would offer the Commission and subsequent report greater credibility across different faiths and cultures.[6] A legitimate criticism that has been posited about the Commission and its membership criteria is that it was established primarily along the lines of interfaith dialogue, something that may have had a detrimental effect on the thinking and shaping of the ideas and thoughts that emerged in the final report. With the Commission having adopted an ethos of interfaith rather than anti-racism those voices that existed outside of the orthodox mainstream of particular faith groups became – inadvertently or otherwise – excluded. Reciprocally, those who were seen to be neither orthodox nor 'mainstream', or were for whatever reason unwilling to participate, failed to find adequate representation or possibly even an adequate voice. As the Inter Faith Network sets out in its guidelines regarding the establishing of groups along these lines:

> It is very important to have participation from the mainstream … Inter faith meetings can quite legitimately be of interest to those who are 'seeking' or who are on the margins of their own faith tradition, but if the leadership of the group does not include a broadly based membership from the mainstream, this can give the group as a whole a marginal feel.[7]

It would seem imperative therefore that the Commission had no dissenting voices what with the potential implications this might have had on the subsequent legitimacy and credibility of the report: a point that in itself is not entirely a negative thing. So whilst interfaith guidelines acknowledge that non-mainstream voices can be problematic, for the Commission it may have been even more problematic had

---

6   From an interview with Dr Zaki Badawi, The Muslim College (3 March 2003).
7   Inter Faith Network for the UK, *Local Inter Faith Guide* (London: Inter Faith Network for the UK, 1999), 24.

there been some dissention from within its ranks. There appeared then a real need to find the right 'mainstream' voice for both the public and political spaces.

The consultation document, *Islamophobia: its Features and Dangers*[8] preceded the main report in March 1997. Being at the time both original and unprecedented, 3,500 copies were distributed to various individuals and organisations in order that the consultation process was as wide and diverse as possible. From this, approximately 140 responses were received of which approximately 90 per cent were positive.[9] These figures however are based on the evidence detailed in the Runnymede Report alone and cannot be independently verified. From those consultation documents that have been verified – through the co-operation of individuals and organisations that have independently provided copies of their responses – whilst many reflect the view that the process was largely positive, a number of constructive criticisms do appear to have been overlooked as in the case of the response of the Islamic Foundation. Describing the document as providing 'much needed objectivity and credibility',[10] it leant its support to the recommendations about legislation, media, social participation and education. However, it questioned the use of 'Islam' rather than 'Muslim' as a marker of identification because of the apparent lack of differentiation between Islamic beliefs and principles, and the practice and action of Muslims as individuals and communities. Similarly, whilst the Revd Dr David Thomas from the Centre for the Study of Islam and Christian-Muslim Relations (CSIC) at the University of Birmingham acknowledged the timeliness of identifying a contemporary anti-Muslim trend, he also argued that the findings would be 'strengthened if you could specify how this form of hostility differs in quality and kind from other instances of xenophobic feeling … crucial to distinguish the various types of Islamophobia (going deeper than listing aspects)'.[11] Whilst there appeared to be a sense that Islamophobia was less than clear, Professor Jorgen Nielsen galvanised the point: 'the term Islamophobia needs to be defined more rigorously'.[12] Nielsen identified an unsystematic shifting between markers of 'Islam' – as an abstract and complex web of ideas, concepts and beliefs – and 'Muslim' – referring to a person or people whose lives are informed and shaped to varying degrees by those same ideas, concepts and beliefs. As he concluded, 'an unfortunate consequence of the paper's justified concern with Islamophobia is that it paints a picture weak on context'.[13]

---

[8]   Runnymede Trust: Commission on British Muslims and Islamophobia (1997).

[9]   Fuad Nahdi, 'Conversation with Professor Gordon Conway', *Q News*, 3–16 October 1997.

[10]   Unpublished response to the document by the Islamic Foundation (March 1997). For more about the Foundation, see http://www.islamic-foundation.org.uk.

[11]   Unpublished letter from the Revd Dr David Thomas to the Runnymede Trust (29 April 1997).

[12]   Unpublished letter from Professor Jorgen Nielsen to the Runnymede Trust (9 May 1997).

[13]   Ibid.

Two other responses however, those of Sharon Imtiaz the then editor of the British Muslims Monthly Survey (BMMS) and the Muslim Educational Trust, were also both largely positive.[14]

Islamophobia, A Challenge for us All: 'to fear or dislike of all or most Muslims'

The Runnymede Report was published in October 1997 and became a landmark in the establishment and development of Islamophobia both as a phenomenon and a concept. In the contemporary socio-political setting, it is a publication that has also influenced not only British ways of thinking about Islamophobia but also those from Europe and beyond. As Conway's foreword notes, it sought to provide:

> a fuller explanation of Islamophobia and of its consequences throughout society, and sets out recommendations for practical action – by government, by teachers, lawyers and journalists, and by religious and community leaders ... a set of proposals which will result in decisive action to eliminate discrimination and prejudice against Muslims.[15]

Acknowledging the limitations and credibility of 'Islamophobia' as a suitable and adequate neologism, it justified its use by suggesting that a new phenomenon of increasing voracity needed a new name. In doing so, the report became the first source to offer a comprehensive definition of Islamophobia: the 'shorthand way of referring to dread or hatred of Islam – and, therefore, to fear or dislike of all or most Muslims'.[16] It is important to note that within the first few pages of the report however this definition changed. In doing so, the report's definition became the 'phobic dread of Islam ... the recurring characteristic of *closed views*'.[17] Still a phobic dread but one that was best understood through the conceptualisation of the Runnymede model itself. Before the report had even established or explained the 'closed views', its relevance and significance had been elevated to such that it was an integral and necessary foundation of understanding. Whilst the 'closed views' will be fully considered, a succinct explanation is offered by Philip Lewis:

> a closed view presents Islam as monolithic and static, an aggressive and ideological enemy to be combated. Muslim minorities should thus be exposed to scrutiny and social control; and there is no need to take seriously any criticisms

---

[14]   Both documents unpublished, letter from Sharon Imtiaz to the Runnymede Trust (4 April 1997) and consultation paper from the Muslim Educational Trust (undated).

[15]   Runnymede Trust: Commission on British Muslims and Islamophobia (1997), iii.

[16]   Ibid., 1.

[17]   Ibid., italics added.

they may make of Western society ... the open view acknowledges that Islam, like Christianity, is diverse, dynamic and in dialogue with wider society.[18]

In raising the profile and giving credence to Islamophobia in the public and political domains, the report not only initiated a discussion about Islamophobia. It also acquired a reputation of authority: one it must be concluded that has been subjected to minimal critical and theoretical analysis. This is not necessarily surprising in that critical and theoretical analyses tend to apply to academic pieces of research and enquiry, something that the Runnymede Report was – at the time of its publication at least – most definitely not. Instead the report was a policy document devised to: raise awareness of what was, at the time, a relatively unknown and unexplored phenomenon across a range of different socio-political spaces; influence and assist policy and decision-makers; and provide a substantial and informed resource for those working in the field of equalities and beyond. As the report suggests, it sought to initiate:

> practical action – by government, by teachers, lawyers and journalists, and by religious and community leaders ... presenting here a set of views which will command widespread support, and a set of proposals which will result in decisive action to eliminate discrimination and prejudice in our society.[19]

Yet whilst the report was far from academic, it was nonetheless a report that had the very specific intention to shape and influence understanding and to make a significant impact, and by consequence, change also.

Response to the Report: 'nice words and exercises in futility'

Following publication, the report's impact was duly acknowledged by a number of different organisations and voices from across Britain's Muslim communities. The UKACIA described it as a 'path-breaking document' where for the first time Muslims were seen to be a 'supra-ethnic' community.[20] To what extent 'supra-ethnic' used in this way reinforces a view of Muslims as unidimensional remains questionable. Nonetheless, the report itself largely substituted the 'supra' for the 'specific' where 'Pakistani' and 'Bangladeshi' became substitutable representatives for all others. Similar sentiments to the UKACIA were voiced elsewhere, as with Nahdi through his mouthpiece publication *Q News*, describing the report as a 'watershed in the relationship between the British establishment and Islam'. Javaid Akhtar of the Pakistan Forum of Britain responded somewhat less eloquently by stating, 'I agree

---

[18]   Philip Lewis, 'Islamophobia: a Challenge to us All', *The Church Times*, 24 October 1997.

[19]   Runnymede Trust: Commission on British Muslims and Islamophobia (1997), iii.

[20]   UKACIA Press release, 22 October 1997.

entirely with this report'.[21] Such responses reflect the positive nature of the mood gauged from the consultation period when as the Muslim National Trust suggested in the *Daily Jang*, 'this is perhaps the first attempt to focus on its scale and depth for the benefit of the wider British community'.[22] Yet whilst the pioneering and groundbreaking nature of the report was clearly welcomed, very few responses made any specific or detailed reference to either the report's contents or findings. Nonetheless, it should be noted that the focusing of attention onto the phenomenon and issues relating to Islamophobia was reason enough to congratulate it, a point that should not be negated in any way.

Other Muslim voices were more dissenting though, including those such as Ghayassudin Siddiqui of the Muslim Parliament who declared that he was 'sick and tired of hearing "nice words" and exercises in futility ...' noting how '... all these things have been said before'.[23] The *Muslim News* through its editor Ahmed Versi, was as equally non-congratulatory and in a number of published articles, openly questioned the report's credibility. One in particular argued that 'the report did not have a free hand to be objective and balanced ... In this respect, it may, in hindsight be viewed as a wasted opportunity'.[24] Versi's views were not isolated and those such as Syed Aziz Pasha, the Secretary of the Union of Muslim Organisations argued that 'the whole exercise is counter-productive ... one that is contributing to Islamophobia, not combating it'.[25] The overall response from Muslim organisations and individual voices was therefore far from categorical. Whilst the pioneering significance of the report was recurrent, some dissatisfaction was also clearly evident.

The IHRC was another organisation to express their ire. Attempting to clarify its position, the IHRC suggested that the report was doomed to fail because of the exclusive attitude of the Commission's construction that excluded controversial or non-mainstream voices from being heard. It argued that as the Commission sought to establish a legitimised and mainstream representative body, certain 'types' of Muslim were more accepted and granted representation. It also argued that the Commission de-legitimised those that were excluded and further marginalised those deemed to be on the fringe.[26] In an interview with Commission member Rabbi Julia Neuberger, not only did she confirm that interfaith principles were key in the formulation of the Commission's make-up but that they were vital to all the key concepts.[27] Unfortunately, the exact selection process and criteria employed for

---

[21]   *Q News*, 1–20 November 1997.

[22]   *Birmingham Evening Mail*, 22 May 1997.

[23]   'No more Muslim apartheid', *Q News*, 1–20 November 1997.

[24]   'Welcome Islamophobia Report Falls into Trap of Demonising Muslims', *Muslim News*, 31 October 1997.

[25]   'Runnymede's Islamophobia Launch Overshadowed by Controversy', *Muslim News*, 31 October 1997.

[26]   'No More Muslim Apartheid', *Q News*, 1–20 November 1997.

[27]   Electronic interview (3 March 2003).

membership of the remains unknown but what with there being some anecdotal evidence in circulation to suggest that certain members of the Commission were hand-picked for mainstream credibility rather than their contribution, it might be that the IHRC's suggestions are not entirely refutable. Anecdotally, some that were close to the Commission have suggested that certain members were mere 'talking heads' and were in place solely because they appealed to those that held political power.

The *Muslim News* continued in an even more controversial vein, claiming that the report demonised the victims of Islamophobia and internalised blame and responsibility, and in some ways, that the report was even pro-Jewish. Whilst the newspaper's allegations may suggest minor sensationalism, some evidence would appear to exist that offers some substantiation. To highlight this issue, *The Muslim News* noted that:

> the report has fallen into the trap of demonising Muslims on various issues … on the one hand it condemns the print media of stereotyping Islam and Muslims, on the other hand it perpetuates it … it regurgitates such views as 'some Islamists support terror', that Islam can be divided into 'political Islam' and 'religious Islam'.[28]

Consequently, it suggested that the report was contradictory where criticisms were simultaneously decried yet also reinforced. Whilst the *Muslim News* appears to overlook the reality that some Muslims do reflect the behaviour and actions of those stereotypes – not however suggesting that such realities either endorse or justify Islamophobia but merely as an acknowledgement that they do exist – its argument relating to the language that is being employed, both by the report's authors and those that the report is challenging, highlights a serious disparity between the Runnymede's Islamophobia and Anti-Semitism Reports.

In *A Very Light Sleeper* no apportioning of blame against its victims can be identified whereas in the Islamophobia Report, this is more open to debate. Throughout the Anti-Semitism Report, a number of non-religious individuals, groups and communities are highlighted as having particular anti-Semitic attitudes or beliefs, one particular example being where Muslims themselves are pinpointed.[29] However the point is best highlighted in the chapter *Reflections and Conclusions* where the report suggests that Christian, Muslim and interestingly Sikh leaders have an ongoing responsibility to ensuring that a positive attitude towards Judaism and its adherents is encouraged and maintained.[30] At the same time though, no Jewish organisations, individuals, religious or community

---

[28]   'Welcome Islamophobia Report Falls into the Trap of Demonising Muslims', *Muslim News*, 31 October 1997.

[29]   Runnymede Trust: Commission on British Muslims and Islamophobia (1997), sections 79 and 80:56.

[30]   Ibid., sections 16–19: 61.

leaders are apportioned any similar responsibilities. By implication therefore, one might assume that anti-Semitic stereotypes would appear to emanate from the perceptions of others about what Jewish people are and what Judaism is rather than from 'Jewishness' itself. Anti-Semitism must therefore exist solely within non-Jewish communities: something that those of Jewish heritage encounter and become victims of and that is it.

In a somewhat more oppositional context however is the Islamophobia Report, where it is implied on a number of occasions that not only do some marginally placed Muslims exacerbate Islamophobia but that Muslims also need to address these 'problems'. Whilst the report states that, 'Hindu and Sikh leaders have important roles to play in combating Islamophobia in their own communities'[31] and that leaders have a responsibility to defeat the Islamophobia that exists within certain Christian denominations, no specific reference to the role of Jews or Jewish communities is made. Unlike the earlier report on anti-Semitism, the blaming of victims albeit implicitly is nonetheless inferred in the Islamophobia Report. Quite significantly therefore, this would seem to suggest that the Islamophobia Report does in some ways internalise the 'problem' of Islamophobia within Muslim communities and indeed within Islam itself. So when the *Muslim News* writes that 'whilst the report accuses Christians, Hindus and Sikhs of fanning Islamophobia, it fails to include the Jewish leadership',[32] such a criticism is to some extent legitimate. Had the Commission employed the use of 'touchstones' as they themselves suggested and urged for journalists, substituting 'Muslim' with 'Jew' and vice versa, they would have noticed a marked disparity between the two reports.

The Muslim community's response to the Runnymede Report was therefore somewhat bi-polar. It was either emphatically supported and endorsed on the one hand, or wholeheartedly questioned and criticised on the other, a pattern that was identifiable in other faith communities also. Whilst responses from Sikh and Hindu communities have been difficult to locate, numerous Christian sources routinely aired their views. Regarding the larger institutional denominations and their representatives, the report was largely welcomed. The Churches Commission on Inter-Faith Relations for example gave its backing to the report,[33] whilst one commentator in the *Methodist Recorder* suggested that it strengthened the processes of bridge building.[34] The response from the *Catholic Herald* was one that not only supported the document but also drew parallels between the attitudes being shown towards Muslims contemporarily and the anti-Papism that Irish Catholics encountered on entering Britain centuries beforehand.[35] Concerning the Church of England, in his role as interfaith advisor to the Bishop of Bradford,

[31]   Ibid., 52.

[32]   'Welcome Islamophobia Report Falls into Trap of Demonising Muslims', *Muslim News*, 31 October 1997.

[33]   *British Muslim Monthly Survey*, Vol. V, no. 10: 2–3.

[34]   Ibid., 2.

[35]   Ibid.

Philip Lewis became a vocal presence in much of its response and subsequent reporting. In doing so, the stress on interfaith and its perceived benefits became recurrent themes that were stressed as being of paramount importance.[36]

Beyond the more institutionalised forms of Christianity, some voices were less congratulatory and supportive. Reverend Patrick Sookhdeo of the Institute for the Study of Islam and Christianity (ISIC), for example suggested: 'the paper is exceedingly weak for a major report of this kind and leaves much to be desired. It does not distinguish enough between ethnicity and religion'.[37] An editorial in the Christian publication, *Third Way*, suggested similar. In the report there was a real:

> failure to demonstrate explicitly that hostility and violence towards Muslims are primarily sectarian as opposed to ethnic. It could have examined the experience of converts to Islam – especially men who do not dress distinctively – to determine whether they had been victims of discrimination.[38]

It would seem that the evidence to substantiate an Islamophobia – based entirely upon markers of Islamic-ness or Muslim-ness – was far from convincing. However, whilst the ISIC and *Third Way* editorial responses both focused on the report's conceptualisation of Islamophobia, a growing unrest within some Christian communities towards Muslims did become apparent. Leslie Newbiggin's article, again in *Third Way*, expressed the view that the presence of Muslim communities in Britain was presenting a very serious challenge to Christians, something they needed not only to engage with but also respond to: '[the report] does not really address the serious issues or the real challenge which Islam is posing'.[39] Similar concerns were also voiced by representatives of the London Bible College (LBC) who suggested in the *New Christian Herald* that the report further exacerbated the 'sense of frustration by British Christians ...' which '... will only lead to resentment and increasing hostility towards the other side [Muslims]'.[40] As with so many of the responses though, very little qualification of such arguments were put forward thus leaving a situation where the causes and sentiments underpinning such resentment remain unclear.

Westophobia: Anti-Western and Anti-Christian Stereotyping in British Muslim Publications

The LBC's Centre for Islamic Studies and Muslim-Christian Relations took their criticism further and even possibly sought to mock the Runnymede Report and

---

[36] *Church Times*, 24 October 1997.
[37] Ibid.
[38] *British Muslim Monthly Survey*, Vol. V, no. 10: 3.
[39] Ibid.
[40] *New Christian Herald*, 19 July 1997.

its notion of Islamophobia. The Centre produced a document that was intended to raise awareness of the 'Westophobia' of Muslims towards Christians and the West. Employing a publishing name extremely similar to the CSIC at the University of Birmingham it produced a short document, *The Westophobia Report: Anti-Western and Anti-Christian Stereotyping in British Muslim Publications.*[41] Almost entirely replicating the first two chapters of the Runnymede Report, the LBC Report merely substituted the words 'West' or 'Christianity', and 'Christian' or 'Westerner' for 'Islam' and 'Muslim' respectively. In doing so, the LBC wrote that the Westophobia Report was a direct response to its Runnymede counterpart. Whilst the LBC appears to have withdrawn the document shortly after its publication, it argued that the Westophobia Report was 'no trivial exercise in "tit-for-tat" one-up-manship'.[42] The reality though might be that that is exactly what the LBC Report was. It could even be argued that the 'tit-for-tat' nature of the LBC Report highlighted those aspects of superficiality that were inherent within the Runnymede Report. Interestingly, the Westophobia Report has recently been in circulation again.

Beyond the thinly disguised somewhat mocking tones of the Westophobia Report there was also some anger that could be identified in the response of others to the Runnymede Report. As with the writers Faye Weldon and Peregrine Worsthorne, both of whom had some of their writing highlighted in the Runnymede Report as examples of Islamophobia, not only were they vehemently opposed to the report but also to the very concept of Islamophobia. Worsthorne himself even went to the extremes of blaming the 'Mohammedans' for Islamophobia.[43] Whilst not necessarily providing a balanced argument, those such as Paul Vallely seemed to voice particularly well what seemed to be the intrinsic dilemma underpinning and subsequently unanswered in the report: how to differentiate between what is and is not Islamophobia:

> many less educated women are oppressed by Islam. That some Shariah laws are barbaric. That Muslim tradition is anti-democratic and, as the Rushdie affair showed, a threat to Western liberal values. That there is something inherently violent about the notion of jihad ... and yet there is something that makes me think that these are the very myths of Islamophobia, planted and nurtured by ignorance.[44]

Similar can be seen in the response of Trevor Phillips, a member of the Commission and one time Chair of the Commission for Racial Equality (CRE), writing in the *Independent* shortly after the report's publication:

---

[41]   London Bible College, *The Westophobia Report: Anti-Western and Anti-Christian Stereotyping in British Muslim Publications* (London: London Bible College, 1999).

[42]   Ibid., 3.

[43]   *British Muslim Monthly Survey*, Vol. V, no. 2: 4.

[44]   *British Muslim Monthly Survey*, Vol. V, no. 10: 3.

the case against Islam rests heavily upon the supposed experience of women. I instinctively find it hard to understand the apparently inferior position of women in many Islamic societies; ... [yet] can one ignore the evidence of many independent, clearly self-possessed Muslim women who say that within their tradition, their status and their rights as women are protected?[45]

For both Phillips and Vallely there appears to be a split between what they personally understand and seemingly dislike about Islam (its inferiority, oppression, misogyny and so on) and that which they see being presented to them by real people (an independence, self-assertion, commitment to equal rights and so on). Whilst one would presume that Phillips would have had greater clarity in his reflection, being a member of the Commission, so it would seem to suggest that not only did a deep-rooted lack of clarity about Islamophobia exist in the wider spaces but that it might have emanated from the thinking of the very people responsible for the report themselves.

Elsewhere commentators such as Polly Toynbee voiced similar concerns to those such as Sookhdeo and the ISIC. Just two days before Phillips' meandering, the problem for her was much clearer: 'racism is the problem, not religion'.[46] Whilst Toynbee might be described as being anti-religion per se, the fact remains that many immediately after the report's publication were far from convinced about the legitimacy of an Islamophobia that was both distinct and real. The question 'what is Islamophobia?' remained a recurrent question, identifiable in the response to the report by the Government also. Launching the document at the House of Commons, the then Home Secretary Jack Straw immediately resisted two of the report's central recommendations: the need for equity between faiths as regards state funded Muslim schools; and second, the call for legislation to protect against religious discrimination. As he said:

> [the Government] do have immediate plans to legislate on racial violence. I am sick to death of the mindless bigotry and thuggery which damages and destroys the lives of so many people in this country ... It is a continuing shame to our society, and as a society, we must not tolerate it.[47]

What this highlighted however was that Straw and the Government had failed to distinguish between race and religion, the very foundations upon which any Islamophobia must be differentiated. As many of the examples provided here illustrate, whilst the report was apparently concerned with a phenomenon that was necessarily based on markers of faith or 'Muslim-ness', the final publication lacked the necessary evidence and argument to convince of this reality. Consequently

---

45   *Independent*, 25 October 1997.
46   *Independent*, 23 October 1997.
47   *Q News*, 1–20 November 1997.

and with hindsight, it might be suggested that the report failed to categorically establish the case for a very real and distinct Islamophobia.

Chair of the Commission Gordon Conway contributed to this and expressed a similar disparity. In an interview following the report's publication, some of his language and terminology was less than straightforward. Whilst acknowledging the contribution of all the Commission's members he stated that 'still too many stereotypes exist about this *strange* "Pakistani/Arab" religion' (emphasis added).[48] Having overseen the research for almost two years, one interpretation of his comments could be construed that Conway was interpreting Islam as a 'strange "Pakistani/ Arab" religion'. Whilst most appropriately he would appear to be paraphrasing prevalent stereotypical misunderstandings, it could be interpreted as putting forward that Islam itself was 'strange' and thus inferring an inherent Otherness to it: possibly 'strange' because it was against the religio-cultural norms of Conway. Whilst these were probably far from Conway's own views, it must be noted that his words could have been misconstrued and by consequence, seen to be counter-productive.

Failings and Flaws: 'looked at in detail'

Evidence would suggest that some criticisms of the report were justified: its failure to differentiate between race and religion and in doing so, its failure to argue for the existence of a distinct and differentiable Islamophobia. Throughout the report the number of times that 'Muslim' was substituted or referred to by a marker of South Asian heritage was 127 times, equivalent to 70.5 per cent of all references in the text. Of these, 'Pakistani' (including 'Paki') was used 60 times, 'Bangladeshi' 36, 'South Asian' 24 and 'Indian' 7. 'Arab' (including 'Middle Eastern' and markers of those countries geographically located in the region) was used 20 times, equivalent to 10 per cent of the total usage. Less than 20 per cent of the text refers to Muslims of non-South Asian or non-Arab descent and even when the report speaks of 'British Muslims' it typically qualifies this by adding additional racial or ethnic markers. The report further exacerbates the situation by heavily focusing on high South Asian heritage Muslim percentage population locales, where Bradford accounts for nearly a third of all examples. Aside from the anomalous case study on Chichester, the evidence employed is therefore undeniably weighted towards those of South Asian heritage. An interesting observation is that 'Black Muslims' – indigenous converts of African-Caribbean heritage – are mentioned only twice whilst 'white Muslims' – indigenous converts of white, British or Irish descent – are completely overlooked.

The dependency upon Muslims of South Asian heritage and the setting of Bradford can be highlighted through the role of Philip Lewis, author of *Islamic Britain: Religion, Politics and Identity among British Muslims*.[49] Having

---

[48]   *Q News*, 3–16 October 1997.

[49]   Philip Lewis, *Islamic Britain: Religion, Politics and Identity among British Muslims* (London: IB Tauris, 1994).

acknowledged that 'the Bradford experience … will be looked at in detail'[50] as part of the Commission's consultative process, in an article written after the report's publication, *Facing Down the Bogeyman of Islam*,[51] Lewis himself blurred the distinctions between religion and race by referring to 'Paki-bashing' as a form of Islamophobia. He again made a similar blurred reference in the *Church Times* at a later date.[52] Whilst the report quotes from Hanif Kureishi's novel, *The Black Album* to highlight the shift in Muslim self-identity since the 1980s quoting the line 'No more Paki. Me a Muslim',[53] it is questionable whether either the report or the Commission wholeheartedly acknowledged this transition for themselves. So whilst the report sought to challenge stereotypical meanings and ideas about Muslims and Islam, evidence would suggest that it was not entirely successful in doing so. Albeit far from deliberate or intentional, a lack of clarity about Islamophobia and its differentiable and constituent components were in evidence from the outset. One must therefore rightly question the report if within weeks of its publication, the understandings that were being gleaned from it and from those individuals that had been integral to its formulation, were unable or unclear about voicing or determining exactly what Islamophobia was.

Despite the influence of the Runnymede Report as noted in the historiography and its permeation through the entirety of thinking about Islamophobia since, from the outset the report failed to differentiate between Islamophobia and other similar phenomena based upon markers of race, ethnicity and so on. Barring one example,[54] wherever statistical data was employed in the report religious markers and identifiers were overlooked to the extent where 'Muslim' repeatedly failed to be either identified or mentioned. Yet still the report claimed that it was challenging and combating the perception that Muslims are 'pictured as undifferentiated, static and monolithic, and as intolerant of internal pluralism and deliberation … [where] sweeping generalisations are then made about all Muslims'.[55] The reality was as Halliday suggests, that the report presented Muslims in such ways that they become a *monist abstraction*, over-simplified and substitutable primarily by the marker 'Pakistani' or even worse 'Asian':[56] 'Asian' being a term that Modood and others had already deemed inappropriate and unworkable. Consequently, both clear evidence and clear understanding of an argument for an 'Islam' or 'Muslim' specific phenomenon failed to emerge from the report and a seemingly unclear phenomenon was – or indeed had – been established in the public and political spaces.

---

50   *Bradford Telegraph & Argus*, 22 February 1997.
51   'Facing Down the Bogeyman of Islam', *Q News*, November 1997.
52   *Church Times*, 25 October 1997.
53   Runnymede Trust: Commission on British Muslims and Islamophobia (1997a), 15.
54   Ibid., table 6: 37.
55   Runnymede Trust: Commission on British Muslims and Islamophobia (1997a), 6.
56   Halliday (2002).

Chapter 5
Runnymede: An Open and Closed Case

Within the first few paragraphs of the Runnymede Report, the definition of Islamophobia was transformed from the 'shorthand way of referring to dread or hatred of Islam – and, therefore, to fear or dislike of all or most Muslims'.[1] Transforming it to an entirely Runnymede-centric understanding, the new definition necessitated Islamophobia as 'the recurring characteristic of closed views'.[2] Both in the report and in the ensuing discourses since, the 'closed views' and to a lesser degree the 'open views' have become not only a recurrent means through which Islamophobia is framed and identified but also conceptualised and defined. What with the report having since permeated all the ensuing debates and discourses of Islamophobia, so the Runnymede model constructed around the closed views has been the foundation upon which the vast majority of understanding and ideas about Islamophobia have since been rooted despite there having been little critical analysis of the report being offered. This chapter will therefore begin to redress this issue, deconstructing the Runnymede model's of Islamophobia in an attempt to better understand what the Runnymede Report established Islamophobia as being.

The End of History: 'a repudiation of the power which stories from the past have'

It would be too simplistic to explain Islamophobia as a mere consequence of a diametrically opposed history with the West. In terms of the Runnymede Report, whilst acknowledging the influence of history's legacy it also identifies Islamophobia as a new and contemporarily specific phenomenon: a new reality that needed naming.[3] As the report went on, 'the task of combating Islamophobia involves a repudiation of the power which stories from the past in general, and the Crusades in particular, do certainly have'.[4] Here the report highlights a markedly different understanding of history to that which was apparent in the Anti-Semitism Report. There it argued that Islamophobia needed to be historically contextualised, suggesting that as with Jews in the contemporary context still being dogged by medieval myths so too were today's Muslims dogged by myths originating from

---

[1]   Runnymede Trust: Commission on British Muslims and Islamophobia (1997a), 1.
[2]   Ibid., 3.
[3]   Runnymede Trust: Commission on British Muslims and Islamophobia (1997a), 4.
[4]   Ibid., 5.

similar historical paradigms.[5] From a position where history is contemporarily relevant to one where its power must be repudiated is something of a major step and one that suggests a lack of consistency between comparable phenomena.

In the Anti-Semitism Report, the power and legacy of the historical evolution of anti-Semitism constitutes a substantial element.[6] Why the power of history is therefore less important to the shaping and determination of Islamophobia is unclear. If as regards Islamophobia, history's power is distracting and irrelevant, then it must be that the contemporary phenomenon exists in a vacuum that is disengaged from the influence of history. The report therefore necessitates the overlooking and removal of history's legacy irrespective of whether there is any interconnectedness or inference with any other historical events or junctures. As regards contemporary anti-Semitism, whilst history and its legacy appear entirely relevant to the anti-Semitic experience – or so the report suggests – in terms of the Islamophobic experience, that similar significance would not appear to have the same value or resonance. Why? Without answering that question – and indeed the report fails to do this – Islamophobia's emergence, development and discourse therefore appear to be attributed with much less relevance and importance.

This is of course quite contentious because whilst there would appear to be some disengagement between the different events and junctures throughout history, they cannot necessarily be entirely rejected or dismissed: repudiated to use the report's language. Whilst it cites Halliday to substantiate their viewpoint, Halliday himself argues something quite different. Halliday states that 'to identify these relics and revivals [of anti-Muslim expression or belief] is not to prove a continuity of culture or politics'[7] but – writing some years after the report's publication – that 'the past provides a reserve of reference and symbol for the present: it does not explain it ...' because '... significant differences of emphasis, prejudice and engagement depending on the colonial histories, the geographical location and the composition of the immigrant community' have emerged.[8] History therefore is be used as a frame of reference to assist and explain contemporary understanding. And this is the function of Chapters 2 and 3 here, to provide the necessary context and framework to better understand the context and setting of the first chapter's historiography of contemporary Islamophobia. Consequently, the report's premise for insisting upon a repudiation of history is both precarious and misappropriated. Shifting understanding from where history is a framework for understanding to one where it becomes detrimental to understanding and highlights a flaw in the report's theoretical premise. Clearly, without a thorough understanding of history and an awareness of its meanings, that which is happening in the contemporary cannot be either fully understood or indeed appreciated.

---

[5]　Runnymede Commission on Anti-Semitism (1994), 55.

[6]　Ibid., 32–41.

[7]　Halliday (1999), 179.

[8]　Halliday (2002), 125.

The Runnymede Model: 'a single set of concepts, a single language'

And in line with this, so the 'closed views' typology appears particularly problematic. Given that the 1997 report offers scant discussion on the construction and origins of the typology, very little was known about this until it was addressed albeit briefly in the Commission's report in 2004.[9] Robin Richardson is able to offer a clearer picture of where the typology came from because, as he put it, it was he who 'translated' the consultations, meetings, discussions and visits into the text of the report.[10] In distilling these findings into a working outline, Richardson initially proposed a document that suggested seven 'features' of Islamophobic discourse in preference to 'views': 'features' that he suggests were extremely similar to the typology in the final publication. From here a Commission sub-group, overseen by Richard Stone, took responsibility for developing these into a tabulated form that would allow for Islamophobia to be clearly and easily understood. As Richardson explained, 'I agreed, but couldn't immediately see how to do this without inviting the criticism that we saw the alternative to Islamophobia merely as, as the term might be, Islamophilia'.[11] The way in which Richardson and the sub-group sought to achieve this was to look at existing typologies of attitudes and beliefs from where Richardson in particular sought to re-evaluate the work of Milton Rokeach, a social psychologist whose research he had encountered years before. It was Rokeach who had first used the concept of the 'closed' or 'open' mind[12] and Richardson found this helpful in explaining how the features of Islamophobia could be tabulated. Using Rokeach as a foundation, it was only Lewis that made any changes to the new typology by suggesting alternative phrasings and a few minor modifications.

With little questioning of Rokeach being apparent from within the Commission, a re-evaluation of his work raises some interesting questions about the Runnymede model of Islamophobia as well as the views of the Commission. Developed between 1951 and 1954 in the US, and to a lesser degree in London, Rokeach's objective was to establish an authoritative typology to understand human psychological reasoning as regards beliefs and values. His goal was to achieve 'a single set of concepts, a single language, that is equally appropriate to the analysis of personality, ideology and cognitive behaviour ... to arrive at a conception

---

[9] Commission on British Muslims and Islamophobia, *Islamophobia: Issues, Challenges and Action* (Stoke on Trent: Trentham Books, 2004).

[10] Personal interview, 2003.

[11] Ibid.

[12] Milton Rokeach, *The Open and Closed Mind* (New York: Basic Books Inc., 1960). Whilst this is the primary source for understanding the open and closed mind, related theories can be further explored in Milton Rokeach, *The Nature of Human Values* (New York: The Free Press, 1973), and Milton Rokeach, *Understanding Human Values* (New York: The Free Press, 1979).

of intolerance and prejudice which is also ahistorical'.[13] In trying to locate and understand those who were 'closed' in their thought or belief using his Dogmatism Scale, his research became heavily influenced by the socio-political and geo-political context of the time. From the perspective of the US, this was one that was externally concerned with the Communist Other and internally with the first throes of the Civil Rights Movement. Rokeach's work therefore seems to be indebted to these contextual factors to the extent that they determine much of his thinking and subsequent outcomes. For instance, throughout his pursuit of analysing the open and closed mind, he significantly differentiates between 'Whites' and 'Negroes'[14] as indeed he does between Americans who have right and left wing political viewpoints, routinely describing those on the left as 'Communists'. So skewed is his understanding that throughout his London-based research, he repeatedly and inappropriately described Labour Party supporters as Communists.

Rokeach's methodological processes and the empirical evidence that he employed to formulate his findings also require some scrutiny. In writing about how the closed views were codified he states, 'some of the statements appearing in the Dogmatism Scale were inspired by spontaneous remarks we overheard being made by persons we thought intuitively to be close-minded'.[15] From such a premise where 'spontaneous remarks were overheard' and where individuals were '*thought* intuitively to be close-minded' (italics added) it might be fair to question the methodological process and in particular any ongoing claims to theoretical relevance. This particular analysis does not however set out to either validate or invalidate such claims, nor is it to underestimate or negate the research of Rokeach within his own specialist field. Indeed as Miguel Farias at the University of Oxford explains, Rokeach's research has been extremely important and a seminal influence.[16] More appropriate is to raise questions about the legitimacy of using Rokeach as a foundation upon which to establish and conceptualise Islamophobia in the contemporary setting.

What is interesting is how Rokeach's typology and its appropriation would seem to have had a determinative effect on the Commission's thinking. What with the 'closed mind' being both the foundation for theoretical development and the definition of Islamophobia, did the Commission understand or interpret Islamophobia as a social psychological phenomenon? Whilst this cannot be answered either way, evidence would appear to suggest that this might have been so, most notably in the similarities between both Rokeach and the Commission's

---

[13]   Ibid., 7–9.

[14]   Ibid. I use the term 'Negroes' here as replication of Rokeach's terminology but acknowledge the inappropriateness of the term in the contemporary context.

[15]   Ibid., 72. The Dogmatism Scale referred to in this reference is the name given by Rokeach to the tabulated form of closed and open distinctions that he established. Dogmatism, for Rokeach, was the name given to individual's and community's intolerance.

[16]   Electronic interview with Miguel Farias, Department of Experimental Psychology, University of Oxford (30 April 2003).

desire to establish a single ahistorical set of concepts. In a very brief and impromptu discussion with the incumbent Chair of the Commission at the time, Richard Stone, he suggested that the closed views of Islamophobia were 'as relevant today as they were then, and will no doubt continue to be'.[17] To some degree, both Rokeach and the Commission's model become quite complimentary in their collaborative purpose. Consequently, one might conclude that the use of Rokeach's theories was either that it concurred with pre-conceived ideas about how Islamophobia was understood by the Commission or that Rokeach's influence was significant in that it shaped the Commission's thinking. It is therefore right to ask whether the term Islamophobia and its emphasis upon 'phobia' was more appropriate to the thinking underpinning the consultation and formulation process than might have previously been apparent.

Closed and Open: 'the features of Islamophobia'

The Runnymede model was clearly conceptualised with the intention of establishing a single set of concepts that could and indeed subsequently have been used to define and identify manifestations of Islamophobia, where 'the features of closed views ...' are entirely equitable to '... the features of Islamophobia'.[18] To fully understand each of the 'closed' and 'open' views, an explanation of each is set out below.

1. Islam is Seen as Monolithic and Static Rather than Diverse and Dynamic

This view suggests that Islam is seen as a single monolithic bloc where Muslim diversity is overlooked both in terms of differences between Muslims and also between Muslims and non-Muslims. Muslims are also seen to be static and unresponsive to new realities and challenges. Sweeping generalisations insist that the negative attributes and characteristics of a few become projected onto all Muslims without differentiation: 'any episode in which an individual Muslim is judged to have behaved badly is used as an illustrative example to condemn all Muslims without exception'.[19] Over-simplifying or ignoring the majority Muslim

---

[17] Paraphrased from a brief telephone discussion with Richard Stone (14 February 2003). Despite numerous requests, Dr Stone felt unable to participate in a full interview regarding his personal involvement in the Commission and was neither able to answer any structured questions in verbal, written or electronic forms, nor indeed were any of his assistants. The telephone discussion was an unscheduled call made by Dr Stone and so any attempt to incorporate structure and/or coherency was limited. In the discussion, Dr Stone was able to give some standard responses to the report and also agreed to send some of his personal writings on the subject, although these have never been received.

[18] Runnymede Trust: Commission on British Muslims and Islamophobia (1997), 4.

[19] Ibid., 5.

experience, such projections draw particular attention to the term 'fundamentalism' and its use in the media as an inappropriate marker of identification.

Little is elaborated upon about the corresponding open view. From its tabulation, open views see Islam as diverse and progressive where internal differences, debates and development are acknowledged. Examples of difference and diversity include the expression of Islam across different geographical locations, different interpretations of the Qur'an, the different experiences of men and women as well as between young and old.[20]

Whilst appearing significant the Commission seemingly overlooked how Muslims were represented in the report itself, disproportionately focusing upon those of South Asian heritage to the exclusion of most other Muslims. Worthy of note also is the way in which 'Islam' was used as a marker for identity within the closed views rather than and in preference of 'Muslim(s)'.

2.   *Islam Seen as Other and Separate Rather than Similar and Interdependent*

Here Islam is seen as the bi-polar opposite of 'the West', where 'Islam' is understood to have no shared values with it or indeed any other culture or religion. This closed view infers that Islam is isolated from other cultures and religions neither influencing nor affecting them in any way. The same stresses the impossibility and implausibility of Islam being 'European', 'British' and so on. Heavily rooted in the theories of Huntington,[21] the 'Islam' and 'the West' differential is strongly reminiscent of Said's 'Orient' and 'Occident'.[22] Whether the terminologies of 'Islam' and 'the West' are Islamophobic themselves is questionable despite such being inferred in the text: 'In the open view it is impossible to assert that … Islam is "East" and Europe is "West"'.[23]

Conversely the open view sees Islam as being interdependent with other cultures and faiths especially those from within the Abrahamic tradition.

3.   *Islam Seen as Inferior not Different*

Embodying the 'us' and 'them' bi-polar differentials that are equally evident in 'Islam' and 'the West', so Islam ('them') is understood to be inherently inferior to 'us'. Incorporated within such processes of stratification is the suggestion that Islam is primitive, irrational, violent, misogynist, sexist, scheming, disorganised, oppressive and barbaric, all of which are inherently deficient to 'Western' norms: 'civilised, reasonable, generous, efficient, sophisticated, enlightened, non-sexist'.[24]

---

[20]   Ibid., 6.

[21]   Huntington (1997).

[22]   Said (1979).

[23]   Runnymede Trust: Commission on British Muslims and Islamophobia (1997a), 6.

[24]   Ibid., 6.

Closed views also suggest that Islamic culture mistreats women, justifies political and military projects, and insists solely literalist interpretations of the Qur'an.

Whilst the report acknowledges how damaging dualistic interpretations of Islam can be, such interpretations are themselves embodied in the Runnymede model that is as equally dualistic in its 'open and closed'. It is therefore difficult to identify the benefit of 'open' and 'closed' for instance over such similar markers as 'us' and 'them'. In reference to Richardson's dilemma previously, whilst the report suggests that closed views cause Islamophobia one must also concede that any reciprocal and equally bi-polar response – open views – attains its validity and understanding by asserting itself as the opposite of Islamophobia. That is, Islamophilia. By differentiating between 'closed' and 'open' to explain 'us' and 'them' the report appears contradictory, embodying the same ideas and meanings but behind only different terminologies.

Problems also exist as regards such blanket assertions that Islam as 'irrational, violent, misogynist, sexist, scheming, disorganised and oppressive' is a closed view. For example, where might one locate an openly misogynist Muslim within this? If such a Muslim is encountered – making the assumption here that a misogynist Muslim is as probable as locating a misogynist person of any other faith rather than an observation about Muslims per se – can the highlighting of such, in the context of this particular closed view, be rather simplistically and superficially deemed Islamophobic? In response to Richardson's apparent concerns about charges of Islamophilia, 'closed' and 'open' would therefore appear to exacerbate rather than solve the problem.

4.   Islam Seen as an Enemy not as a Partner

Here Islam is seen to be largely violent, aggressive and firmly committed to terrorism against the West, reinforcing the theories of those such as Huntington et al. The report uses the example from Peregrine Worsthorne to illustrate this: 'Islam was once …' a great civilisation worthy of being argued with … [now] it has 'degenerated into a primitive enemy fit only to be sensitively subjugated'.[25] Open views suggest Islam as an actual or potential partner at international, regional or national levels where it should be encouraged to engage in co-operative and shared processes to solving problems. Beyond an understanding that interprets 'Islam' as a 'monolithic entity' it is unclear as to whom or what is meant by the marker of 'Islam' across the different international, regional and national contexts.

Such a point highlights a condition that permeates the entire report. Despite castigating Worsthorne for his inappropriate use of 'Islam' and 'Islamic' to describe 'Muslims' and 'Muslim communities', the report itself repeatedly does exactly the same. Likewise despite Richardson's fears of incurring charges of Islamophilia through the 'open views', such charges are possible in those instances where a Muslim openly espouses anti-Western views or is supportive of terrorism: would

---

[25]   Ibid., 7.

the legitimate and valid description of such a person – that is a 'closed' view of such a person – therefore be necessarily deemed Islamophobic? Unfortunately, no explanation or clarification is put forward by the report as to how such a situation might be alleviated. Legitimate debate therefore – somewhat against the Commission's wishes – could realistically become stifled.

5.   Muslims Seen as Manipulative not as Sincere

Closed views suggest that Islam is used for strategic, political and military advantage as opposed to it being a sincere and honest religion. Muslims are seen to be instrumental in using Islam as a political or ideological weapon.[26] Open views necessarily oppose this, where traditions and adherences are seen to be genuine and where Muslims practice their faith with conviction and sincerity. This closed view would appear to significantly interchange and overlap with others from within the model as seen in the examples given in Box 5 that illustrate the how Islam is 'seen as enemy not as partner': 'Muslims co-opt religious observance and beliefs to bolster or justify political and military projects'.[27] It is unclear from the text where the necessary differentiation exists.

6.   'Racial' Discrimination Against Muslims Defended Rather than Challenged

Such views identify Islamophobia as being initiated by and overlapping with other forms of racism. In doing so, Islamophobia becomes manifested through violence and harassment on the streets as well as in direct or indirect discrimination in the workplace. It notes how the media give legitimacy to such racist sentiments and expressions by highlighting how in the *Sun* newspaper 'Asian' and 'Muslim' became confused and blurred.[28] Open views prefer that debates and disagreements with Islam should neither hinder nor diminish attempts to combat wider forms of discrimination and exclusion.

   This closed view again has a resonance with the way in which the report itself fails to differentiate adequately between race and religion, something that is at times quite overwhelming. In noting such an overlap and interchange, it is therefore necessary to question whether the report provides sufficient evidence to substantiate an independent and distinct Islamophobia, as was suggested previously in the example of verbal abuse directed towards a 16 year old 'British Asian': 'Oi, Paki!...Wotcha doin' in our country? Go back where you belong'.[29]

---

[26]   Ibid., 8.
[27]   Ibid., 7.
[28]   Ibid., Box 7: 9–10.
[29]   Ibid., 38.

7. Muslim Criticisms of 'the West' Rejected not Considered

When criticisms of the West made by Islam are rejected without valid reflection or consideration, especially those made against liberalism, modernity and secularism, so the model suggests this as a closed view: one that excludes Muslims from being active participants in societal debates, dialogues and deliberations. As the report elaborates, 'Islamophobia prevents Muslims from being invited or encouraged to take a full part in society's moral deliberations and debates'.[30] Open views quite simply suggest the opposite to this, where criticisms of the West put forward by Muslims and the Islamic world should be both considered and debated instead of just being 'dismissed out of hand'.[31]

8. Anti-Muslim Discourse Seen as Natural not Problematic

Here it is noted that anti-Muslim expression is increasingly 'a natural, taken-for-granted ingredient of the commonsense world of millions of people every day'.[32] The media are highlighted as being prone to this as indeed are 'liberals' who the report suggests would normally campaign against such prejudices and discriminations if targeted at non-Muslims. The academic field is similarly criticised. Being unlike its predecessors, this view is much less a 'view' than a consequence or culmination of the preceding views: much more a statement of fact, conclusion or even a reason for undertaking the research rather than much else.

Islamophobia: 'part of the fabric of everyday life in Britain'

The final view concludes that, 'Islamophobic discourse, sometimes blatant but frequently subtle and coded, is part of the fabric of everyday life in Britain in much the same way that anti-Semitic discourse was taken for granted earlier in the century'.[33] With correlations again being drawn between Islamophobia and anti-Semitism, so the disparities between the two interlinked Runnymede Reports approach each of the phenomena is once more brought into focus. Whilst anti-Semitism was modelled on three broad and quite fluid categories,[34] Islamophobia became a much more dualistic process. Despite numerous reminders in the report of the similarities between Islamophobia, anti-Semitism and racism, little explanation is offered about why different models and typologies might be – and indeed were – required for each.

---

30   Ibid., 10.
31   Ibid.
32   Ibid.
33   Ibid., 11.
34   Runnymede Commission on Anti-Semitism (1994), 23–7.

The closed views may be best categorised into three types: perceptional, prejudicial or naturalised. The first five views form the first type, constructing a neat basis from which negatively evaluated perceptions of 'Islam' and 'Muslims' can be identified. These five also appear to be most appropriate to the description of being 'views'. The sixth and seventh views form the prejudicial type, whereas the final view falls into the naturalized type alone in that it is much more distinct: more an observation of the current climate rather than a specific perception, prejudice or indeed 'view'. The latter 'views' would therefore seem to require the need for some questioning about their appropriateness especially when the corresponding 'open view' for the final 'closed view' is little more than the identification for the need for good practice. As such, the 'views' are inconsistent and possibly even incoherent when considered as a typology.

Contesting Open and Closed: 'the mistake of those opposed to anti-Muslim prejudice'

The 'closed-open' differential therefore establishes a series of dualisms that appear, to some degree at least, to reinforce many of the 'closed views' themselves. As 'closed' and 'open' are largely interchangeable with 'negative' and 'positive', so the assumption must be that the report suggests that Islam be both understood and engaged with 'openly' or indeed 'positively', irrespective of whether any 'closed' or 'negative' realities exist to the contrary. Through the 'repudiation of the power'[35] of historical stories and events, so the meanings of the 'closed' views are such that they become isolated from the histories and historical contexts within which they might given meaning to, thus overlooking the reasons, events and issues of why and indeed how these meanings came about in the social consensus. This of course is worrying particularly given the fact that the report has acquired such authority whilst at the same time having had so little analysis undertaken of its findings. One of the few to have done so has been Halliday, whose criticisms have ranged from the construction of the Commission[36] through to the etymological reductionism of the term Islamophobia.[37] What is most relevant at this particular juncture is his criticism of the use of 'Islam' as an adequate identifier, something that would appear to have been identified – and subsequently overlooked – in the Commission's consultative endeavours by those such as Nielsen amongst others.

For Halliday, the report's use of 'Islam' as a marker ensures that it is little more than a unitary object, something of a relative abstraction.[38] The importance of differentiating between 'Muslim' and 'Islamic' has previously been discussed, but when a model is established that suggests that the 'closed

---

35   Runnymede Trust: Commission on British Muslims and Islamophobia (1997a), 5.
36   Halliday (2002), 60.
37   Halliday (1999).
38   Halliday (2002), 123.

views' are against 'Islam' as opposed 'Muslims', only two conclusions can be drawn. The first is that the dynamics of the phenomenon are against the actual religion of Islam, where it is the religion that is hated, feared, disliked and so on; the second being that if the model assumes a shared identity of all Muslims without differentiation behind a homogenising marker of 'Islam', so the diversity of Muslims and their respective communities is reduced to a single abstraction that is neither representative nor real. If the first is to be assumed, then questions must be asked about the validity of both the terminology and model because as Halliday suggests, whilst historically it is has been Islam that has been the focus for hostility and conflict, in the contemporary setting that focus has shifted much more towards a phenomenon against Muslims.[39] This would appear true where despite Islam remaining misunderstood in the current climate, it is the proximity and closeness of Muslims – real people in real environments – that are much more the focus of today's hostility.[40] As Islam is therefore no longer the primary focus, it is therefore questionable as to how applicable and relevant the neologism of Islamophobia is. Consequently, Halliday's preferred terminology appears to be 'anti-Muslimism'.[41]

Similar problems exist as regards the second conclusion faced by the deployment of 'Islam' as an identifier behind which a shared identity is assumed. Without the necessary and real diversity of Muslims being made known, so the inherent and somewhat necessary diversity of Muslims becomes reduced. Muslims are therefore reduced from a vibrant and myriad number of religiously affiliated peoples and communities to an over-simplified and uni-dimensional marker. As such, employing 'Islam' ensures that Muslims and all that this subsequently entails become irretrievably and irrefutably reduced. Through these processes of reductionism, the first closed view – the very same thing that the entire report is purporting to challenge – actually becomes manifested and underpinning of the report's own model of what Islamophobia is. And given the concern about the report's marginalisation of fringe Muslims through the 'mainstreaming' lens of the Commission, so this reduced 'Islam' also becomes the acceptable or legitimate face of Islam: the 'real' or 'true' Islam that has recently gained institutional legitimacy.[42] As Halliday suggests, 'the mistake of those opposed to anti-Muslim prejudice has been to accept, as the one true answer, particular and often conservative versions

---

[39]   Ibid.

[40]   Chris Allen, 'Undoing proximity: the impact of the local-global nexus on perceptions of Muslims in Britain', *The Globalisation and Localisation of Religion: EASR Congress 2003*, 11 May 2003 (University of Bergen: Norway).

[41]   See Halliday (1999) and (2002).

[42]   Laurent Bonnefoy (2003), 'Public Institutions and Islam: a New Stigmatization?', *International Institute for the study of Islam in the Modern World* no. 13 (December 2003), 22–3.

[of the Islamic religion]',[43] conforming to imposed and external understandings that exclude those who cannot or maybe do not wish to adhere to such.

Essentialised Muslims: Transforming Particularities into Universalities

In elaborating upon the processes underpinning the establishment of 'Islam' as a shared identity that all Muslims can be accommodated within, so a process of essentialisation ensues. To explain this, Sayyid's extrapolation of the essentialism within Orientalism is particularly useful.[44] One critique of the concept of Orientalism is that Orientalists showed little interest in overcoming or removing the limitations of their enquiry that in turn constructed a framework where gross generalisations were made and indeed became the norm. Through the embedding of the diversity of Muslim communities into a single entity defined solely by 'Islam' therefore, so the Runnymede Report appears to have been doing something similar to those Orientalists, something where the personal, human and real becomes lost, or at least hidden from the actuality of understanding. What with the report's premise of the implied exclusion of those Muslims that do not fit into its version of 'Islam', so an essentialised understanding and imposition of that which is 'Muslim', either individually or collectively, is put forward, one that assumes conformity in word, action and deed. If such conformity is correct, then it is both possible and indeed probable that the characteristics necessary for 'open views' to be legitimate will be somewhere in evidence, simultaneously negating those who do not adhere to such. It is only this *essentialised Muslim* therefore that sits within the marker of 'Islam' as established in the Runnymede model, whilst all others – those that do not conform – become overlooked and excluded. Those Muslims who cannot – or do not want to – match the ideals and qualities of the essentialised Muslim therefore become essentially 'inessential'. As with those Muslim voices who are unable or unwilling to adhere to the ideals of the Commission's interfaith constructed consultative process, so the possibility arises that these and even more Muslims thus become inessentialised and so remain outside the scope and remit of those campaigning against Islamophobia. Unlike these excluded groups and individuals, the essentialised Muslims are drawn from particular and acceptable cultural, historical and theological expressions of Islam; live their life and practice their faith in particular ways; engage in society and hold world-views that reflect the requirements of the 'open views'; and generally fit the frames and contexts that the model imposes upon Muslims in order to achieve the shared identity necessary to succeed.

---

[43]   Halliday (2002), 127.

[44]   Bobby Sayyid, *A Fundamental Fear: Eurocentrism and the Emergence of Islamism* (London: Zed Books, 1997). My explanation of the formation of an 'essential' Muslim draws heavily upon the work of Sayyid and his observations about the formation of an essentialised Islam, Said (1979).

The qualities and characteristics of these essentialised Muslims therefore transform particularities into universalities that subsequently become normatively attributed to all Muslims without differentiation. In a somewhat inverse effect from the processes of 'closed views' and of Islamophobia per se, whilst Islamophobia is purported to have the effect of attributing all Muslims with such views as barbarism, misogyny and irrational behaviour, so the essentialised attributes homogenise all Muslims with opposite qualities and characteristics. The essentialised Muslim therefore becomes the blueprint for all Muslims, where the mainstreaming of the essentialised Muslim becomes the universally idealised standard. Consequently, the Muslim becomes an entirely passive actor in the process. Those who do not fit or match the essentialised Muslim therefore become lesser or illegitimate thus justifying their exclusion from such processes as interfaith dialogue, political engagement and societal participation. As Sayyid concludes, 'the consequence ... is erasure'[45] leaving those that do not conform to the demands of the essential Muslim to be seen as the antithesis of everything that is deemed to be the 'true', 'authentic', 'mainstream' and so on.

In expanding upon Richardson's insight into the consultative process, he stated that the:

> big topic we decided we couldn't address at all directly was the behaviour and mindset of some British Muslims. 'To what extent and in what ways may Muslims themselves exacerbate Islamophobia?'... that is a key question we simply did not know how to address.[46]

One must first ask why it was felt that such a question could not be addressed. Whilst initially acknowledging that '*some* British Muslims' may exacerbate the problem, the question shifts to a much broader and homogenous understanding of how '*Muslims themselves* exacerbate Islamophobia'. To whatever extent this 'problem' was subsequently addressed within the Commission leaves one wondering whether the construction of an essentialised Muslim was indeed done so to coerce, overcome or eradicate not only those marginalised and inessentialised Muslims, but also those Muslims who were seen to 'exacerbate Islamophobia'. Maybe the premise was that if all Muslims were unidimensional – in terms of the 'open views' at least – then Islamophobia would not be a problem and on an extremely simplistic level, easier to address. But again, we are left with the recognition that some Muslims can neither be located, nor indeed would wish to locate themselves within the pre-requisites of the report's essentialised model. How for example does one 'openly' view those Muslims who preach messages of hate, for example Abdullah el-Faisal, Abu Hamza, Omar Bakri Mohammed and Abu Izzadeen amongst others? Likewise, how might the processes involved in establishing the open views accommodate groups such as the Supporters of

---

45   Ibid., 10.
46   Personal interview, 2003.

Shariah or Islam4UK, both of which are alleged to have been splinter groups of the now proscribed al-Muhajiroun? How for example does the 'open views' accommodate the views of such groups? When on their websites, they espouse such messages as:

> Islam does not recognise freedom … democracy is also anathema to Islam, since Muslims do not believe in the rule of the majority or in elections every four or five years or in sovereignty for anyone or anything other than Allah, whether that is the people, their government or any constitution, be it the UN, OIC or any other body. As for secularism, Islam considers anyone adopting this to have committed an act of apostasy ….[47]

Whilst it is surely far from being Islamophobic to acknowledge and consider such examples, to assert the fact that some Muslims – recognising that these individuals undeniably identify themselves as being Muslims and speaking in the name of 'Islam' – are intolerant of other faiths – even of other interpretations of the religion of Islam – could however, through the Runnymede model at least, be legitimately construed as being Islamophobic. Similarly, as regards al-Muhajiroun's declaration, to suggest that an open view of these may enable better engagement with them is both questionable and obviously problematic. If one is in disagreement with their particular views, irrespective of whether those same views were being put forward by either a Muslim or non-Muslim voice, it cannot be equated that disagreement and criticism are the same as prejudice or discrimination. Disagreement and prejudice are of course quite separate, and given that legitimate disagreement and debate was one of the things not to be stifled by the report, so the report would appear to have failed. Whilst in the Commission's 2004 report they state that 'legitimate disagreement and criticism, as also appreciation and respect, are aspects of open views',[48] from the original report – and incidentally without any further elucidation in later reports or publications – such an accommodation is not necessarily clear. There is also an acknowledgement here by Richardson that whilst asking such questions about some Muslims may indeed be relevant and valid, what the Commission had achieved with its 1997 report was to create a scenario where they themselves had stifled their own debate and discussion, fearful of the consequences if they suggested openly that *some* Muslims may appear to exacerbate the situation. The problem therefore was rather more self-imposed and self-created – and indeed internalised – than it ever really needed to be.

---

[47]   Al-Muhajiroun, *Al-Muhajiroun*, 24 October 2002 <http://www.almuhajiroun.com/pr/uk/24_10_2002b.php>.

[48]   Commission on British Muslims and Islamophobia (2004), 22.

The 'Problem' of Islamophobia: Hierarchical and Far from Being All-Inclusive

Not all Muslims therefore can be located within the compartmentalised and essentialised requirements of the Runnymede 'open and closed' model. And because these Muslims have become inessentialised and as a result, excluded from the context of the Runnymede model, these same Muslims have been banished from the debates about Islamophobia. It is an extremely tenuous argument to suggest that if some within an extremely broad identifier go against the norm, then not only are they exacerbating the prejudice, discrimination and hostility already directed at some, but in some way this might also be legitimised or justified. Therefore whilst *some* Muslims *do* reflect the negative stereotypes, this should not be allowed to imply that they are rendered any lesser Muslim than those whose reflect the characteristics of an imposed and essentialised Muslim. No hierarchy of victim, based upon adherence to essentialised or inessentialised norms must therefore be established. In developing this line of reasoning, so it becomes right to suggest that those such as Abu Hamza or Anjem Choudary for example might be exacerbating Islamophobia. Yet it must also be right to suggest that it is Islamophobia if *anyone* is subjected to prejudice, discrimination or violence solely on the basis of their Muslim-ness, perceived or real. Ultimately therefore, Islamophobia cannot be determined, differentiated and defined by the 'type' of Muslim being victimised. It has to go beyond this and take into account the recognition of an actual or perceived 'Muslim-ness'.

Take for example the statements and actions made recently by Islam4UK that have included suggesting that Queen Elizabeth II converts to Islam, that Buckingham Palace be transformed into a mosque and that they have protested at marches by soldiers returning from fighting in Afghanistan. Whilst mainstream voices – both Muslim and non – were able to dismiss their claims by arguing that they fail to reflect the true nature of Islam, had any of Islam4UK's members or supporters become victims of an Islamophobic attack, the Runnymede model could have been used as a means of justifying such attacks given they were widely seen to be exacerbating the situation. At the same time, had a perceivably essentialised Muslim been attacked, then this, within the bounds of the Runnymede model, would have been rightfully condemned. Hypothetically though, both attacks could have been motivated and underpinned solely by the victim's Muslim-ness and quite irrespective of anything else. Both attacks would be as equally abhorrent in both motivation and purpose. But the Runnymede model makes assumptions about the nature of Islamophobia where they feel that such instances and attacks are made because of the views and beliefs of some rather than the Muslim-ness of its victims, thus assuming that the perpetrators are informed and have a purpose that is reasoned and in some ways rational. It is therefore the model and its creators who reinforce the construct that an essentialised Muslim exists – and is indeed necessary – in order that this same Muslim becomes the idealised foundation from which the combating of Islamophobia begins. The 'problem' of Islamophobia therefore becomes projected entirely onto its victims, simultaneously deflected from both society and its perpetrators.

So when Richardson suggests that this confronted the Commission with the 'big topic … in what ways may Muslims themselves exacerbate Islamophobia?' he highlights the extremely precarious and naive way the Commission and its report approached and established their model of Islamophobia. Within the British context, whilst the vast majority of the population would understand that racism motivated the killers of Stephen Lawrence, there would be no credibility in suggesting that such a killing was in any way legitimated because *some* black males exacerbate racist stereotypes or misgivings. The two are completely independent and have no associative justification whatsoever: even the contemplation of the seeking of a connection between the two is absurd. Yet despite this absurd precept, a logical extension of the Runnymede Report would suggest that until all Muslims become essentialised, Islamophobia will fail to be tackled and will not go away. This is of course a serious weakness in the way in which the Runnymede model not only approaches Islamophobia but also theoretically and conceptually tries to explain it.

Consequently Islamophobia becomes reduced to a phenomenon that is both overly simplistic and largely superficial, defined more by the characteristics of the victims than the motivation and purpose of the perpetrators themselves. In addition, it also fails in neither embodying the necessary clarity of thought or concept, nor the analytical or empirical credibility required to substantiate Islamophobia as a distinctly separate and identifiable phenomenon, one that is as credible and equitable with such correlative phenomena as anti-Semitism or racism. Despite this, the report and its model continues to have a major influence and impact on the discourse of Islamophobia. Yet having undertaken a critical analysis of the report, neither it nor its model would appear to either substantiate or provide the necessary answers to knowing exactly what Islamophobia is. Instead, and as Sayyid suggested previously, that which emerges from the blank spaces, the ambiguities and all that is left unsaid about Muslims and Islam is what defines understanding. All that exists within these generalised terms, and indeed all that is excluded, are merely reduced to nothing, where a mere abstraction – concerning 'Islam' and 'Muslims' – is all that remains. And what equally emerges from this is an Islamophobia that is abstract in its understanding, definition and conceptualisation, dependent upon both the views and perceptions of non-Muslims as well as the very condition, actions, beliefs and behaviour of some rather than all Muslims themselves. One must therefore rightly question the influence and impact, both ongoing and retrospectively, of the Commission and the report on the shaping of the discourse and narrative of Islamophobia. If the Runnymede model of Islamophobia is therefore incomplete or inadequate in explaining Islamophobia, what then might Islamophobia be?

To begin the process of answering this question, the following chapters start to put Islamophobia into context: first in the setting of the UK; second in the setting of Europe. Having done so, it will be necessary to try and ascertain exactly what Islamophobia might be and how it might be better defined and conceptualised.

PART 4
Islamophobia in Context

Chapter 6
'They're All the Same':
Islamophobia in the Context of the UK

Understanding the British context is vitally important to understanding contemporary Islamophobia, not only because it was in Britain that today's Islamophobia was first recognised but also because of the impact of the Runnymede Report. Irrespective of the failings of the Runnymede model, as the report noted, Islamophobia in Britain was becoming increasingly 'more explicit, more extreme and more dangerous'.[1] At the time of its publication, an event the magnitude of 9/11 could not have been comprehended. Amid the sheer hyperbolic overstatement surrounding these events, the resonance of merely the terms 'Islam' and 'Muslim' had a deep and possibly irreversible impact across a vast range of social, economic, political and cultural strata. Add into this the more recent memory and fallout from 7/7, the failed terrorist attacks of 21/7 and at Glasgow Airport, various terror raids and plots to behead serving British Muslims soldiers amongst other incidents and it may be that the impact is irreversible: only history will allow for such an evaluation of this statement to be made. Nonetheless, 9/11 and its aftermath – the period of urgent history that we continue to try and make sense of a decade after it happened – provides an unprecedented and quite unique perspective from which to try and contextualise, as well as better understand, manifestations of Islamophobia in a given setting. So whilst we have clearly seen and understood that Islamophobia is something that has a distinctly pre-9/11 context, so it would seem that Islamophobia also has a distinctly post-9/11 context also. This and the following chapters therefore will seek to move the historiography forward and explore Islamophobia in the twenty-first century, in a post-9/11 setting.

From 9/11 to 7/7 and Beyond: 'you want killing for what you did in America'

Since the events of 9/11, Islamophobia and its acknowledgement has been ever more recurrent and increasingly more prevalent across the public and political spaces in Britain. First coined by Jorgen Nielsen, urgent history can be extremely problematic given the fact that it does not allow any reflection and analysis over a given period of time. Unfortunately, this urgency is ever increasing in Britain, necessitating politicians, commentators and community representatives to respond in such ways that we seem to want to demand exactly what our future histories will

---

[1]   Commission on British Muslims and Islamophobia (1997), 1.

be as a means of indeterminably shaping the future. Unlike Halliday's insight, no longer would it seem that in the UK at least, will the past be used as the framework within which we understand the present. Instead, urgent history necessitates that we act in the present to ensure that the future is put in place well in advance of the future actually taking place.

Whilst the long-term effect remains both problematic and open to contestation, what can be substantiated is that following the attacks of 9/11 a significant rise in Islamophobia was an unwelcome consequence. Whilst the EUMC 9/11 Report noted a backlash of Islamophobia across the entire breadth of the European Union including the UK, it was those such as Dr Lorraine Sheridan at the University of Leicester in her research entitled: *Effects of the Events of September 11th 2001 on Discrimination and Implicit Racism in Five Religious and Seven Racial Groups*,[2] that more accurately noted the effects in the UK. Those such as FAIR, the IHRC and the *Muslim News* all compiled dossiers of evidence in the aftermath of 9/11 whilst others such as the European Muslim Research Centre and the Muslim Safety Forum have continued to do so more recently. To contextualise attitudes following 9/11, it is interesting to consider the findings of a YouGov poll conducted shortly afterwards.[3] The poll showed that:

- 84 per cent of British people tended to be more suspicious about Muslims after 9/11
- 35 per cent stated that their opinion of British Muslims had gone down since
- 82 per cent believed that Muslims were too isolationist
- 56 per cent felt that they generally had nothing in common with Muslims
- 63 per cent suggested that Muslims did little to promote tolerance between themselves and others
- and finally, one in six said that they would be 'disappointed' if Muslims became their neighbours.

More recently, the 2010 British Social Attitudes Survey suggested that 52 per cent of respondents believe that Britain is deeply divided along religious lines. In addition, it noted how 45 per cent of people believe that religious diversity is having a negative impact on society, and that more than half would oppose the building of a large mosque at the end of their road as opposed to 15 per cent who would object if it was a church.[4] It is worth stressing that whilst these attitudes are

---

[2]   Sheridan, Lorraine, *Effects of the Events of September 11th 2001 on Discrimination and Implicit Racism in Five Religious and Seven Ethnic Groups: a Brief Overview* (Leicester: University of Leicester, 2002).

[3]   Poll conducted by YouGov in October 2002 on behalf of the Islamic Society of Britain as part of their Islam Awareness Week 2002. Further details and information relating to this can be found posted on their website at http://www.isb.org.uk.

[4]   National Centre for Social Research, British Social Attitudes Survey 2010 26th Edition (2010, http://tinyurl.com/yeo48hf).

not in themselves Islamophobic per se, it would be difficult to argue against there being a strong link between the findings of the YouGov poll and the most recent British Social Attitudes Survey.

In reflecting the wider European landscape, Muslim communities in the UK are not only the second largest faith community but so too are they the most visually recognisable, with traditional Islamic attire or even just mere aspects of the tradition being easily identifiable across many of Britain's towns and cities. Because of this, Muslims can be easily identified on the recognition of 'difference'. From this recognition of difference has emerged a wider demarcation that embodies Muslims with notions of Otherness and inferiority:[5] more precisely, Otherness and inferiority that are seen as being counter to or even against the 'norms' of British society. At the same time as the socio-religious icons of Islam and Muslims have acquired a greater visual immediacy, so this immediacy has also been simultaneously contextualised and understood via largely negative evaluations. With 9/11 as a catalyst, so the situation following both 9/11 and 7/7 has simultaneously intensified and deteriorated: intensified because the visual identification and subsequent difference of Muslims per se came under greater scrutiny at the same time as becoming increasingly recognisable; deteriorated given that same visual identification and difference underpinned a raft of negatively perceived attitudes and acts.

And this greater scrutiny has been closely aligned to policy responses to anti-terror and security issues. Despite some attempts by politicians and others to argue that these policies are not Muslim-specific, many view the current counter-terrorist legislation and policy agendas to the contrary. From seeking to curtail and control radicalism, proscribing 'extremist groups', and introducing a raft of new offences that include 'acts preparatory to terrorism', 'encouragement to terrorism' and the 'dissemination of terrorist publications', research has shown that not only has this the potential to isolate and alienate Muslim communities[6] but so too has it reinforced the wider fears and anxieties about Muslim cultures and traditions that already exist. Against this backdrop, policies such as the *Preventing Violent Extremism* (PVE) programme have been implemented in the hope of encouraging better relations between Muslims and mainstream society. And as before, not only is it being suggested that these policies and initiatives are making Muslim communities feel increasingly under pressure[7] but so too is it being suggested that they are liable to bring about greater feelings of anger, alienation, mistrust, and radicalization.[8] In many ways, a self-perpetuating cycle appears to have been established.

---

[5]   Pnina Werbner and Tariq Modood, eds, *Debating Cultural Hybridity: Multi-Cultural Identities and the Politics of Anti-Racism* (London: Zed, 1997).

[6]   Rachel Briggs, Catherine Fieschi and Hannah Lownsbrough, *Bringing it Home: Community-Based Approaches to Counter-Terrorism* (London: Demos, 2006).

[7]   Khaleda Khan, *Preventing Violent Extremism (PVE) and PREVENT: a Response from the Muslim Community* (London: An-Nisa Society 2009).

[8]   Briggs et al. (2006).

Muslims in Britain: 'terrorists warring against the West, or apologists defending Islam'

Post-9/11, post-7/7 processes have therefore both 'newly established' and 're-established' Muslims as chimerical Others. Consequently, British Muslims have dangerously found themselves being identified in pre-determined and bi-polar ways, and even more dangerously, having to do the same in terms of self-definition also. As Sardar suggested, Muslims are contemporarily identified as either terrorists warring against the West, or apologists defending Islam as a peaceful religion.[9] Given the negative recognition British society has of Muslims, both types of Muslim have through the same lens become increasingly non-differentiated: in essence, whether 'terrorists' or 'apologists' all Muslims in the UK have become virtually identical. All have become indiscriminately characterised by the same negative and stereotypical attributes, where all Muslims have the capability to either be terrorists or at least be supportive of terrorism. In such ways, the first – and most permeating Runnymede closed view of Muslims as a monolithic and static entity – has been clearly present in the way that all Muslims have come to be understood.

Given the climate of fear and threat posed by 9/11 and more pertinently due to the close proximity of 7/7, so the demarcation of difference has meant that Muslims have been further characterised in terms of 'them' and 'us': increasingly in terms that present 'them' being undeniably *against* 'us'. So when the media report of the alleged threat posed by such media-speak defined 'sleepers' or 'fifth columnists' that are 'in our midst', all Muslims come to be seen to be both realistically and conceptually capable of posing the same threats, exacerbating the climate of fear and suspicion even further. It is for this reason that in the immediate aftermath of 9/11, Muslim (and Sikh) men that resembled Usama bin Laden – however insignificantly, possibly only having a beard or wearing a turban – were attacked thousands of miles away from where he himself was alleged to have been. Visual difference and the meanings attributed to this therefore transcends geographical boundaries and proximities thus making all Muslims along with the visual identifiers of Islam legitimate targets for hatred and abuse. This can be highlighted by an article that appeared in the *Manchester Evening News* entitled, 'A cultural divide breeds suspicion'.[10] On seeing an image of bin Laden on the front of a newspaper, the writer reflected upon how he was alleged to look 'not unlike many devout Muslims in our midst'. In developing the old British racist adage that 'all blacks look the same', transferring this onto Muslims in contemporary Britain it might more appropriately be that 'all Muslims *are* the same'.

---

[9]   Ziauddin Sardar, 'The Excluded Minority: British Muslim Identity after 11 September' in Phoebe Griffith and Mark Leonard, eds, *Reclaiming Britishness* (London: Foreign Policy Centre, 2004) 51–6.

[10]   'A Cultural Divide Breeds Suspicion', *Manchester Evening News*, 18 September 2001.

In an attempt to try and offer some theoretical underpinning, Barker's 'new racism' model might be useful.[11] As noted in the historiography, following the legislative protection rightly afforded to minority communities and ethnic groups in the early 1980s, those such as Barker began to acknowledge a shifting focus away from more traditional markers of race to newer and legislatively unprotected markers based upon cultural and religious difference. It was this same demarcation of difference that following 9/11 attained a greater immediacy of recognition. However, unlike older forms of racism, 'new racism' sought to elaborate upon the differences identified in much less explicit ways, where the markers of difference do not underpin explicit hatred and hostility but instead implicitly infer and establish direct challenges and threats, where 'difference' poses challenges and threats to 'our way of life'. With such threats therefore, a situation emerges where prejudices and their subsequent impact are triggered by the perception that something is either presenting, or seen to be capable of presenting a threat. In this case, that threat was against – as Barker's framework might term it – 'us'. This of course is rather simplistic but does offer a useful tool to illustrate the process through which Muslims have become seen as being Other to British values and norms. A further exploration of Barker's theories and new racism as a concept are considered later.

The evolution of such a theoretical understanding can therefore be seen in the post-9/11 period where Islam and Muslims have been clearly presented in terms of being incompatible with the norms of 'our' (British) society and 'our' (British) way of life. In today's populist understanding, the 'threat' that Muslims are seen to present – not just in terms of terrorism or the widely convoluted 'clash' thesis – is one that has a myriad manifestations. As such, in recent times, questions about state schools; freedom of speech surrounding the cartoons furore, the role of women, radicalism and extremism, and finally issues surrounding the future of multiculturalism and community cohesion have been just a few of the issues where Muslim 'difference' has been understood to be threatening or at least challenging the British 'way of life'. This is none more evident than in an article by the former Chancellor of the Exchequer, Norman Lamont espousing the death of multiculturalism.[12] From analysing the arguments put forward, its is concluded that Lamont – like many others – believes that multiculturalism is dying – is possibly even dead – as a consequence of the threat that has been posed to 'our way of life'. As an analysis of Lamont's article concludes:

> In today's public and political spaces, the 'threat' that Muslims are most commonly seen to present is typically framed ... [and] becomes evident along the lines of new racist discourse where 'Islam' and 'Muslims' are seen to be

---

[11]   Barker (1981).

[12]   Norman Lamont, 'Down with Multiculturalism, Book-burnings and Fatwas', *The Daily Telegraph* (8 May 2002).

incompatible with the dominant or perceived overriding culture and its heritage: that is, being 'British' and being 'us'.[13]

Essentially, Muslims are seen to be indiscriminately different.

And it is the markers of difference that are seen to be presenting challenges to the British and in the wider sense, Western way of life. As such, that which is seen to be different is also seen to be problematic, and that which is problematic is also seen to be challenging. The impact of 9/11 and 7/7 have therefore both heightened awareness of these differences – or problems depending upon one's particular perspective – and subsequently intensified them many times over. And so as the threats and challenges are nowadays seen to be much greater than ever before, so a sense of justification emerges that suggests that rather than Islamophobia being an unfounded hostility, in many ways becomes an informed reality. So when Islamophobia becomes disseminated in the public domain, a greater receptivity to such ideas not only means that they become increasingly normalised, but that a greater rationalism emerges. And with rationalism comes the belief that such ideas and attitudes appear to be correct.

I.S.L.A.M.: 'intolerance, slaughter, looting, arson, molestation of women'

Since 9/11, and undoubtedly bolstered by 7/7, the BNP have used the climate to acquire social and political legitimacy, both of which have been undertaken on the back of this increasing receptivity to Islamophobia in the British, particularly English domain, not least founded upon notions of both fear and threat. Much of this has been through inciting and encouraging provocation and division, employing language and images that encourage and invigorate prejudice and discrimination. However, the BNP has always stressed the legality of its actions, referring back to the legislative anomaly that allowed it a window of opportunity to be overtly anti-Muslim and anti-Islamic without prosecution. Under one of its first successful political campaigns shortly after 9/11, entitled *Islam out of Britain*, the BNP declared its clearest objectives, where it sought to expose 'the threat Islam and Muslims pose to Britain and British society' in a leaflet entitled, *The truth about I.S.L.A.M.*: 'I.S.L.A.M.' being used as an acronym for 'Intolerance, Slaughter, Looting, Arson and Molestation of Women'.[14] Widely distributed, it used highly inflammatory reasons for justifying hating Muslims suggesting that 'to find out

---

[13]   Chris Allen 'Down With Multiculturalism, Book-burning and Fatwas', *Culture and Religion* (8:2,125–38, 2007).

[14]   This leaflet was widely distributed across parts of the UK where high percentage populations of Muslim communities were in existence from early 2001 through till mid 2002. It was also available to download from the party's website although this was removed once the BNP were reported to the House of Lords Select Committee on Religious Offences in October 2002. The BNP also removed all links to its 'Islam out of Britain' campaign.

what Islam really stands for, all you have to do is look at a copy of the Koran, and see for yourself … Islam really does stand for Intolerance, Slaughter, Looting, Arson and Molestation of Women'. Dismissing those apologists that Sardar identified as one half of the bi-polar perceived Muslim, by selectively quoting the Qur'an the BNP painted the most despicable picture of Muslims adding – in clear new racist rhetoric – that, 'no-one dares to tell the truth about Islam and the way that it threatens our democracy, traditional freedoms and identity'.[15]

The BNP also went on to suggest that understanding the Qur'an could provide context to a whole raft of different events, from the 2001 disturbances in the North of England[16] through to the global events of 9/11, two events the BNP stressed were inextricably linked. By linking these events – the local and the global – the differences that were seen in one context therefore became attributed to all whereby any differentiation became increasingly blurred. The BNP also rooted this 'problem' into the context of an Islamic theological one, where an 'anti-*kafir*' framework sought to both reinforce and demarcate further the difference between 'Muslims' and '*kafir*' – in more simplistic terms, 'them' and 'us' – as being rather more derivative of Muslims or Islam than it was of the BNP. This shifting of the focus meant that the BNP could adequately suggest that it was neither them nor indeed any non-Muslim that was saying that a 'them and us' dichotomy existed but more so, Muslims themselves. For the BNP it was Islam that caused the problems and for the benefit and wellbeing of all in British society, the BNP were merely highlighting the point.

As a direct consequence of the inroads made by the far-right and the deepening receptivity in society to anti-Muslim ideas and expressions, and in identifying the way that the visual markers of difference were being used in the contemporary climate, Muslims also became targeted by other minority communities too. Following anecdotal evidence that youth groups of Indian descent in Manchester were adopting an overtly Hindu identity in order to deflect any potential anti-Muslim backlash, the BNP capitalised upon this and exploited intra-'Asian'

In addition to this leaflet, a full range of other equally inciting literature was also readily available from the website, see, http://www.bnp.org.uk.

[15]   Ibid.

[16]   Throughout the summer of 2001, a number of disturbances erupted across the North of England undertaken primarily by young Muslim men of South Asian descent. Primarily being in Bradford, Burnley and Oldham, smaller occurrences were also witnessed in Hanley and Leeds too. Despite various official reports into the disturbances, the role of the far-right including the BNP was largely dismissed as being irrelevant to the tensions that emerged. However the BNP were actively campaigning in all of these areas at the time of the respective disturbances, and the BNP leader, Nick Griffin, had been addressing a meeting of supporters in Bradford the night before the Bradford disturbances, incidentally the worst disturbances of their kind in recent British history. For a fuller consideration of the Bradford disturbances and its aftermath, see Chris Allen, *Fair Justice: the Bradford Disturbances, the Sentencing and the Impact* (London: FAIR, 2003).

tensions by issuing an audio resource entitled, *Islam: A Threat to Us All*.[17] The venture, undertaken in conjunction with fringe Sikh and Hindu organisations, was created to provide 'insider' validation – by which one must assume this means 'Asian' – of both its own skewed view of Islam and the need to rid Britain of Islam. As the press release stated, it sought to:

> Give the lie to those who falsely claim that we are 'racists' or 'haters'. We sympathise and identify with every people in the world who want to secure or preserve a homeland for themselves, their traditions and their posterity. And we demand and strive for that same basic human right for the native English, Scots, Welsh, Irish and Ulster folk who together make up the British.

The demarcation of Muslims from all others is clearly present, and in line with new racist theories that purport a threat to 'us' and 'our way of life', the BNP denounce any claims that they themselves are racists. The employment of new racist rhetoric and perspectives therefore allows for disclaimers to be made that are initially difficult to refute. One way of seeing through this is to acknowledge that the BNP do not identify or include their Sikh and Hindu partners in what they define to be 'British'. Nonetheless, when communities that can be identified in terms of racialised markers unite to further demarcate Muslims, it highlights the hatred for Muslims that exists across contemporary British society. So great therefore was the need to demarcate themselves from Muslims, that those Sikh and Hindu groups found adequate justification to join forces with an overtly racist organisation that had in very recent history been targeting Sikh and Hindu communities on the basis of their skin colour rather more than their religion. So great was their unifying cause – the single, common denominator – that other contentious and previously oppositional factors were ignored or overlooked. Islamophobia therefore, whether from the perspective of the BNP, those fringe Sikh or Hindu groups, or the growing numbers voting for the BNP found within the anti-Muslim expression and rhetoric something that they felt was justified. Currently, the BNP appear to be in negotiations with a British Sikh man about becoming the first non-white member of the Party.

Since 9/11 and its aftermath, the BNP have continued to grow, exacerbating the sense of insecurity and fear that has once again emerged following 7/7. Focusing on the alleged differences between the 'aboriginal' communities – a term sometimes employed by the BNP to describe what it recognises as the real British people – and Muslim communities, within days of the atrocities the BNP had produced a leaflet showing the bombed out carcass of the bus in Tavistock Square emblazoned with a message that adopted the tone of 'we told you so'. Shortly after, the BNP produced

---

[17]   This resource was widely distributed to the media and received significant media coverage across 2001 and 2002. Contemporarily though, and as with the earlier mentioned anti-Muslim literature, this resource is very difficult to obtain due to the actions deployed by the BNP following the House of Lords Select Committee.

another leaflet that placed a picture of one the cartoons of the Prophet Muhammad from the Danish *Jyllands-Posten* alongside a photo of a cartoons inspired protest in London where a number of aggressive young British Muslims held some of the most despicable placards that urged violence against those who insulted Islam. The BNP leaflet simply asked, 'Which do you find offensive?'

Despite public and political outcry at the inappropriateness of the leaflets, that year the BNP successfully fielded around 350 candidates in municipal elections across the country. Under a campaign entitled 'Islam Referendum Day', they asked, 'Are you concerned about the growth of Islam in Britain?'. The BNP made unprecedented gains across the country: 33 candidates were initially declared to be winners with a further 70 being declared in second place. However it was in Barking and Dagenham, a diverse and densely populated area of East London, where its success was most notable. Winning eleven of the thirteen seats it contested, the BNP became the first far-right party in British history to be the official party of opposition in a British council chamber. At the first meeting of Barking and Dagenham Council in May 2006 after its electoral gains, the BNP attempted to try and force through an amendment to change the nature and emphasis of the council's commitment to anti-racism. Later that same evening outside the tube station in Barking, a man of Afghan origin was repeatedly stabbed by four men who left a flag with the St George's Cross emblazoned on it draped across his body before running off and leaving the man to die.[18]

The exploitation of the perceived threat posed by Muslims to 'our' way of life has been one that has to some degree taken the mainstream of British politics by surprise. Potentially more worrying however is the extent to which this message has seemingly been accepted by a growing number of people across all of Britain's diverse communities. As research undertaken by Democratic Audit at the University of Essex stated, in those parts of England where the BNP was targeting most of its resources, around one in four voters were considering voting for them. In some parts of London, this figure was shown to be around one in five.[19] Emanating entirely from the successes gained on the back of their openly anti-Muslim campaigns, the BNP have found a much greater, near country-wide quasi legitimacy that has seen their popularity mushroom into a party that many believe now offer a real political alternative. Targeting their seats directly and specifically, the BNP now have elected councillors across England, from Grays in the South, through Sandwell and Dudley in the Midlands, to its first stronghold in Burnley in the North. Current estimates suggest it has around 56 local councillors. More significantly for the BNP though has been the recent successes in London and Europe. In 2008, they won one of 25 seats in the London Assembly having gained approximately 5.3 per cent of the capital's vote. Then in 2009, the BNP further consolidated its position when it won

---

[18]   *The Observer*, 26 May 2006.

[19]   Peter John et al., 'The BNP: the Roots of its Appeal' (Colchester: Democratic Audit, University of Essex, 2006).

two seats in the European Parliament with 9.8 per cent of the vote in Yorkshire and Humber and 8.0 per cent in the North West.

Without any doubt whatsoever, the growing success of the BNP has been achieved via its clear and acknowledged shift towards a more explicit anti-Muslim, anti-Islam agenda that both taps into and feeds the fear of threat. As the Party's leader, Nick Griffin told a group of activists in Burnley in March 2006:

> We bang on about Islam. Why? Because to the ordinary public out there it's the thing they can understand. It's the thing the newspaper editors sell newspapers with. If we were to attack some other ethnic group – some people say we should attack the Jews ... But ... we've got to get to power. And if that was an issue we chose to bang on about when the press don't talk about it ... the public would just think we were barking mad ...
>
> ... It wouldn't get us anywhere other than stepping backwards. It would lock us in a little box; the public would think 'extremist crank lunatics, nothing to do with me'. And we wouldn't get power.[20]

What is interesting is the way that Griffin acknowledges how 'it's the thing the newspaper editors sell newspapers with': Muslims as threat, Muslims as other, Muslims as against 'our' way of life. As Griffin put it on another occasion, 'We should be positioning ourselves to take advantage for our own political ends of the growing wave of public hostility to Islam currently being whipped up by the mass media'.[21]

And as with the BNP, so too have other far-right groups sought to capitalise on the situation and climate. Consequently groups such as the National Front, Combat 18, the White Wolves and the White Nationalist Party amongst others have developed similar anti-Muslim campaigns. Even what might be termed a more traditional right wing political party in the UK Independence Party (UKIP) has adopted similar campaigns, with its councillor in Dudley being highly vociferous in opposing the building of a new 'super-mosque' on wasteland on the outskirts of the town. As a marker of the campaign's success, a petition of more than 22,000 names was submitted to Dudley Metropolitan Council. But it is the English Defence League (EDL) that has grown rapidly and most successfully. Formed in June 2009, the group claim they did so as a response to the frustration felt at the lack of action by the British Government against what it describes on its website as 'extremist Muslim preachers and organisations'.[22] Whilst many – somewhat

---

[20]   BNPtv Films, *Nick Griffin Speaking at Burnley Branch Meeting*, March 2006 (2 September 2009) http://video.google.co.uk/videoplay?docid=1269630805284168668#.

[21]   Nick Griffin, *By their fruits (or lack of them) shall you know them*, 21 March 2006 (3 October 2008) http://web.archive.org/web/20071014195717/http://www.bnp.org.uk/columnists/chairman2.php?ngId=30.

[22]   For more about the English Defence League, see their website at http://www.englishdefenceleague.org.

inaccurately – suggest the EDL are merely the 'foot-soldiers' of the BNP, the group are far more specific about their aims and causes. For them, they believe they are necessary as a bulwark against Britain's 'politically correct culture' which panders to what the group describe, 'Jihadist preachers'. It cites its evidence as being the fact that nativity plays in schools have been banned, that *halal* meat is served as an only option in many schools, that Englishness is marginalised, and that the national flag – the St George's cross – has apparently been banned by some councils. But it was the sight of a handful of Muslims vociferously and offensively protesting when the Royal Anglian Regiment returned to Luton from duty in Basra, Iraq that was, as the EDL put it, 'the final straw'. Claiming they comprise 'ordinary, non-racist citizens of England and supporters who have had enough of being treated as second-class citizens to the Jihadis in our own country', the EDL in less than a year have mobilised significant numbers of supporters to march across a number of British towns and cities. Normally attracting violent protests against their marches, the group would appear to be continuing to garner support and have further marches planned for the foreseeable future.

Closing the Gap between Left and Right: 'swamping our schools'

One key observation to have come out of the period since 9/11 is how the gap between the opposite poles of the extreme political right and left, when concerned with attitudes and perceptions of Muslims at least, would appear to have become much closer. With similar sentiments, the apparently centre-left former Home Secretary, David Blunkett, verbally attacked those young British Muslims in Bradford peacefully campaigning against the harsh sentencing of their friends and family convicted of involvement in the 2001 disturbances, by openly calling them 'whining maniacs'. In addition, Mr Blunkett also ensured widespread media coverage when he aired his endorsement of the more 'rational' claims of the assassinated Pim Fortuyn, suggesting that Muslims should accept and assimilate into 'our culture' and 'our ways'; and that immigrants and asylum seekers – a group that are becoming increasingly interchangeable and indistinguishable from Muslims in the contemporary setting – were 'swamping our' schools'.[23] Echoing similar suggestions made by the then Prime Minister, Margaret Thatcher some twenty or so years beforehand, this particular statement by Thatcher was deemed to be a formative moment in the development and transition of the 'new racist' ideologies of the early 1980s. Could Blunkett's equivalent therefore be the precursor confirming the phenomenon of anti-Muslimism as the 'new' racist ideology emergent in the early twenty first century?

Since the events of 7/7 other prominent members have followed suit. Despite Blunkett having left the front bench of British politics, many members of the British Government have both spoken to and openly criticised Muslims and their

---

[23] Allen (2003).

communities. In his first public speech to a Muslim audience after becoming Home Secretary, John Reid addressed a community group in East London by calling for Muslim parents to look out for the tell-tale signs of extremism in their children. As he put it, 'our fight is not with Muslims generally ... [but a] struggle against extremism'. He went on, 'There is no nice way of saying this. These fanatics are looking to groom and brainwash children, including your children, for suicide bombings, grooming them to kill themselves in order to murder others'.[24] At the event, Reid was heckled by the highly mediatised and well-known Abu Izzadeen, someone who came to fame through commending the 7/7 suicide bombers. Shouting at Reid, Izzadeen decried former Prime Minister Tony Blair as a murderer and accused the British government of killing Muslims all over the world.

The event was unsurprisingly shown across all the television networks as an example of what Reid was trying to convey in his message to Muslims, yet within hours of the event many were asking questions about the complicity of both Reid and Izzadeen in staging the event. Many were asking how a well-known and allegedly violent 'extremist' from an organisation that had been proscribed by the Government and who was very well known to Special Branch and senior police officers had been allowed within touching distance – and for a considerable period of time – of the Home Secretary. Following Izzadeen being given airtime by the BBC the next morning in which he called for the establishment of *sharia* law in the Islamic state of Britain, race commentator Darcus Howe voiced the opinion of many in a similar position: 'the Sky News clash was staged by Reid and his cohorts at the Home Office. They organised the meeting, Abu Izzadeen was invited in advance – his performance guaranteed – and the press was alerted to film and report the confrontation'.[25]

And as with Blunkett and Reid, so other politicians have contributed to the debates that have covertly shaped and determined a climate of anti-Muslim suspicion and attitudes. For example, ministers at the Department of Education issued guidelines to lecturers and university staff urging them to spy on Muslim and 'Muslim looking' students who they suspect might be involved in Islamic extremism or prone to supporting terrorist violence due to the belief that university campuses had become 'fertile recruiting grounds' for Muslim extremists.[26] Elsewhere, the former Communities Secretary Ruth Kelly announced that Muslim organisations that refused to defend core British values and failed to be 'pro-active' in the fight against extremism were to lose access to millions of pounds of Government funding. Using what can only be described as potentially loaded

---

[24]   BBC Online, 'Reid heckled during Muslim speech' (http://news.bbc.co.uk/1/hi/uk/5362052.stm) 20 September 2006.

[25]   Darcus Howe, 'John Reid's dirty little one-act play', *The New Statesman* (6 October 2006).

[26]   Vikram Dodd, 'Universities urged to spy on Muslims', *The Guardian* (16 October 2006).

language, Kelly stated that a *'fundamental* rebalancing' was required.[27] Shortly before this, Kelly had also called for Islamic schools that sought to be isolationist to be immediately closed down.[28]

In a period that appeared to repeatedly focus on the 'problem' of Britain's Muslim communities, it was the former Foreign Secretary and Leader of the Commons Jack Straw that gained the most attention by suggesting that Muslim women who wear the *niqab* could make relations between communities more difficult. He also revealed that he asked Muslim women who visit him and are wearing the *niqab* to consider removing it. Whilst such statements can be considered in isolation, it was – given the large amount of debate about Muslims in the period of Straw's comments – as the BBC News' Home Editor Mark Easton argued: 'not some reflective little observation from Jack Straw about the protocols of MP/constituent meetings in a multicultural world. This was a quite deliberate foray into what is becoming a real debate within Westminster: Does Britain's brand of multiculturalism work?'.[29] In addition to various telephone polls in both the broadcast and print media that showed overwhelming support for Straw's comments, so all the main political players added their agreement including: Tony Blair, Gordon Brown, Harriet Harman, and Bill Rammell amongst others, all of whom held positions of importance within the Labour Government at the time. Whether this can be construed as being Islamophobia is unclear but what it achieved was to further reinforce the notion in the public and political spaces that Muslim 'difference' was something that was causing 'us' problems.

The ongoing debate about Muslims and Islam in Britain's public and political spaces continues to be intensive and highly inflammatory. Since 7/7, the shooting of the innocent Brazilian national Jean Charles de Menezes for suspicion of being a suspected suicide bomber and the raid of a house in Forest Gate, London where an innocent Muslim man – 23 year old Mohammed Abdul Kahar – was shot due to being suspected of owning a chemical weapon vest, the intense scrutiny that Muslims have been placed under has incorporated numerous dawn raids, allegations of racist plots, the burgeoning anti-terror legislation, the holding of a number of Muslims without trial in London's Belmarsh prison, and the numerous other plots, conspiracies and allegations made against various Muslim individuals, groups and organisations. As a whole, such events have gone some way to suggesting that a somewhat institutionalised and pan-political anti-Muslim ideological foundation has ensued. Whether any or all of these events and undertakings amount to Islamophobia – explicit or otherwise – remains open to debate especially given the lack of valid understanding or definition about what Islamophobia is. However,

---

[27]   Toby Helm, 'Back British Values or Lose Grants', Kelly tells Muslim groups, *Daily Telegraph* (12 October 2006).

[28]   BBC Online, 'Close Extremist Schools – Kelly' (26 August 2006) http://news.bbc. co.uk/1/hi/uk_politics/5290338.stm.

[29]   'Analysis: Straw's Veil Debate' (5 October 2006) http://news.bbc.co.uk/1/hi/uk/5411642.stm.

what cannot be denied is the fact that numerous events, incidents and undertakings – as well as the events of 9/11 and 7/7 amongst others – have all contributed to a climate where the immediacy of recognition and acknowledgement of Muslim and Islamic difference, the growing receptivity to anti-Muslim ideas and expressions, and the sense of justification that is recurrently evident, is increasingly being seen to 'make sense'.

The British Media: 'I am an Islamophobe and proud'

The language, terminology and ideas circulated in the public and political spaces relating to Muslims however do not only emerge from the political elites. Increasingly important and pertinent in the circulation and dissemination of such ideas has been the role played by the media, not least by Nick Griffin previously. As identified in the Runnymede Report:

> closed as opposed to open views of Islam are routinely reflected and perpetuated in both broadsheets and tabloids, in both the local press and the national, in both considered statements and casual throwaway remarks, and in editorials, columns, articles, readers' letters, cartoons and headlines as well as in reports of events.[30]

It added that negative representations of Muslims and Islam were 'an ingredient of all sections of the media'.[31] This is particularly problematic given the findings of research that suggested that 74 per cent of Britons claim that they know 'nothing or next to nothing about Islam'. Amazingly, 64 per cent of the population also claim that what they do know is acquired through the media.[32] However, it is important to remember that as the EUMC Report concluded:

> the role and impact of the media is one that is contentious and debatable…to try and explain the media's role therefore remains difficult. None of the reports suggested that the media directly caused or, indeed, were responsible for any reported or identified act of aggression or significant change in attitude. However, this is not to dismiss their impact in any way, and despite there being no direct evidence to suggest otherwise, the media continue to play a major role in the formulation and establishment of popular perceptions in the public sphere.[33]

---

[30] Runnymede Trust: Commission on British Muslims and Islamophobia (1997), 20.

[31] Ibid., 1.

[32] YOUGOV, *Attitudes towards British Muslims*, Islam Awareness Week (4 November 2002).

[33] Allen and Nielsen (2002), 46–8.

It cannot therefore be legitimately suggested that, 'the media directly caused or, indeed, were responsible for any reported or identified act of aggression or significant change in attitude'.

Nonetheless, quantitative data that is available can be employed to highlight the problematic nature of the media and the impact that it potentially has. Following 9/11 in Britain alone, more 13 million people bought a national newspaper everyday.[34] In total, the *Times, Telegraph, Guardian, Independent, Financial Times* (FT), *Daily Mail, Daily Express, Daily Star, Mirror* and *Sun* added an additional 2.5 million copies to their normal combined print runs, all of which sold out on a daily basis.[35] The disseminative audience of the British press was therefore much wider immediately following 9/11 than on what might be termed a 'normal' day prior to it. So as per Whitaker, from the 1 January to the 9 September 2001 inclusive, the number of articles that were identified in the national newspapers:[36]

Newspaper	No. of articles
Guardian	817
Independent	681
Times	535
Daily Telegraph	417
Daily Mail	202
Mirror	164
Daily Express	139
Sun	80
Daily Star	40

Undertaking the same process from the 20 June 2001 to the 19 June 2002, a period that included 9/11, these numbers dramatically rose thus becoming:[37]

Newspaper	No. of articles	% increase
Guardian	2,043	250%
Independent	1,556	228%
Times	1,486	278%
Daily Telegraph	1,176	282%
Daily Mail	650	322%
Mirror	920	561%
Daily Express	305	219%
Sun	526	658%
Daily Star	144	360%

---

[34]   Michael Bromley and Stephen Cushion, 'Media Fundamentalism: the Immediate Response of the UK National Press to September 11th', in *Journalism after September 11*, eds Barbie Zelizer and Stuart Allan (London: Routledge, 2003), 160–77.

[35]   Ibid.

[36]   Brian Whitaker, 'Islam and the British Press', Hamid and Sharif (2002), 53–7.

[37]   Ibid., 54.

Whilst unfair to suggest that all of these articles were either negatively evaluated or anti-Muslim, if the observation that the Runnymede Report's 'closed views' are recurrent in the British press, then it might be fair to assume that any Islamophobic content had a similar proportional increase also.

For Poole, she identified different approaches being adopted towards 'British Muslims' and 'global Muslims', where 'the associative negative behaviour [of global Muslims] is seen to evolve out of something inherent in the religion, rendering any Muslim [global or British] a potential terrorist'.[38] What was being attributed to Muslims therefore, irrespective of their whereabouts, became transcendent and irrespective of conceptual or physical geography, overlooking all differentiation and proximity. Recalling Sardar's observations concerning how Muslims became identified either as terrorists warring against the West or apologists defending Islam, from Poole's research so it be concluded that irrespective of which 'type' is being put forward via the media, so a lack of necessary clarity insisted that all Muslims thus became whether visually or conceptually indistinguishable and identical, blurring the demarcations and differences that had underpinned the somewhat previously perceived bi-polar understandings of good/bad, local/ global Muslims, culminating in the process of understanding where all become indiscriminately homogenised with the same attributes, qualities, capabilities and characteristics.[39]

Almost a decade on from the publication of the Runnymede Report and five years from the undertakings of Whitaker and Poole, research undertaken on behalf of the Greater London Authority (GLA)[40] suggested that the situation had further deteriorated. Based on an analysis of the representation of 'Islam' and 'Muslims' in the British press between Monday 8 May 2006 and Sunday 14 May 2006 inclusive, the research sought to establish what the a 'normal' week looked like. It was termed a 'normal' week because there was no evidence to suggest that it would be any different from any other randomly selected week, from the point of view of the coverage of events related to Islam and Muslims. Comparing it to existing research from 1996,[41] it was estimated that the newsworthiness of Islam and Muslims, as measured by items in the national press, had increased by about 270 per cent. In comparison to Poole's earlier observations, so a shift towards a more 'British' rather than 'international' focus had seemed to have been undertaken, where 45 per cent of articles had a British focus compared to the 52 per cent international equivalent. Despite this, it was noted that it was however becoming increasingly difficult to differentiate between where 'British' and

---

38   Ibid., 4.

39   Ziauddin Sardar, 'The Excluded Minority: British Muslim Identity after 11 September', in *Reclaiming Britishness*, eds Phoebe Griffith and Mark Leonard (London: Foreign Policy Centre, 2002), 51–6.

40   Chris Allen, 'A "Normal" Week in Muslims in the Media', ed. INSTED (London: GLA – published in 2007).

41   Poole (2002), 23, 57.

'international' begins and ends, possibly a culmination of the process identified about the increasing homogenisation of all Muslims per se.

During that 'normal week', of the 19 national newspapers analysed, 12 were identified as having entirely negatively framed or associated representations of Islam and Muslims and, across all newspapers, 91 per cent of all representations were deemed to be negative. Almost 50 per cent of all of these referred to Muslims and/or Islam as posing a 'threat' whilst a further 34 per cent were related to crises. A significant majority (84 per cent) represented Islam and Muslims either as 'likely to cause damage or danger' or as 'operating in a time of intense difficulty or danger'. In doing so, Islam and Muslims were repeatedly represented as being the antithesis or Other of 'the West' through having contrasting belief systems, actors, characteristics, attributes, qualities and values. Because of the nature and recurrence of such representations, it was noted that it was highly probable that those who are repeatedly exposed to such representations would begin to accept them as 'truths'. Another consequence noted was that if Muslims were continued to be represented as an ineluctable Other, then it might be difficult for both Muslims and non-Muslims alike to see how Islam and Muslims can be ever be or fit into that which is deemed to be 'British' or take an equal participatory role in that which might be seen to be 'our' way of life. Consequently, far from being seen to be less problematic as regards its role and responsibilities, contemporarily the role of the media would appear to have become ever more important in communicating and disseminating ideas and meanings about Muslims and Islam.

Representing Islam: 'absolutely nobody having any fun whatsoever'

At times, the messages that are disseminated through the media about Islam and Muslims are done so in such ways that they are possibly meant to garner specific reactions in order to reinforce what those media outlets expect of Muslims. One particular example can be seen in the decision by the *Daily Star* to run a spoof newspaper entitled the *Daily Fatwa* that was to include an editorial column that was blank and stamped 'censored' alongside semi-nude female models as part of its '*Burka Babes*' special. The entire *Daily Fatwa* was to run under the headline 'How your favourite paper would look under Muslim law'.[42] Before going to print however, the National Union of Journalists stepped in and blocked its publication fearing for the safety of the journalists who had been required to work on the spoof piece. Yet within a few days, men's magazine – or 'lad's mag' – *Zoo* had taken up the mantle and printed a double-page spread featuring headlines such as 'Public stonings!', 'Beheadings!' and 'Absolutely Nobody having any Fun Whatsoever'. It also featured a full-page picture of a woman in a *niqab* alongside the headline,

---

[42]   *Socialist Worker* (London, 21 October 2006). The article can also be accessed at the following web address: http://www.socialistworker.co.uk/article.php?article_id=9977.

'A girl! As you've never seen her before … Pending approval under *shariah* law'. The article went on to add:

> Maybe shariah law isn't so controversial after all … Muslims who practise it to the letter are able to divorce their wives (up to four allowed) by text message. Wives are banned from being in a car with a man who is not a blood relative. And – common sense a-go-go – women aren't allowed to drive cars anyway! And hey, maybe the stricter Muslim woman is happy to hide her face and fleshy bits from public view? Been getting it all wrong with bikini-wearing babes, all-seeing Sex-Ray Specs and the pro-flesh Hot List? So for one week only, we proudly present your all-new, veil-friendly Zoo ….[43]

Whilst distasteful to Muslims, it is unclear whether such incidents in reality ever initiate or promote Islamophobia to its disseminative audience especially given that the *Zoo* article went largely unnoticed beyond its limited readership. Nonetheless, such approaches to Muslims and Islam would seem to be undertaken to deliberately garner a reaction that would seem to reinforce not only widespread views and attitudes that are already in circulation but also reinforce the ideas that the piece more openly suggested itself: that Muslims and Islam are those not 'having any fun whatsoever'.

Muslims therefore do not necessarily need to be named for the same ideas and meanings about them to be understood. All it needs is for there to be some reference to their inherently perceived and made known 'difference'. This difference neither explains nor justifies why Islamophobia occurred or indeed occurs – or even what Islamophobia is – but does highlight how embedded and receptive people are to such anti-Muslim, anti-Islamic messages. Islamophobia is therefore not explained or better understood from this particular perspective – more theoretical deconstructions need to be undertaken in order to begin to achieve this – but it does offer an insight into the catalysts, processes and motivations underpinning and influencing such manifestations and attitudes. Nonetheless, since the onset of the contemporary period of urgent history, so the recurrence of issues relating to Muslims and Islam as well as the presence of Islamophobia have been important and possibly even hugely significant in the way in which each of these component entities and associated phenomena have been both shaped and understood in the British context.

---

[43]   AIM (London, 21 October 2006). This article can also be accessed at the following web address: http://www.asiansinmedia.org/diary/?p=15.

Chapter 7

Different Forms of Discourse, Speech and Acts: Islamophobia in Europe

It is almost inconceivable that at the turn of the twenty first century both the term and concept of Islamophobia had little discursive resonance or value across most of Europe. Today however, the same could be no further from the truth. Contemporarily, Islamophobia emerges from a myriad range of sources and settings across Europe. But as was seen in both the historiography and in the British context previously, rarely is there any clear thinking or understanding employed as regards usage or understanding. From the high profile murder of Theo van Gogh in the Netherlands and the backlash against Muslims that ensued through 'direct democracy' votes against the building of minarets to verbal abuse against Muslim women and children in various European locations, these myriad and disparate events and incidents are – whether rightly or wrongly – regularly and repeatedly incorporated into the discursive landscape of Islamophobia. Islamophobia therefore is at times little more than an indiscriminate and all-encompassing term that is employed to satisfy or appease a vast spectrum of commentators, actors and perpetrators in varying different ways.

A Changing Europe: 'all kinds of different forms of discourse, speech and acts'

With the term now being widely used in the public and political spaces across a number of European states, Islamophobia has found a resonance or presence in the increasingly mediatised societies that we constantly and increasingly inhabit. Yet this is occurring at the same time that the media is being earmarked as one of the most virulent producers and disseminators of those stereotypes and misunderstandings of Muslims and Islam that seem to underpin such discourse and understanding. So too in the political spaces also: from Berlusconi's infamous remarks about Islam being a backward civilisation through the controversy surrounding Geert Wilders' film *Fitna* to the wide ranging debates that have raged in France, the Netherlands and elsewhere around the wearing of one or other of the *hijab*, *niqab* and *burqa*. In each setting, allegations abound that a piece of material can in some way establish a barrier to being French, Dutch and possibly even European or Western. It is not only in countries where larger Muslim communities are in evidence but in Belgium also, where headscarves and other forms of Muslim dress have been banned in some in schools. Irrespective of geographical or national setting therefore, it would be unlikely that some claim of Islamophobia, or counter-claim against that same thing or event being most definitely *not* Islamophobia, has been played out through the media, political or public spaces in the past five or so years. Few would have been able to avoid the growing menace that either Islam and Muslims are perceived to be presenting or possibly on the other hand, the growing menace of Islamophobia that seems to be spreading across Europe. Either way, the viewpoint is entirely subjective and open to both debate and disagreement.

One possible consequence – or possibly even cause – of this has been replicated across Europe in the same way that it has in Britain, where the roles and responsibilities of Europe's Muslim communities have come under greater scrutiny and interrogation. Beyond the mainstream political spaces – and in some settings within it too – there has been a catalyst that has seen a more virulent discourse about Muslims and Islam emerge and find a more willing and receptive audience: the debates and discussions surrounding the dramatic and near universal increase in 'security' and 'anti-terror' legislation that has occurred across Europe since 9/11 being a case in point. Yet at the same time, and possibly as a series of measures to balance what might be perceived to be the targeting of Muslim communities, various other legislative measures, political debates, reports and initiatives have sought to challenge and potentially halt what is seen in some circles to be a rapid and downward spiralling acceptance of negative attitudes and ideas about Muslims. The situation is therefore far from one-sided and one cannot apportion blanket blame against all Europeans and their governments as indeed some commentators and agitators most definitely have. From within Muslim communities themselves also, a similar two pronged response has similarly emerged where despite there being an ever worrying trend towards – if security sources are to be believed – the radicalisation of Muslim youth in particular, Muslim communities have also begun to respond to a growing recognition of Islamophobia much more positively. Since the turn of the century therefore, the situation affecting and informing the European landscape is one that has significantly changed.

Yet despite or possibly even because of these rapid and significant changes having occurred, Islamophobia continues in the European context to be a contested concept.[1] Underpinning all of these events as well as the discourse and rhetoric, understandings and meanings that have ensued exists a highly fluid, protean and largely inconsistent phenomenon, one captured by Maussen's observation that '"Islamophobia" groups together all kinds of different forms of discourse, speech and acts, by suggesting that they all emanate from an identical ideological core, which is an "irrational fear" (a phobia) of Islam'.[2] With so many disparate events, activities, actions and attitudes either emerging from or being expressed as a consequence of Islamophobia, so overly simplistic definitions and

---

[1]   Chris Allen, *Islamophobia: Contested Concept in the Public Space* (Ph.D diss., University of Birmingham, 2006).

[2]   Jocelyne Cesari, *Securitization and Religious Divides in Europe: Muslims in Western Europe after 9/11 – Why the term Islamophobia is more a Predicament than an Explanation* (Paris: Challenge, 2006), 6.

simplified terminologies have failed to adequately provide enough explanation or understanding of a phenomenon – whether real or otherwise – despite it having had such a dramatic impact both on Europe's extremely diverse Muslim and non-Muslim communities. So despite there being signs of an anti-Muslim, anti-Islamic phenomena existing, so there also appears to be a sense of contestation about meaning, interpretation and ownership at its core: a situation that appears to have been largely overlooked and subsequently undervalued. This first became apparent in the findings of the EUMC's *Summary Report into Islamophobia in the EU following 11 September 2001*.[3] At this juncture, it may therefore be useful to consider this report in more detail.

The EUMC Report: 'indiscriminate victims of an upsurge of both verbal and physical attacks'

The EUMC Report was the synthesis of 75 nationally focused reports, five from each EU member state that closely monitored reactions against, and any changes of attitude towards Muslims following the attacks on the US. Of the 75 nationally focused reports, the first 15 were commissioned within 24 hours of the attacks, putting in place the necessary mechanisms to closely track the situation faced by Muslims across each of the EU's members. The project ended at the end of the 2001 calendar year. As there was little if indeed any concrete evidence at the juncture of the project's implementation of any actual changes in attitude or backlash against Muslim communities, the immediacy of this response points towards a sense of expectation, or even inevitability, that such a reaction would ensue. In recognising the response of the various presidents and prime ministers of Europe who also took immediate action to stress the need for understanding that this was not 'Islam' or 'Muslims' per se that had perpetrated the attacks, the report itself noted that there was an almost unspoken acknowledgement that a clear and unequivocal pre-emptive response was required.[4] Unfortunately, despite the attempts by some of Europe's political elite to diffuse the situation, the summary report concluded that, 'Muslims became indiscriminate victims of an upsurge of both verbal and physical attacks following the events of 11 September'.[5] From its findings, a new dynamism emanating directly from the attacks on the US saw manifestations of anti-Muslim and anti-Islamic expression become both more extreme and explicit, and much more widely tolerated.

As regards violence, aggression and changes in attitude, the report concluded that across the entire spectrum of the EU, incidents were identified where a negative or discriminatory act was perpetrated against Muslims or a material entity

---

[3]   Allen and Nielsen (2002).

[4]   Ibid., 43.

[5]   Taken from the press release from the EUMC at the launch of the report's publication, 15 May 2002.

associated with Islam. Numerous mosques, cultural centres and Islamic schools were either targeted of threatened, with probably the most distasteful being a mosque in Exeter, England where seven pigs heads were left impaled on spikes outside it and where what purported to be pigs blood was smeared over the outside of the building and its entrance. What emerged across the EU however was that irrespective of the varying levels of violence and aggression that were identified and documented, underpinning this were, as the report itself termed it, visual identifiers of either Muslims or Islam, or both.[6] Whilst these were not necessarily the reason for such changes or attacks, they were the single most predominant factor in determining the foci for whom or what necessitated retaliatory action or response. The visual identifiers provided a social stimulant that offered an outlet for the venting of rage, revenge or any other denigratory sentiment or action.

It is no surprise therefore that when these visual identifiers held such primacy in determining who or what became the targets for discrimination, abuse, violence and aggression, that it was Muslim women in particular – possibly the most visually identifiable religious adherents in contemporary Europe – who became the primary foci for retaliation. So for example, the report stated that Islamophobic incidents were identified in Denmark where a Muslim woman was thrown from a moving taxi; in Germany, where Muslim women had their *hijabs* torn from their heads; and in Italy where a bus driver repeatedly shut a Muslim woman in the bus' doors much to the amusement of an on-looking and cheering crowd. Numerous other similar instances were recorded elsewhere. Interestingly, in those countries where it was uncommon for Muslim women to wear traditional attire, in Luxembourg for example, no incidents were reported as being targeted towards women. In this particular setting however, the focus shifted towards the more physical visual identifiers of Islam where Luxembourg's sole Islamic centre was vandalised and attacked.

Neither were Muslim men exempted from this process and in line with the heavy media rotation of images of bin Laden and the Taleban following the attacks, turban-wearing men became indiscriminate targets, identifying – somewhat inaccurately – turbans as a visual identifier of Muslims. Because of this, a rise in attacks against Sikh men was reported but this can only be attributed to ignorance and misinterpretation rather than any rise in anti-Sikh behaviour or attitudes. Similarly, men with beards – again incorporating Sikh men – were also targeted for attack and violence in certain locations although in a much lesser degree than other forms of targeting, as indeed were the everyday visual symbols across society that would normally be ignored or unnoticed. The last aspect relating to visual identifiers was the attacks on the physical entities of Islam where, as mentioned beforehand, mosques, schools and cultural centres were identified. Included in this were general threats, through vandalism and material damage, to more serious concerns purporting to bomb and death threats. Across Europe, many Islamic schools closed for a number of days due to the fear of threats being fulfilled or the

---

[6]   Allen and Nielsen (2002), 34–7.

possibility of a spontaneous attack. At times of prayer also, many mosques had increased security and many local police authorities agreed to increase patrols in response to requests from some Muslim communities that had received threats of violence and worse.

Removing Difference and Diversity: 'all muslims are the same'

The report stated that prejudices and distrust appeared to be extended to all individuals whose looks may have either affiliated or associated them with Islam, quite irrespective of whether or not they were indeed Muslim. Consequently, the role of the visual aspects of Islam and Muslims cannot be overlooked because embodied within the common identifiers that are today readily recognised and acknowledged, there is also an embodiment of a view that not only essentialises all Muslims through the common denominator of Islam that simultaneously infers that all Muslims bear some form of collective and homogenous responsibility. One way of elaborating upon this, if somewhat coarsely, is to reiterate the previously amended old racist adage that 'all Muslims *are* the same'.[7]

The report also noted an upsurge in ethnic xenophobia, especially those that were either historical or pre-existent to 9/11, typically also either nationally or regionally constrained.[8] So whilst this happened across the spectrum of the EU, different manifestations were identified in different settings, dependent upon the Muslim communities themselves and their particular histories, nationalities, status and ethnic backgrounds. As the report put it, the attacks on the US provided a catalyst of fear that sought to reaffirm and renew old – and indeed enhance new – prejudices that exaggerated the potential of the perceived 'enemy within'. The impetus of a greater awareness, a previously unacknowledged vulnerability, and a fear and dread of both old and new enemies, all sometimes being supported and reiterated by voices in both the media and political spheres, contributed and compounded the problem where as the report suggested, both latent and active prejudices found a catalytic reinvigoration.[9] So in Spain for example, the widespread survival in Spanish folklore of the 'el Moro'[10] found greater credence, where a greater emphasis on 'el Moro's' Muslim-ness became readily apparent. Similarly in Greece, the centuries old enemies that were previously described as being either Turkish or Albanian were subsequently described, in the post-9/11 global context, as Turkish Muslims or Albanian Muslims.

---

[7]   Chris Allen, 'From Race to Religion: the New Face of Discrimination' in ABBAS, ed., *Muslim Britain: Communities Under Pressure* (Aldershot: Ashgate, 2004).

[8]   For a more detailed exposition of the findings of this section, see Allen and Nielsen (2002), 40–41.

[9]   Ibid., 40.

[10]   Nino Del Olmo Vicen, 'The Muslim Community in Spain' in Gerd Nonneman et al., eds, *Muslim Communities in the New Europe* (Reading: Ithaca, 1995), 303–14:307.

The distinctions between religion and ethnicity therefore became increasingly blurred and the primacy of an enemy's 'Muslim-ness', whether relevant or not, became stressed in order to reinvigorate and reaffirm historical foes albeit in a contemporary frame of reference and understanding. So whilst these types of xenophobia were not anything new and were distinctly pre-9/11 phenomena, through the overlapping of Muslim-ness and the previously racialised or ethnicised Otherness that such enemies previously had, those fears and attributes that were already in circulation in those particular settings became not only subsequently reinforced but also transitionally found an increased resonance through a seeming confirmation of the fears and beliefs that those societies and communities previously held, albeit somewhat inactively or suppressed. The atavistic stereotypes of historical enemies – the historical Others that much of Europe and European society had learned to define itself in opposition to – that were deeply embedded in the experience and culture of various different races, nationalities and communities were being reinvigorated – and possibly re-justified – by contemporary events: a reminder of how history provides the framework within which contemporary thinking and thought are understood.

In identifying these broad findings from the EUMC Report, it is imperative to note that whilst the report was the culmination of the largest ever monitoring project into Islamophobia (and indeed continues to be to the present day) it was not entirely conclusive and so it would be wrong to constrain the focus to this. Indeed since that report, a handful of others have been published that have reinforced and further evidenced the situation across the European landscape. So for instance, the EUMC published two reports simultaneously in 2007: one considered the evidence that showed that since 9/11, European Muslims had become seriously affected by an increasingly hostile social climate,[11] the other reported the findings from 58 in-depth interviews with members of Muslim communities in 10 EU countries with significant Muslim populations.[12] In the first, it noted how Muslims '… are vulnerable to manifestations of prejudice and hatred in the form of anything from verbal threats through to physical attacks on people and property'.[13] In the second, the reports set out how many Muslims felt that they had been placed under intense scrutiny and that there had been an increase in open incidents of everyday hostility. Most agreed that the situation had deteriorated in recent years and that this had the effect of generating disaffection and alienation.

A few years later in 2009, the European Union Agency for Fundamental Rights (FRA) published its *Data in focus: Muslims Report* which provided some additional interesting observations.[14] Looking specifically at Europe – excluding the UK – the report reiterated many of the findings from earlier reports, mostly in terms of the

---

[11]   European Monitoring Centre for Racism and Xenophobia (2007a).

[12]   European Monitoring Centre for Racism and Xenophobia (2007b).

[13]   European Monitoring Centre for Racism and Xenophobia (2007a), 8.

[14]   European Union Agency for Fundamental Rights: *Data in Focus Report: Muslims* (Vienna: FRA, 2009).

levels and likelihood of Islamophobia and anti-Muslim discrimination. However, it challenged some also. As regards experiencing discrimination, the report noted how approximately 34 per cent of Muslim men and 26 per cent of Muslim women in Europe had experienced discrimination in the past year. Whilst going against research that has suggested that it is Muslim women who are likely to experience discrimination more readily, the report added that of victims of both genders who had experienced discrimination, it was likely that they had experienced an average of eight incidents each over the past 12 months.[15] Again against previous research, the report added that being 'visible', for example wearing Muslim clothing and so on did not make someone more likely to become a victim, going against the findings of the EUMC's research in particular. Further exploring the type of person likely to become a victim, the report suggested that someone between the ages of 16 and 24 were most likely to become a victim, with that likelihood seeming to reduce with age. Of those who did become a victim, 79 per cent were unlikely to report their experience of discrimination. The main reasons given for not reporting discrimination was that 'nothing would happen or change' by reporting their experience of discrimination (59 per cent), while many (38 per cent) did not see the point of reporting discrimination, as it was just 'part of their normal everyday existence'.[16] More worryingly, around 80 per cent of victims could not name either an organisation or institution – official or otherwise – where they offered support or advice to people who have been discriminated against.

Beyond 9/11: 'we cannot say that we have a grasp on the "real" object in front of us'

The question to ask therefore is: what are, or indeed what have been the conditions upon which this spread or development of Islamophobia occurred? To answer this it is important to consider the backdrop of Europe since the turn of the century, one that has been punctuated and dictated by various terrorist atrocities, the ongoing mediatisation of knowledge and understanding, and the burgeoning 'war on terror' as both a myth and reality. It has been – and indeed it might be suggested remains – one that is given context through Baudrillard's 'close up photography' analogy:

> When we get 'too close' to an object, we sometimes have trouble even distinguishing what the object is. In that sense, we cannot say that we have a grasp on the 'real' object in front of us. The hyperreal, in relation to this analogy, is like the extreme close up and an extreme long distance photograph at the same time. That is to say, there is no longer a third, normative position of realistic

---

[15]   Ibid., 3.

[16]   Ibid.

perspective. The notion of total involvement or immersion combined with alienating detachment is also perceived.[17]

To some extent, the conditions for this emergent and developing Islamophobia have been ones where there has been a collapse of perspectival space, contextualized and informed by a period of intense and urgent history as well a climate of fear and anxiety. At the same time, as the historically known physical and conceptual proximities of Muslims and Islam as external, distant and 'out-there' have been systematically eradicated through patterns of mass migration and the onset of global media networks, so the critical – even conceptually 'safe' – distance that existed previously no longer exists. Consequently, the historically and mythologically distant Muslims of old remain the enemy Other but are also nowadays the enemy 'within'. In addition, as the EUMC Report noted, this does 'not explain why some EU citizens felt the need to exact revenge or engage in some retaliatory act' but what with the 'contemporary context with international tensions and uncertainties relating to the ongoing 'war on terrorism' being high in the consciousness of many in the West', then this was identified as a possible catalyst. Given that this has continued and indeed arguably deteriorated, further events and incidents have merely sought to remind us of the closer proximity of Muslims and Islam to Europe and Europeans. As the EUMC Report went on, 'Islamophobia and anti-Muslim sentiments will continue to be founded for the foreseeable future'.[18] Unsurprisingly, this is the situation that Europe may be continuing to face.

One important means through which these conditions have become played out has been through the media, where terrorism, violence and anti-Westernism have been recurrent themes. Despite the EUMC 7/7 Report noting that, 'the media appears to have avoided linking directly the Muslim faith or Muslim communities in general with terrorism or radical groups. In many cases, mainstream media made particular efforts to differentiate between the pseudo-religious justification of terrorism and the Muslim faith …', it did go on to add that '… this distinction has sometimes been blurred by inflationary language and headlines such as "Islamic terrorism", and in many cases the use of terms "Islam", "Muslim", [and] "fundamentalism" seems to confuse rather than educate the reader'.[19] Whilst still not explaining the causes or reasons for the potentially voracious spread of Islamophobia, the framework of conditions within which such developments have occurred would appear to be becoming clearer.

It is also worthy of note that these conditions are the same conditions through which Islamophobia has been responded to at the European level. If one considers the response to Islamophobia at the pan-European level, it is this same backdrop that has initiated the various reports and monitoring projects that have been put in place and undertaken. As such, it is not surprising that the EUMC has produced

---

[17]   Richard J. Lane, *Jean Baudrillard* (London: Routledge, 2001), 98.
[18]   Allen and Nielsen (2002), 37.
[19]   Ibid., 43.

reports following the events of 9/11 and 7/7 or that other organisations have followed suit. This is not a negative process because it is through these sources, and the activities that have emerged from them, that things have gone some way towards helping familiarise and endorse both the term and concept on a European platform. They have therefore attributed Islamophobia with some much needed legitimacy and credibility. In acknowledging the positives it is also worth noting the negative flipside to this situation and acknowledge how – at the pan-European level at least – activities that have been proactive towards Islamophobia have been near non-existent. To compound the problem, rarely whether socially or politically has either the term or the concept of Islamophobia been dealt with in such ways that a critical analysis or better understanding emerge, a criticism that that might to some degree be posited at the academic sphere also.

Having set out the situation that emerged following 9/11 in an attempt to try and contextualise this, given the consideration of the conditions relating to the spread of Islamophobia across Europe since, now it is necessary to consider some of the events, incidents and occurrences – and consequences – that have occurred since. To do so, it is necessary to contextualise these within a series of broad themes. In this way, a broad panoramic landscape can be set out rather more so than the minute detail of each individual setting. It is important to stress however that these events, incidents and occurrences are in isolation not Islamophobic but are instead informed or initiated by an ideological understanding or meaning that is Islamophobic. So for example, the act of spitting at someone is in isolation far from Islamophobic per se but actually spitting on someone because they are Muslim would be something that was informed by the ideological premise of Islamophobia. As with the visual identifiers therefore, in Europe it is the recognition of 'Muslim-ness' or 'Islamic-ness' and the ideological meaning informed by this that might be constituted as being Islamophobic and nothing more. This distinction is necessary as it somewhat different to how a literalist interpretation of the Runnymede model of Islamophobia might be understood.

General Attitudes Towards Muslims: 'threatening the consensus of values'

The growing presence or more so, the recognition of the presence of Muslims has meant that the issue of integration has become something of a recurrent feature of the discourse surrounding the roles and responsibilities of Muslims. In turn, this has lead to many questions being asked about the 'place' of European Muslims or more worryingly, the Muslims in Europe. Besides Muslims themselves, the most significant victim of many of these debates has been the previously upheld social model of multiculturalism, something that is particularly relevant in the British and Dutch contexts. Broadly speaking, arguments against the ongoing validity of the multiculturalism model have suggested that its continuation will dilute or even eradicate notions of European identity, an identity that is being increasingly framed in terms that are primarily white and Christian. An interesting insight into this can be seen in rhetoric of both the Austrian Freedom Party leader, Jorg Haider and the Flemish separatist Vlaams Blok (now Vlaams Belang): 'the increasing fundamentalism of radical Islam which is penetrating [Europe], is threatening the consensus of values which is in danger of getting lost' whilst Muslims and Islam present 'a threat to the Flemish people and culture'. To some degree, similar discursive meanings can also be identified in the rhetoric surrounding Turkey's proposed accession to the EU.

In those countries across Europe where multiculturalism has been heralded as the social model of choice this has resulted in the complete overhaul of thinking about society, identity and immigration. One consequence of this has been the oft repeated question of whether it is now possible to be both 'Dutch' and Muslim, 'Danish' and Muslim and so on. In some ways, many of the recent attacks on multiculturalism have been little more than a thinly veiled attack on Muslims themselves and the notion of what a Muslim identity is. Whilst in the Netherlands – a country whose liberal multiculturalism was until very recently regularly touted as being a model that other countries should emulate – the focus has seen a much greater emphasis being placed on cultural assimilation where 'good citizenship' and 'civic integration' have become important policy goals.[20] The fears, anxieties and perceived threats that have been associated with or underpinning of much of this discourse has nowhere been as articulately and decisively aired as by the assassinated Pim Fortuyn. Being vociferous and widely reported about the need to maintain the liberal values and ethics of the Netherlands, Fortuyn directed much of his rhetoric towards Muslims and the religion of Islam: as he put it, 'if it were legally possible, I'd say no more Muslims will get in here'.

For Fortuyn, both Islam as a religion and the culture brought with Muslims had failed to undergo the necessary process of modernisation that was required if Islam and Muslims were to become a part of Dutch society. For him, this meant that both lacked either the ability or even the willingness to accept certain tenets of a Western society. Regarding multiculturalism, his position was possibly most persuasively put when in a televised debate with an imam in 2002 he baited the imam with his homosexuality. As the imam eventually exploded with rage and denounced Fortuyn in a rage of homophobia, he calmly turned to the camera and addressing viewers directly, told them 'this is the kind of Trojan horse of intolerance the Dutch are inviting into their society in the name of multiculturalism'.[21] Having been voted the greatest ever Dutch man to have lived during a television poll in 2004, his words and views have had a resonance across Europe and in many ways, ongoing through those such as Geert Wilders and his Partij voor de Vrijheid (Party for Freedom). Having won municipal elections in Almare with around a fifth of all votes cast in 2010 and coming second in The Hague – where Wilders has since taken a seat on the council – commentators are suggesting that Wilders, the Partij voor de Vrijheid and all of its associated campaigns and causes – including those

---

20   Cesari (2006).

21   Rod Dreher, 'Murder in Holland' (*National Review*, 7 May 2002).

relating to Muslims and Islam – will dominate the political landscape in the run-up to the parliamentary elections later this year.

Safeguarding Europe: 'terrorists' and 'fifth columnists'

The tightening and implementation of new anti-terror and security legislation and measures have been significantly impacting, throwing a shadow of suspicion over Muslims across the entire breadth of Europe. In this setting, issues relating to anti-terror and security have far too often been equated with issues relating to immigration where internal and external security policies have become conflated or even interchangeable with each other. Because of this, Muslims have become understood in frames that both acknowledged and perpetuated an ongoing Otherness, one that is inherently foreign, alien and enemy and regularly interchanged with those populist notions of Muslims as 'terrorists' and 'fifth columnists' amongst others, as has been the case in the UK also. Consequently, and at the same time interestingly, the nations of the EU have arrested more than twenty times the number of terrorist suspects than the US since 9/11.[22] Across Europe therefore, high profile and large-scale 'terror raids' have become a recurrent feature gaining particular expediency in Germany and Italy as well as elsewhere. Despite political and populist attitudes being such that many would suggest that they were most at risk from Muslims, terrorism in Europe since 9/11 has been far from confined to radical Islamists. In France and Spain for example, many more Basque nationalists have been arrested than Islamists where of the 358 inmates accused of terrorism in France, only 94 are Muslim.[23]

Under increased legislation that is on one level identified as being vital to increase security and protect the homeland and its people, other impacting consequences have also ensued. Take Germany for example, various pieces of legislation have been passed that have allowed for a number of Muslim organizations to have been banned, for mosques to be searched with seemingly little justification, and a new data-mining technique has been introduced that seeks to identify what has been termed the 'quiet' radicals.[24] As a driver for this, two identical suitcase bombs were planted on two commuter trains in Dortmund and Koblenz in 2005 but failed to explode and it is alleged that Hamburg was a base for one of the cells responsible for the attacks of 9/11. Somewhat unsurprisingly, Germany has also witnessed a growing number of 'terror raids' in locations such as Ulm, Neu Ulm, Freiburg, Frankfurt, Dusseldorf and Bonn amongst others. Across Europe therefore, three significant consequences appear to have emerged out of this situation. The first is that there has been a dramatic increase in the amount of intelligence surveillance and police activity being undertaken specifically as

---

[22]   Cesari (2006).

[23]   Alexandre Caeiro, 'French Report', Cesari (2006), 203.

[24]   Yasemin Karakasoglu et al., 'German Report', Cesari (2006), 148–9.

regards Muslims and their respective communities. Second, there has been the banning of various Muslim groups and organisations on the premise of them being 'radical', 'fundamentalist' or 'extremist' in some ways. And finally, there has been an increase in the deportation of those identified or deemed to be – in line with the proscribed groups and organisations – radical, fundamentalist or extremist. Each of these consequences has indeterminably affected Muslim communities more than any other even though they have not – in many of the given situations – been explicitly identified or even linked with Muslims or Islam.

Across Europe, it has been commonplace for immigration policies to have been tightened, at times where the overlap between security issues and concerns are increasingly indistinguishable from those relating to immigration. For some countries, such as Germany and France for example, the prospect of high numbers of low skill workers migrating to their respective countries has become untenable. In response, they have sought to address the increasing trend by putting policies in place that make it easier for more highly skilled immigrants to enter the countries at the same time as reducing the possibilities of others. In France, Nicolas Sarkozy's call for a more selective immigration policy has been responded to with policies and legislation being introduced in May 2005. In highlighting the blurring of boundaries that exist between immigration and security and their incorporation of Muslims and Islam, throughout this process Sarkozy quite openly referred to Islam in his rhetorical justifications, arguing that any new migrants to France must be willing to accept the publication of religious cartoons in newspapers and for women to have identity photographs taken without wearing the *hijab* or *niqab*, two direct references to Muslims and Islam. In reinforcing his argument, Sarkozy made reference to the role of Muslims and Islam in his denunciations of the riots of 2005 that constituted a significant part of his melee of anti-immigration arguments.[25]

As in the UK, so the gap between the right and left of the political spectrum has come markedly closer since the events of 9/11 in terms of views and discourses about Muslims.[26] In France it has been noted how those from the left have also contributed to the debates especially as regards the issue of gender. Malek Boutih, ex-president of the anti-racism organization SOS-Racisme and prominent member of the Socialist Party, defended a policy of immigration with 'laïcité' and the acceptance of gender equality as a precondition for migration.[27] From an equally liberal perspective, the Dutch Ministry of Aliens Affairs and Integration recently produced a film which is intended to assist with the screening of immigrants by showing them the extremes of Dutch gender relations and sexuality. In doing so, the film shows images of naked beachgoers and homosexuality in public as well as assertive female characters.[28] Similar citizenship tests elsewhere have become

---

[25]   Caeiro (2006), 198.

[26]   Allen (2005).

[27]   Caeiro (2006), 197.

[28]   Marcel Maussen, 'Anti-Muslim Sentiments and Mobilization in the Netherlands: Discourse, Policies and Violence', Cesari (2006), 122.

de rigueur if somewhat less controversial. So in the German state of Baden-Wurtenberg for example, moral questions have been asked about the obligation to ensure that all children participate in swimming lessons. As Spain and Italy have only recently introduced newly developed policies about immigration, it is too early to determine whether or indeed how these might affect Muslims rather than all immigrants. Although as a potential pre-cursor in 2000, the spokesman of the Association of Moroccan Immigrant Workers (ATIME), Mustafa Mrabet, had already begun to highlight the disparity between the 52 per cent of citizenship applications from Moroccans that were settled compared to Latin Americans who had more than 80 per cent acceptance rates.[29]

It is important to point out that in many settings, changes to immigration law and the perceptions attached to it should be understood in the context of changing perceptions and attitudes to immigration and not merely a climate of Islamophobia. To highlight a situation from the UK for example, in recent years there has been much debate in both the political and media spaces about the widening of the EU and the influx of migrants from Bulgaria and Romania. This debate follows closely the same debate that has been played out in the public spaces about the influx of Polish and other economic migrants from Eastern Europe as well as the scourge of 'Sangat' and its asylum seeking 'folk devils' that pre-dated 9/11.

Public Enemy Number One: 'resentments, fears and constructions of the enemy ... have now come to the surface'

It is worth revisiting the observation by the EUMC 9/11 Report that 'across the entire spectrum of the EU member states incidents were identified where a negative or discriminatory act was perpetrated against Muslims or an entity that was associated with Islam'.[30] However, due to the lack of reliable and effective national and Europe-wide monitoring systems and procedures at the time, it was difficult to determine the exact scale or nature of the violence, damage and discrimination that was being directed against Muslims and Islam. This has in many ways remained a serious problem, one that has been further compounded by the fact that it is not only difficult to differentiate between what might in many circumstances be 'racist' as opposed to 'Islamophobic' but also because of a widespread apparent unwillingness amongst Muslim communities – irrespective of location – to come forward and report such incidents. Because of this, evidence tends to be largely anecdotal and thus easily challenged and by default, easily dismissed so does not accurately reflect the true depth and breadth of the situation.

As with the immediate aftermath of 9/11 however, events or incidents that are in some way understood to be 'Muslim' or 'Islamic', or are attributed to either of these, would seem to act as a catalyst for a dramatic rise in the number of

---

[29]   Jose Maria Ortuno Aix, 'Report on Islamophobia in Spain', Cesari (2006), 253.
[30]   Allen and Nielsen (2002), 33.

retaliatory attacks and responses both physically and materially. So in addition to those events such as 9/11, following the 7/7 London tube and Madrid train bombings backlashes against Muslims have again been in evidence. So in Austria and Ireland for example, Muslim women have become increasingly targeted for verbal and physical abuse. Similar incidents – though varying in number – have also been recorded in other locales including Belgium, Finland and Luxembourg. Following the murder of Theo Van Gogh in the Netherlands, more than 80 incidents against Muslims were recorded there including a bomb being placed at a Muslim school, another being burnt down, and a place of worship in Helden being destroyed following an arson attack begun by neo-Nazis.[31] Drawing upon the British setting to provide a more detailed insight into the backlashes that ensued after 7/7 police records from Sheffield in the North of England show how from the beginning of 2005 to 6 July 2005, only one 'Islamophobic' incident had been reported, whereas in the two weeks following the 7/7 bombings, the same records show how more than 30 incidents were recorded: a rise of 3,000 per cent.[32] To further illustrate the dramatic rises that occur following such events, since the end of July 2005 figures have once again returned to normal even though tensions at 'street' level have remained high.

As a consequence of the pressure applied on Europe by such issues as terrorism, immigration and the widening of the EU's boundaries, there has been a growing incidence of right-wing and nationalistic rhetoric and discourse. The 'Muslim' issue has added to this and as an Austrian source noted, 'resentments, fears and constructions of the enemy, which have formed to historic burdens and a lack of information, [have] now come to the surface'.[33] More recently in Austria, the more extreme right of the political spectrum has made significant inroads. In 2008, Heinz-Christian Strache and his *Freiheitliche Partei Österreichs* (Freedom Party), both of whom were accused of xenophobia and waging an anti-Muslim campaign, won around 18 per cent of the electoral vote whilst Jörg Haider and the *Bündnis Zukunft Österreich* (Alliance for the Future of Austria), won just over ten per cent. More recently, Strache actively campaigned against the planned extension of a mosque in Vienna warning that it would lead to greater 'religious indoctrination'. Elsewhere, other right wing parties have also been using anti-Muslim and anti-Islamic discourse and ideas, see the *Schweizerische Volkspartei* (Swiss People's Party), *Sverigedemokraterna* (Sweden Democrats) and the *Lega Nord* (Northern League) amongst others.

However, it is not only Islamophobia that has been on the rise as a result of this shift towards the right, other forms of discriminatory practices including racism by colour, xenophobia and anti-Semitism have also been noted as having

---

[31]   Maussen (2006).

[32]   Unpublished resources acquired from West Yorkshire Police Force (Sheffield), November 2006.

[33]   Unpublished document as part of the EUMC monitoring programme into Islamophobia following 11 September 2001 from the Austrian National Focal Point.

increased in recent years.[34] Numerous examples of this can be seen across Europe such as in Italy where Forza Nuova has laid claim that Italy is by history and character irrevocably and essentially Catholic. Forza's argument continues that because Muslims are not Catholic, then Muslims cannot either be or indeed ever become Italian and so cannot be citizens let alone 'good' citizens.[35] Elsewhere the Lega Nord has switched its rhetoric to take advantage of anti-Muslim sentiment, deploying slightly modified versions of traditional anti-Semitic devices as weapons against Islam and Muslims, in many ways highlighting the pool of hatreds and hostilities that such concurrent phenomena draw upon.

Likewise in Denmark – a country placed under the international spotlight following the publication of cartoons of the Prophet Muhammad in January 2006 – a similar shift can also be seen. With its Prime Minister having publicly criticised the Muslim community for unnecessarily taking up to 'four' prayer breaks at work each day even prior to the events of 9/11, Denmark was the first European country to have governmental elections following the attacks. Maybe somewhat unsurprisingly, political capital was sought by focusing on the presence and role of Muslims in Denmark via debates about immigration, terrorism, security and the role of 'foreigners', a term that has become increasingly equitable and substitutable in the Danish vernacular with 'Muslims'. Following the *Dansk Folkeparti* (Danish People's Party) being reported to the police for hate speech crimes, the Danish political spaces continued to be dominated by tests of loyalty: the requirement of Muslims to pledge their allegiance to the Danish constitution over and above the Qur'an; the establishment of legal criteria to restrict Danish citizens or residents from bringing spouses into the country from elsewhere in the world; and the need for all immigrants to show a stronger cultural connection to Denmark than any other country or entity. Without going into the debates about the publication of cartoons in the Jyllands-Posten at this particular juncture, what is interesting is that one year after the original publication of the cartoons a video was aired in the Danish media that showed youth members of the Dansk Folkeparti engaged in a contest to draw pictures that insult Muhammad. Whilst the government roundly condemned the video's contents, a group named 'Defending Denmark' claimed that they had made the video to expose the extreme right wing associations of the party and its ongoing vitriol against Muslims and Islam. Just this year, the Prime Minister Lars Loekke Rasmussen has joined in the debate about Muslims and Islam by asserting that the 'face veil' has no place in Denmark.

The examples given here are therefore indicative rather more so than exhaustive of the vast changes that have occurred and are indeed continuing to occur across Europe. Without any doubt, it is now possible to make openly anti-Muslim, anti-Islamic and anti-immigrant statements in such ways that would have been deemed inappropriate and unacceptable in the political spaces of Europe had they

---

[34]   European Monitoring Centre on Racism and Xenophobia, *Anti-Semitism – Summary Overview of the Situation in the European Union 2001–2005* (Vienna: EUMC, 2006).

[35]   Mirna Liguori, 'Report on Islamophobia', Cesari (2006), 308–9.

been made against other minority or religious groups. Whilst vitally important to understanding the landscape and context, two other trends are also worthy of note. The first is the increasing differentiation between 'good' and 'bad' Islam increasingly couched in terms of 'mainstream' or 'moderate' and 'extremist' or 'radical' respectively.[36] Rarely in any of the political settings of the European setting is the term Islam or Muslim used neutrally. Given that the distinctions of 'good', 'moderate', 'mainstream' and 'true' amongst others are regularly made, underlying this is the assumption that Muslims and Islam are inherently and normatively problematic and that stressing their 'good', 'moderate' or other characteristic is something of a necessity. The second is the increasing deployment of Muslim voices to air criticisms of Islam and Muslims. Reflecting the process used so successfully by the BNP in employing the 'legitimate' voices of Sikhs and Hindus, so the deployment of Muslim voices has provided similar justification elsewhere where speaking from 'inside' Muslim communities allows those same voices to be much harsher and far more critical than those located on the 'outside'. Possibly the most notable – and notorious – of these on a European platform has been in the Netherlands by Ayaan Hirsi Ali. Questionably established as an expert on Islam, she has moved her political alliances from left to right as her prominence has increased. In doing so she has declared moderate expressions of Islam as being fundamentally incompatible with a liberal democracy and most controversially, the Prophet Muhammad as 'a paedophile' and 'perverse tyrant'.[37]

Stereotyping Muslims and Islam in the Media: 'an almost necessary part of the reporting process'

As seen elsewhere, so Islam and Muslims are regularly presented in the media in terms of being a problem through discourses of violence, terrorism, misogyny and so on. This is clearly identifiable and recurrent across the entirety of Europe. To illustrate this, Geisser's study of the media in France notes how it typically prefers to adopt populist public attitudes and prejudices rather than trying to be informative and balanced. Whilst Tévanian shows how the media helped construct the 'problem of the *hijab*' by deciding which voices should be included in the debate. All social scientists, feminists, teacher, and civil actors not opposed to the *hijab* were excluded, leaving the ensuing debate being played out through the media between bearded foreign stereotypical Muslim men defending the *hijab* against women who had chosen not to wear it, supported by a number of secular male intellectuals.[38] In Spain, a similar climate exists where the role of the media has constructed Muslims as an 'internal enemy' which deserves an exceptional

---

[36]   Laurent Bonnefoy, 'Public Institutions and Islam: a New Stigmatization?', *International Institute for the study of Islam in the Modern World* no. 13 (December 2003), 22–3.

[37]   Maussen (2006), 128.

[38]   Caeiro (2006), 208–9.

criminal system[39] whilst in Italy, Gritti has noted how the vast majority of the country's media coverage is built around the myth of Islamic martyrdom and national fanatics.[40]

The second incident has already been touched upon, namely the publication of cartoons of the Prophet Muhammad by the *Jyllands Posten*. Whilst certain conspiracy stories are in circulation about why the cartoons were published, it was the debates about freedom of speech and the boundaries associated with this that spread from Denmark out across Europe and beyond, contemporarily seen in those emanating the 'dog Muhammad' drawings by the Swede, Lars Vilks and the subsequent 'death sentence' placed upon him. With the newspaper being accused of abusing freedom of speech by various Muslim groups and a number of non-Muslim Danes, many others jumped to the defence of the newspaper. For many, this debate was one that epitomised the entire 'clash of civilisations' thesis: a clash of values, practices, beliefs, ethics and most importantly, a clash of Muslims against the secular West. Beyond the confines of Europe, the controversy resulted in the withdrawal of the ambassadors of Libya, Saudi Arabia and Syria from Denmark, as well as consumer boycotts of Danish products in a number of Islamic countries. Various Danish embassies were firebombed in the aftermath and many violent protests were broadcast by the media, typified in the recurrence of images of Muslim men burning Danish flags. Despite apologising to Muslims, the newspaper maintained its right to print the cartoons, saying that Islamic fundamentalism cannot dictate what Danish newspapers can and cannot print. An interesting development however was when it emerged that in April 2003 a different editor of the newspaper had rejected a set of unsolicited Jesus cartoons on the grounds that readers would dislike the cartoons and that they might provoke a public outcry. For many who opposed the printing of the cartoons, this was merely evidence that the newspaper – and indeed the West – applied double-standards when it came to Muslims and Islam.

These examples are useful in that they reinforce the observation set out in the EUMC 9/11 Report. In the first instance, whilst distasteful to Muslims, it is unclear whether such incidents in reality ever initiate or promote Islamophobia. In the second, whilst the number of incidents against Muslims rose in Denmark as a result, it is again difficult to establish whether these were a direct result of the printing of the publications or whether the response from non-Muslims was merely because this was another 'Muslim' incident that seemed to reinforce widespread views and attitudes already in circulation. The observation from the EUMC 9/11 Report referred to in the previous chapter seems as equally valid here as indeed it was there:

---

[39]   Jose Maria Ortuno Aix, 'Report on Islamophobia in Spain', Cesari (2006), 253.

[40]   R. Gritti da Torri, 'Comunicazioni, Media e Nuovi Terrorismi dopo l'11 Settembre' (Rome: Fillenzi), 278–9.

To try and explain the media's role therefore remains difficult. None of the reports suggested that the media directly caused or, indeed, were responsible for any reported or identified act of aggression or significant change in attitude. However, this is not to dismiss their impact in any way, and despite there being no direct evidence to suggest otherwise, the media continue to play a major role in the formulation and establishment of popular perceptions in the public sphere. So when certain media were identified as representing Muslims both negatively and stereotypically – sometimes as an almost necessary part of the reporting process – in a situation that was volatile, a greater willingness to be responsible and accountable would have been welcomed. However, some media sectors were responsible and accountable, while others sought to remain balanced and objective, and for this those sources should be congratulated. So whilst no evidence exists to suggest that medias are influentially causal, they also cannot be completely dismissed either.[41]

Responding to Islamophobia: 'a greater willingness to be responsible and accountable'

The same conditions that initiated a greater receptivity towards Islamophobic and anti-Muslim attitudes have therefore also been the same conditions that have significantly framed the responses that have occurred at the pan-European level to try and tackle Islamophobia. This is not to negate what has been undertaken in any way but to merely put it in its rightful context. What might be termed 'anti-Islamophobia initiatives' are therefore much better understood when considered within the typically national or local settings within which they function and operate. As such, despite various politicians from across the European political spectrum having at some time or another called for solidarity with Muslim communities and the need to differentiate between Islam and 'Islamism' or 'Islamist terrorism', little of these calls have been undertaken at the European level. Instead, and as highlighted by those such as Tony Blair and the Irish Taoiseach Bertie Ahern amongst others, political leaders have preferred to air such concerns and make any visible gestures towards Muslims within their national contexts.[42] Whether this is intentional remains open to debate because when national politicians have made much more derogatory or negative comments about Islam and Muslims these have to a greater extent been reported as though they are of European concern. Maybe this observation suggests more about the role and representation of the media than it does the politicians themselves.

Efforts to combat Islamophobia, its effects and consequences have however begun to emerge across a number of different countries. As yet, much of this has been locally initiated and largely exempted from state or other governmental

---

[41]   Allen and Nielsen (2002), 52–3.
[42]   Allen and Nielsen (2002).

influence. A number of different Muslim communities and their organisations have sought to strengthen their organisations, not only in attempts to monitor and keep records of Islamophobic incidents but to also push towards official recognition being afforded to the growing problem and reality of Islamophobia and its consequences. One such example was the establishment of the Islamic Anti-Defamation League of Italy in 2005.[43] Other notable responses have been the many initiatives that have emanated from within wider faith communities, identifiable particularly in the growth and development of interfaith dialogue between Muslims and Christians. Such initiatives have been both important and influential as in Greece where Archbishop Christodoulos, the head of the Church of Greece, quickly brought together leading figures from the Christian, Jewish and Muslim traditions as a show of solidarity to the Greek public. Shortly after, the Orthodox Ecumenical Patriarchate organised an interfaith summit in Brussels to challenge the legacy of historical enmity that continues to shape the way in which people from different faiths continue to view each other in the contemporary setting.[44] Many more localised initiatives have also been undertaken and include those such as the multifaith prayer events held in Senate's Square, Helsinki and the oration for peace organised by the Pax Christi in Lisbon.[45]

In those countries where there have been no national efforts to tackle Islamophobia directly, as in Germany, interfaith initiatives have provided invaluable opportunities for communities to come together and discuss the issues. The *Christlich-Islamische Gesellschaft* (Christian-Islamic Society) is a national organisation that sponsors such dialogue and has in recent years, established groups in a number of cities across Germany.[46] Similarly, the *Deutsches Islamforum* (German Islamic Forum) has begun to mediate between Muslims and non-Muslims whilst the Central Council of German Muslims declared 3 October – German reunification day – as Open Mosque Day, in order that people from different communities have the opportunity to visit mosques and speak with Muslims in a non-confrontational way. A similar initiative is organised in Austria. As with earlier issues and the overlap between issues relating to 'Muslims' and 'immigrants' so in Spain a council has been established to give advice and information to the Spanish government about questions of immigrant integration whilst in March 2006, the Spanish Observatory on Racism and Xenophobia was set up to monitor and report on racism and xenophobia. Incorporated in its remit is the issue of Islamophobia albeit not in an overt or obvious way.[47] Elsewhere as in the Netherlands, a Commission on Equal Treatment has been established to help implement the 1994 Equal Treatment Law. Likewise, there is the National Bureau

---

[43]   Liguori (2006).
[44]   Allen and Nielsen (2002).
[45]   Ibid.
[46]   Karakasoglu et al. (2006).
[47]   Ortuno Aix (2006).

Against Racial Discrimination that was set up to provide the expertise required to prevent the growth of racial – and by default religious – discrimination.[48]

Regarding the consequences of Islamophobia, the situation or landscape is not as easy or straightforward as stating that the situation has merely deteriorated or worsened since 9/11. Whilst the Runnymede Report may have suggested a decade ago that Islamophobia was becoming 'more explicit' it may well be that something of the opposite has occurred, where contemporary Islamophobia has become far less explicit and much more natural and normal: obscured by debates, events, incidents and occurrences that are – at times at least – seemingly unconnected to earlier concepts or notions of Islamophobia. Many of the examples given and discussed here therefore may not necessarily be overtly Islamophobic, but underpinning them – sometimes in a relatively invisible way – is an anti-Muslim, anti-Islamic ideology that informs, explains and causes such consequences to ensue.

Despite the failings of the term and the lack of clarity that exists, it would appear that Islamophobia is here to stay and that it will no longer be able to be discarded from the various languages and discourses that form part of the pan-European lexicon. The most important task therefore is to locate some way in which Islamophobia might be defined as clearly as possible, setting out what one means by Islamophobia and as equally importantly, what one does not. Little consensus about this is in evidence at present. Despite being a term that had limited discursive value or resonance at the turn of the century, the spread of Islamophobia both discursively and conceptually into the public and political spaces of Europe has meant that whilst one may not necessarily always be able to articulate exactly what Islamophobia is, it is a phenomenon that is conceptually at least, a social reality. Having noted the changes that have occurred across Europe and having contextualised this alongside the British setting also, the task now therefore is to seek out what exactly Islamophobia might be.

---

[48]   Maussen (2006).

PART 5
Towards a New Theory and Definition of Islamophobia

Chapter 8
What is Islamophobia?

Before beginning to answer what might appear to be a simple question – 'what is Islamophobia?' – it is necessary to go back and address those seemingly basic but repeatedly overlooked questions that were set out at the start of this book.

Does 'Islamophobia' Exist?: 'a 19 year old woman wearing the *hijab* was beaten around the head with a metal baseball bat'

It might appear nonsensical to fundamentally question at this stage, a decade and a half after the publication of the Runnymede Report, the existence of something that the preceding chapters have focused upon. But what with the flawed nature of the Runnymede model and its inability to substantiate or explain Islamophobia, it is indeed quite valid and somewhat necessary to return to this basic premise, not only to ensure the legitimacy and justification for this research but also to begin the process of providing greater clarity and insight. From the Runnymede Report, a largely ambiguous phenomenon emerged, at times indistinguishable from other similar phenomenon, at times both nondescript and indistinct. Very little of its content or theory argued either a 'Muslim' or 'Islam' element as its catalytic essence, where inappropriate and inaccurate evidence was repeatedly cited as indicative and substantive of Islamophobia, undermining the necessary distinctiveness that Islamophobia must surely have albeit with overlaps and inter-linkages with other similar phenomena but not being entirely synonymous. Consequently, Islamophobia emerges from all of this as a phenomenon that is little more than an anecdotal assumption.

Having stated this, it is also true that in both the British and European settings however, there is evidence to suggest that manifestations of an anti-Muslim, anti-Islamic phenomenon are apparent, albeit at times as something of a causal influence underpinning a myriad of expressions and forms. To explore this further, it might be useful to firstly consider the data that is available relating to anti-Muslim incidents that have been collated by a number of different organisations. Rarely though has this been undertaken by governmental institutions or at either national or regional levels, or indeed when 'events' have just occurred and so problems with the data that is available does clearly exist. Due to the centrality of the UK in its recognition and development of understanding about Islamophobia, so the data collated in the UK will form the basis for the initial part of this consideration. One organisation that had some data available is the IHRC which claimed that 674 attacks on

Muslims were recorded following 9/11.[1] Ranging from psychological pressure and harassment, both verbal and written, through to physical violence and material damage, the IHRC verifies its evidence as 'concrete proof of Islamophobia'. The IHRC attempts to contextualise the scale of the problem noting, 'the vast majority of incidents including serious physical assaults go unreported'[2] suggesting that the 674 recorded were merely one part of a greater, more serious whole. Whilst the IHRC posits this as substantive evidence, there are some potential problems with this. Not only is the IHRC primarily a London-based organisation but some might suggest that it operates outside what might be, albeit inappropriately terminology-wise, the 'mainstream' and so would immediately undermine the validity of their data. It is worth adding that the IHRC might wish to contest both of these assumptions. Nonetheless, it is fair to suggest that they are well known in certain sectors of Muslim communities of which many of those would, one must presume, approach them when attacked. However, whilst it might have been that the same figures would have been replicated elsewhere or indeed nationwide had similar research been undertaken, it is debatable as to how far outside of London the IHRC was able to reach thus necessitating a less than categorical conclusion to be drawn, where the evidence and figures provided could be legitimately challenged and possibly even dismissed.

FAIR also drew similar conclusions from its monitoring programme that was in operation prior to 9/11. Post-9/11, FAIR reports that the number of incidents increased by a staggering 600 per cent.[3] Although as with the IHRC, whilst the data would seem to validate the existence of a virulent anti-Muslim, anti-Islamic backlash, they too are a largely London-only organisation. Consequently, despite both sets of data being put forward to substantiate Islamophobia, empirically and methodologically they can only realistically be seen to be indicative, especially when one considers that neither organisation appeared to have any baseline criteria of what might reasonably be deemed or categorised as 'Islamophobic'. Both projects therefore fail to provide the necessary statistical evidence at least required to prove a distinct anti-Muslim anti-Islamic phenomenon subsequently again reinforcing the anecdotal nature of Islamophobia. Whilst clearly indicating that anti-Muslim anti-Islamic incidents did occur, both FAIR and the IHRC fail to provide any insight into whether this was evidence of Islamophobia or indeed, what that Islamophobia might be. Making such a statement neither diminishes nor derogates the work of either organisation, but it does make an observation about the data and the methodologies employed.

An unpublished document that drew extensively upon these data sets however was the former Commission for Racial Equality's (CRE) second monitoring

---

[1]   Islamic Human Rights Commission, *The Hidden Victims of September 11: the Backlash Against Muslims in the UK* (Wembley: Islamic Human Rights Commission, 2002), 8.

[2]   Ibid., 8.

[3]   Statistics taken from unpublished documents made available by FAIR between the period October 2001 and August 2003.

report for the EUMC.[4] What with much of this data being geographically specific, the CRE sought to counter this by broadening its context, incorporating media reports as well as incidents that were reported through their own regional offices. Resultantly, a more balanced if not necessarily complete picture was constructed even though the report itself was largely inconclusive, being far too broad at times and far too sporadic at others. Under 'Physical Attacks' for example:

> in the Northeast of England a 20 year old Bangladeshi man suffered from a broken jaw after being beaten by a gang of youths … a 19 year old woman wearing the *hijab* was beaten around the head with a metal baseball bat by two white men in Swindon. Prior to the attack one of the men was reportedly heard to say 'here's a Muslim'.[5]

As with evidence of Islamophobia previously cited, whilst the second example acknowledges a 'Muslim' marker as a catalyst, the first does not, leaving doubts about how 'Islamophobic incidents' and 'racist incidents' are categorised and subsequently differentiated between. Most worryingly however, of all the 'Islamophobic' incidents cited throughout the document, a third failed to acknowledge any 'Muslim' or 'Islamic' markers, fluctuating from serious examples of a seemingly distinct anti-Muslim, anti-Islamic nature to those that were vague and indistinguishable from traditional forms of racism. Consequently, it is difficult to substantiate or conclusively identify something distinctive from the evidence.

Broadening the focus to Europe and returning to the EUMC's post-9/11 Islamophobia Report that was deconstructed in the preceding chapter, so some interesting insight and context as to whether Islamophobia exists can begin to be undertaken.[6] Remaining the largest monitoring project into Islamophobia to have been undertaken anywhere in the world, it is worth reminding ourselves that the report noted how, 'Muslims became indiscriminate victims of an upsurge of both verbal and physical attacks following the events of 11 September'.[7] Beyond this

---

[4]   Commission for Racial Equality, *Anti-Islamic Reactions in the EU After the Terrorist Acts against the USA: United Kingdom Second Country Report* (London: CRE, 2001). Collated between the period 14 September 2001 and 19 October 2001 inclusive, the report was the second in a series of five that the EUMC required each of its National Focal Points (NFPs) produced – the CRE being the British NFP – to monitor any changes in attitude and/ or acts of violence or aggression towards ethnic, cultural or religious minorities especially Muslim communities in the wake of the 9/11 attacks. Whilst the report in its entirety was never published, so of its findings, data, evidence and conclusions would have been a part of the final UK report produced by the EUMC and available to download at the website http://www.eumc.eu, as indeed it would have featured in the final, EU-wide synthesis report that incorporated a section on each of the various national contexts.

[5]   Ibid., 2.

[6]   Allen and Nielsen (2002).

[7]   Press release from the EUMC at the launch of the report's publication (14 May 2002).

however, the report established a firm basis upon which a distinct anti-Muslim, anti-Islamic phenomenon appeared to be apparent, seeking to ground its own evidence in preference of making inflationary claims or conclusions. As it stated:

> these explanations are neither exhaustive nor conclusive but attempt to clarify some of the common trends and themes that were apparent in the wake of September 11. No single explanation can completely account for the events that followed those in the US, but this does allow an insight to certain identifiable phenomenon ... In this respect therefore, the explanations must be considered both in isolation, largely as they have been presented here in the text, but also as corroborative contributions as well. What many of them do highlight however is the deep seated nature of Islamophobia ... Expressions of Islamophobia have certainly in some instances been a 'cover' for general racism and xenophobia, in some countries offered legitimacy by the statements of politicians and other opinion leaders. However, there have also been instances in which such expressions have been selectively targeted at visibly perceived manifestations of Islam ... In general terms, however, anti-Muslim sentiment has emanated from a vast array of sources and taken on a range of manifestations building upon premises that were already pre-existent to the events of September 11 and may even have been strengthened by them.[8]

Most significantly, the report acknowledged that an anti-Muslim anti-Islamic phenomenon that was pre-existent to 9/11 was reinforced by the attacks in the US. Similarly, the report noted that its findings were neither exhaustive nor conclusive, with questions remaining about how this phenomenon was distinct from other similar and inter-related phenomena, making it incongruent as a phenomenon defined and conceptualised through over-simplified means.

A clear understanding and argument for the existence of Islamophobia was therefore being established that was both grounded and realistic. Whilst the evidence in the EUMC Report was methodologically inconsistent,[9] the report did not make claims beyond its findings, setting out and acknowledging its limitations and weaknesses, but at the same time identifying what it saw as a distinct phenomenon, one that had a firm and necessary 'Muslim' or 'Islamic' component to it but without conflation or claims to authority whatsoever. The report therefore categorically and justifiably concluded that a 'certain identifiable phenomenon'

---

[8] Ibid., 49.

[9] For a fuller exposition and critical analysis of the data collection processes and methodologies employed by both the EUMC and its NFPs, see: Chris Allen, 'A Critical Appraisal of the Comparability of Data Aollection Processes and Methodologies Implemented by the National Focal Points of the European Monitoring Centre on Racism and Xenophobia', *European Monitoring Centre on Racism and Xenophobia Colloque*, 25 June 2002 (EUMC: Vienna).

was evident.[10] In this context, that same 'certain identifiable phenomenon' could only have been Islamophobia. In doing so and in opposition to previous conceptualisations, the report differentiated between the manifestations or forms that the phenomenon acquired and what might possibly be the phenomenon itself, neither concluding nor making the assumption that the manifestations or forms of that 'certain identifiable phenomenon' were either that which constituted it or in any way subsequently defined it. The report was therefore clearly different in its conceptualisation of Islamophobia than those which had gone before. But was this justification enough to conclude that 'Islamophobia' exists?

Dismissing Islamophobia: 'a popular anti-Muslim racism did not happen'

This question again brings about contestation because despite the EUMC, others suggest that this same 'certain identifiable phenomenon' fails to exist. Such dismissals typically appear through the press – identifiable in the writing of Toynbee[11] and Burchill[12] to name a few – although consideration should not be limited to these more traditional forms of media. For example, the online periodical *Spiked* has a number of articles that bring into question the validity and existence of Islamophobia.[13] Employing the very evidence that was put into the public domain in an attempt to 'prove' Islamophobia, referencing both the IHRC and FAIR, Josie Appleton unequivocally states that, 'a popular anti-Muslim racism did not happen', interesting also in her reluctance to use or refer to 'Islamophobia'.[14] As with earlier observations about this particular data, Appleton stresses the unconvincing nature of the evidence, abruptly dismissing it as an 'over-sensitivity' on the part of Muslims. Whilst it is difficult to agree with her claims of 'over-sensitivity', what Appleton does justifiably highlight is that evidence and research into Islamophobia is largely inconclusive and limited: an argument that cannot be denied.

As Richardson has since written because the evidence is largely inconclusive and limited, easy dismissals and rejections of the existence of Islamophobia can be made against almost any data, incident, event and so on because of the subjectivity inherent in defining Islamophobia through the existing definitions

---

[10]   Allen and Nielsen (2002), 49.

[11]   *The Guardian*, 5 October 2001.

[12]   'Some People will Believe Anything', *The Guardian*, 18 August 2001.

[13]   See: Josie Appleton, 'Who's Afraid of Islamophobia?', *Spiked*, 2 July 2002 (12 November 2002) <http://www.spiked-online.com/Articles/00000006D95B.htm>. Mark Hume, 'Whatever happened to RIP?', *Spiked*, 2 June 2003 (10 September 2004) <http://www.spiked-online.com/Articles/00000006DDD5.htm>. Josie Appleton, 'Islam on the Brain', *Spiked*, 11 August 2004 (10 September 2004) <http://www.spiked-online.co.uk/Articles/0000000CA662.htm>.

[14]   Appleton (2002).

and conceptualisations.[15] When Islamophobia is defined as 'unfounded', immediately the evidence, manifestations and consequences of such are subjected to an interpretive understanding: what is unfounded to one may not necessarily be unfounded to another thus resulting in a situation where individual, group or communal subjectivities prevail over a somewhat invisible and difficult to establish objectivity. Thorough subjectivity, clarity never exists thus rendering the phenomenon invalid within individual, group or communal frameworks, all of which must be arguably accepted. Thus whether Islamophobia is dismissed by Burchill, Appleton or the BNP, that it is defined and categorised as unfounded allows for detractors, irrespective of the criticisms and dismissals they put forward, to argue them as subjectively valid, and by consequence, founded. Existing conceptualisations therefore have little, if indeed any grounding in reality or objectivity, and can, resultantly, be either appropriately or inappropriately dismissed or countered thus rendering the phenomenon invalid and illegitimate, if not entirely objectionable. It is the existing conceptualisations and resultant processes therefore that leaves wider society unconvinced: unconvinced of the existence of an Islamophobia that is distinct and 'real'.

This sense of being 'unconvinced' once again returns us to the opening historiography, where a similar sentiment might underlie the findings and conclusions of a number of projects and reports made reference to by it, where the argument or inference of a distinct and separate Islamophobia is less than evident. For example, whilst Sheridan identifies that Muslims more than other minority groups increasingly experience racism and discrimination based on their religion and identity, she failed to differentiate as to whether this 'racism' was in any way different to what these same communities were experiencing based upon their Pakistani, Bangladeshi or other heritage.[16] The Open Society Institute's (OSI) investigation into Muslims in the UK was similar. Whilst recognising that, 'following the events of 9/11 Muslims and those perceived to be Muslim have faced unprecedented levels of attacks and violence',[17] it could be argued that despite suggesting the likelihood of an anti-Muslim, anti-Islamic phenomenon, it fails to either define or identify it, thus either overlooking or deliberately not employing the term – and by consequence the concept – of Islamophobia. In the Home Office Report into religious discrimination,[18] again whilst it acknowledged that Muslims experience prejudice and discrimination for being Muslim, the authors failed to define it as Islamophobia. Interestingly, and despite the report focusing upon religious discrimination, it failed to tackle Islamophobia or any

---

[15]   John E. Richardson, *(Mis) Representing Islam: the Racism and Rhetoric of British Broadsheet Newspapers* (Amsterdam: John Benjamin, 2004), 24.

[16]   Lorraine Sheridan, *Effects of the Events of September 11th 2001 on Discrimination and Implicit Racism in Five Religious and Seven Ethnic Groups: a brief Overview* (Leicester: University of Leicester, 2002).

[17]   Choudhury (2003), 73.

[18]   Weller et al. (2001).

other potential anti-Muslim, anti-Islamic phenomena in any significant way. The term Islamophobia was though employed in the text, in brackets once in the main text, in a footnote relating to Muslim organisations, and in a 'vox-pop' from a postal survey,[19] used only through the words and voices of others and not in the words or voices of the authors.

Elsewhere, whilst the term Islamophobia was repeatedly used and the concept referred to by a number of different representative groups and organisations submitting both oral and written evidence to the House of Lords Select Committee on Religious Offences in England and Wales,[20] there was no direct reference to Islamophobia in its final report. What with the term being repeatedly used and bearing in mind that the religious offences bill was largely seen to be a piece of legislation affording protection to Muslims, the fact that it was missing from the final report must demand serious question be asked about how convinced the Committee were, not only of whether it was significantly or distinctively different from racism but more worryingly, of the reality of Islamophobia.[21] Some years beforehand, a similar process occurred in the *Parekh Report* where instead of referring to Islamophobia, 'anti-Muslim racism' was used instead.[22] What was interesting about this though was that the Parekh Report was undertaken under the auspices of the Runnymede Trust yet still seemingly failed to be convinced of Islamophobia. What emerges throughout therefore, irrespective of context or setting, is the feeling that despite evidence to suggest that anti-Muslim, anti-Islamic incidents and attitudes are clearly identifiable and that the terminologies and concepts are discursively and conceptually in circulation, many are far from convinced of Islamophobia as a distinct and viable phenomenon.

The question of whether Islamophobia exists therefore is an entirely legitimate one: legitimate but not, as yet, openly asked. If however it has been asked, then it must be either that it is yet to be convincingly answered or ultimately that Islamophobia does not exist. In responding to this, the EUMC Report is essential what with its identification of a 'certain identifiable phenomenon'. This identification and recognition therefore does not suggest that the products, manifestations or consequences of that largely ambiguous, widely interpretive and entirely subjective Islamophobia that have been posited previously and established as the

---

[19]   Ibid., 15 and 53 respectively.

[20]   House of Lords Select Committee on Religious Offences in England and Wales, *Select Committee on Religious Offences in England and Wales, Volume II – oral evidence (HL Paper 95–II)*. (London: The Stationary Office, 2003); House of Lords Select Committee on religious Offences in England and Wales (*Select Committee on Religious Offences in England and Wales, Volume III – written evidence (HL Paper 95–III)* (London: The Stationary Office, 2003), respectively.

[21]   House of Lords Select Committee on religious Offences in England and Wales, *Select Committee on Religious Offences in England and Wales, Volume I – report (HL Paper 95–I)* (London: The Stationary Office, 2003).

[22]   Parekh (2000).

concrete and static basis for all understanding equates to this 'certain identifiable phenomenon', but instead merely reiterates – and confirms – that a 'phenomenon' exists. In acknowledging this, such an assertion is neither overblown nor unfounded but instead grounded in the research and evidence available. What has previously ensued is the putting forward of a phenomenon that has neither been empirically proven nor has it stood up to critical analyses of its concepts, theories or function in practice, resulting in the establishing of a phenomenon that is easily derogated and dismissed by way of its own weaknesses and subjectivities. Reflecting the 'anti-racism problematic' Stuart Hall acknowledges regarding racism, simplistically imposing positive images over negative ones will never combat anything: 'since the binaries remain in place, meaning continues to be shaped by them. The strategy challenges the binaries – but it does not undermine them',[23] hence the reason why Islamophobia remains weak and unconvinced in the public space because it was never accredited with any substance or theory that went beyond the merest of positive images. If the existence of a 'certain identifiable phenomenon' is therefore acknowledged, based only upon the evidence and research at hand, assuming that this is 'Islamophobia', the logical question to ask must therefore be: what then is 'Islamophobia'?

What is Islamophobia?: 'the instrument does not measure up to the theory'

To answer 'what is Islamophobia?', it is essential to clarify how this differs from what has gone before. From the analyses undertaken previously, the means of defining and conceptualising Islamophobia are both subjective and societally questioned, and entirely over-simplified and unable to accommodate anything more than the most basic of concepts, meanings and understandings. Whilst touched upon previously, a critique of Rokeach highlights one of the serious problems with defining and conceptualising Islamophobia in such ways. As Leyens, Yzerbyt and Schadron recognise, not only is Rokeach's work less than 'content-free' but 'the instrument does not measure up to the theory'.[24] Regarding Islamophobia, the same is brutally true: the instrument for identifying Islamophobia neither measures up to the theory nor is it entirely content-free.

So far therefore, the theory of Islamophobia has been weak, to the consequence where the 'products' are equitable with the very phenomenon itself as well as being the means to definition also. In this way, Islamophobia (the 'phenomenon') has been explained, understood and at the same time identified through its more obvious and explicit manifestations and forms ('products'), thus excluding any potential or actual consequence that either or both may individually or collaboratively initiate. At this particular juncture it may be appropriate to describe these consequences

---

[23]   Hall (1997), 274.

[24]   Jacques-Philippe Leyens et al., *Stereotypes and Social Cognition* (London: Sage, 1994), 37.

in terms of 'exclusionary practices', the prejudicial, discriminatory and excluding processes, amongst others, that may emanate or ensue from a particular phenomenon. So far, when data or incidents have been put forward as evidence of Islamophobia, rooted in the products rather more so than anything else, so the motivation, cause, product and consequence have been indistinguishable, simultaneously negating and obfuscating that 'certain identifiable phenomenon'. Consequently, whilst the EUMC Report put forward different incidents and events ('products') as evidence, never did it suggest that these products were Islamophobia ('the phenomenon'). To the contrary, the EUMC Report suggested that the products were motivated by them, a subtle but hugely important distinction. The EUMC Report therefore differentiated between the products and the phenomenon whilst also touching upon the possibility of some form of consequential or exclusionary practice, as in the rise of political campaigning against Muslims and Islam.[25] In differentiating between these different constitutive components, the report initiates the possibility of a new means of conceptualising Islamophobia.

In the report therefore, the incidents, events and expressions – 'products' – were presented in terms of being manifestations or forms that initiate Islamophobia, clarifying that 'these were not necessarily in themselves the reason for any attacks ...' but '... a stimulant' underpinning their manifestation and realisation.[26] As such, a clear distinction between product and motivation was made. In its concluding observations, the subtle distinction between the phenomenon and the 'expressions of Islamophobia' was again made.[27] What with the established and previously authoritative models of Islamophobia having been so necessarily and unequivocally challenged, it is the EUMC's basis of understanding that will from hereon become the foundation upon which answering the question 'what is Islamophobia?' will begin to be explored and hopefully developed. To do so therefore, it must be accepted and acknowledged that to answer 'what is Islamophobia?' at this stage at least, Islamophobia then can be nothing more than that 'certain identifiable phenomenon' acknowledged in the previous section.

Phoney and Patronising: 'wrong' for no other reason but being 'wrong'

In addition, and in referencing Hall et al., it is necessary that any answer to this question also has the ability to counter the 'race relations problematic', convincing of the reality and existence of an Islamophobia. For Hall, if this is not achieved, then a situation will emerge where the acceptance and subsequent theories of such become overwhelmed and obfuscated by phoney and patronising definitions that simultaneously over-inflate, homogenously accuse, and wallow in the negativity of reminding everyone 'just how bad Islamophobia is' but without making a

---

[25]   Allen and Nielsen (2002), 43–6.
[26]   Ibid., 34.
[27]   Ibid., 49.

conclusive justification for it. That is, not beyond the somewhat naïve and immature argument of just 'because it is'.[28] In this way, any answer to 'what is Islamophobia?' must ensure that it is neither over-inflationary, accusatory nor merely regurgitate positive stereotypical frames and arguments, all of which can have little grounding or apparent justification. If this is not overcome, then any subsequent definition, theory or conceptualisation may be rendered largely meaningless. This rendering of meaningless can be seen in the way that Islamophobia is employed by Green Party MEP, Jean Lambert: 'the UK is institutionally Islamophobic'.[29] Whilst numerous sources have inferred that Islamophobia is in evidence in the UK, to indiscriminately suggest the UK as 'institutionally Islamophobic' is as equally overblown and homogenising as suggesting that all Muslims are supportive of terrorism. Even more problematic is that Lambert neither contextualises nor grounds her statement, instead rooting it in Hall's problematic, where Islamophobia 'is wrong' for no other reason but being 'wrong'. Thus her statement has little or no meaning or value, a completely worthless statement that is over-inflationary, accusatory and indiscriminately negative and ultimately contestable.

And because of this, as with others who employ the term and concept in equally meaningless ways, detractors can readily contest or dismiss both her statement and Islamophobia by rendering it entirely subjective, devoid of meaning and substantiation, being grounded in a complete lack of any real or concrete evidence. Branding the UK as 'institutionally Islamophobic' therefore has no value whatsoever and would appear, on the surface at least, to be nothing more than an attempt to attract the ever growing and politically important 'Muslim vote' in the UK, a 'cause celebre', or a headline grabbing sound-bite for the media, all of which hopefully would credit Ms Lambert with some publicity in her quest for votes. Being just one example of many, Islamophobia both as a term and as a concept is in public discourse without any real clarity or conviction, where those that are themselves speaking about and employing Islamophobia, do so without any real meaning, understanding or concept which in turn further compounds the problem and bi-polarises the already existent gulf between the 'advocates' and 'detractors' of Islamophobia further. The longer it continues, the wider the gulf and the more difficult it will become to not only begin to define and conceptualise the reality of Islamophobia, but also to negotiate a process to convince both the advocates and detractors of its reality and existence and overcome the contestation that exists between the two.

One further way of answering this question might be to consider the few substantive pieces of research that have been directly – rather than peripherally – undertaken into Islamophobia, steeping back to use and contextualise the findings from the defining exercise the EUMC undertook in 2001, highlighted in

---

[28]   Stuart Hall et al., 'Policing the Crisis: Mugging, the State and Law and Order (London: Macmillan, 1978).

[29]   Green Party, 'UK "Institutionally Islamophobic" MEP Warns', *The Green Party*, 1 June 2004 (15 September 2004) <http://www.greenparty.org.uk/index.php?nav=news&n=1439>.

the chapter beforehand.[30] In attempting to establish operable EU-wide definitions for racism, anti-Semitism and Islamophobia, the EUMC sought to collate a range of definitions in order to codify them into a set of standards that would be universally accepted, whether socially, politically and legislatively. Having questioned the different NFPs, the project found that in seven of the fifteen, no clear or known definition of Islamophobia was operable, either through a lack of usage or a lack of conceptual recognition.[31] Of the fifteen, two acknowledged that whilst the term was non-operational they could still provide a definition,[32] three directly referenced the Runnymede model,[33] whereas three others offered different if not sometimes correlative definitions.[34] So whilst the term Islamophobia was being used at the international level by the UN at this time, across the EU at least just under half of the member states had no formal concept or meaning of it, and elsewhere, little consensual agreement was identifiable. Again the ambiguous nature of Islamophobia becomes apparent.

Aside from the Runnymede rooted definitions, including both the British and Irish, some of the alternatives offered were however interesting. For the Belgian NFP, Islamophobia was an articulation of the ideology of racism, a distinctive component of a greater whole. In France, whilst noting that the concept was primarily of British origin and having been coined by Tariq Modood, they suggested that as a concept and operable term it was largely unknown there but would have similarities with French discourses towards North Africans and Arabs, defined as anti-Algerian and anti-Arab racisms respectively. Likewise the Dutch suggested that Islamophobia was largely unused, consequently having little discursive value. Nonetheless, it suggested that Islamophobia might be:

> defined as: any ideology or pattern of thought and/or behaviour in which [Muslims] are excluded from positions, rights, possibilities in (parts of) society because of their believed or actual Islamic background. [Muslims] are positioned

---

[30]   Named the RAREN 3 data collection project, this project was undertaken in late 2001, early 2002 and sought to establish universally accepted definitions for 'racism', 'xenophobia', 'Anti-Semitism' and 'Islamophobia'. Overseen by Dimitria Clayton on behalf of the EUMC, the findings of this report were distributed to those participants of the RAXEN NFP meeting held in Vienna on the 24 and 25 June 2002. Further developments of this project and the problems experienced in trying to establish a universally accepted definition were explored in: Dimitria Clayton, 'Data Comparability, Definitions and the Challenges for Data Collection on the Phenomenon of Racism, Xenophobia, Anti-Semitism and Islamophobia in the European Union' *European Monitoring Centre on Racism and Xenophobia Colloque*, 25 June 2002 (EUMC: Vienna). Neither the findings of the RAREN 3 project nor Clayton's paper were published.

[31]   Denmark, Finland, Germany, Greece, Italy, Luxembourg and Portugal.

[32]   France and the Netherlands.

[33]   Austria, Ireland and the UK.

[34]   Belgium, Spain and Sweden.

and treated as (imagined/real) representatives of Islam in general or (imagined/real) Islamic groups instead of their capacities as individuals.[35]

Whilst un-operational, the Dutch definition incorporates rather more complexity than the Runnymede version, where a separation between manifestations (products) and consequences (exclusionary practices) becomes implied if not stated outright. Both the Dutch and Belgian definitions refer to Islamophobia being ideological also. Of the remaining definitions, the Swedish suggested Islamophobia was the adherence to ideas and actions directed against the interests, legal rights and religious practices of Muslims, whilst Spain suggested the phenomenon be better understood as a set of attitudes suggesting the hatred and rejection of Muslims and Islam, additionally attributing it with a retrospective dimension also. From this process therefore little consensus was established, thus explaining why a universal definition was not therefore put forward and possibly also why the comparability between the various national reports used to compile the post-9/11 synthesis report similarly failed to offer an adequate definition of Islamophobia.

Nonetheless, some useful and important points for further consideration, when contextualised by the synthesis report, do emerge as regards answering 'what is Islamophobia?'. Firstly, it would seem that the 'certain identifiable phenomenon' is neither consistent nor uniform, neither in its products nor in the way that it is conceptualised or defined, possibly even suggesting a plurality of 'Islamophobias' – or more so a multiplicity of understandings and interpretations – rather more than a single, all encompassing entity. Secondly and despite being asymmetrically shifting between notions of anti-Muslim and anti-Islamic, the phenomenon was not always seen to be Islamophobia, thus suggesting some overlap with other phenomena that either may or may not be acknowledged as distinct or differentiable. Thirdly, both the nature and products of the phenomenon would appear to be shaped and determined by the national, cultural, geographical and socio-economic conditions within which any such phenomenon is identified, being different in Germany where such might focus upon Turkish communities whereas in Britain the focus would be upon South Asian communities. Fourthly, Islamophobia would appear to have the possibility of having a historical legacy from which it draws information, relevance, understanding and meaning. Fifthly, it would appear essential that a distinct 'Muslim' or 'Islamic' identifier or identification process be present and underpinning, albeit explicitly or implicitly, direct or indirect, either expressly acknowledged or not. And finally, it would appear that despite the discursive prevalence that the neologism Islamophobia has attained, Islamophobia has significantly failed to permeate all settings and contexts, and even where it has achieved greater social and public permeability, understanding and meaning remains confused and lacking in clarity and where other terminologies and associative phrases are sometimes preferred or employed to describe and highlight similar if not the same.

---

[35]   Unpublished data incorporated in the RAREN 3 data collection project.

Having set out what is now known about 'that certain phenomenon' therefore, maybe it might be more appropriate at this juncture to consider whether 'Islamophobia' is an appropriate neologism or whether alternative terminologies are required?

Are New Terminologies Required?: 'the rhetoric is against people, not religion'

As identified by Clayton in terms of the RAREN exercise, one of the most significant problems was that Islamophobia was neither operational nor fully understood in some of the member states and by consequence, significant swathes of Europe. However, she did identify in her research that similar concepts and phenomena were named in some contexts as 'anti-Islamism', 'anti-Muslim racism' and even just 'racism'.[36] Whilst the first two have failed to attain the same discursive prevalence and the latter has been employed only correlatively as regards Islamophobia, it might therefore be useful to consider whether any of these might be more appropriate for naming the phenomenon.

Indeed Halliday had already raised questions about the appropriateness of Islamophobia as a name for the phenomenon even before the Runnymede Report was published. Suggesting 'anti-Muslimism' as more appropriate, Halliday argued that what with such phenomena being almost entirely anti-Muslim, naming it 'Islamophobia' was both misleading and inaccurate.[37] Post-Runnymede, Halliday re-examined this and succinctly concluded that:

> Islam as a religion *was* the enemy in the past – in the Crusades of the *reconquista*. It is not the enemy now ... the attack now is against not Islam as a faith but against Muslims as people ... the term 'Islamophobia' is ... misleading. The rhetoric is 'anti-Muslim' rather than 'anti-Islamic'. The rhetoric is against people, not religion.[38]

Whilst evidence would suggest that 'anti-Muslim' phenomena and events would outnumber those that might be deemed 'anti-Islamic', one point of contestation with Halliday's argument against Islamophobia is that from the EUMC Report's perspective, both anti-Islamic and anti-Muslim phenomena were in evidence, with the foci repeatedly switching between Muslims to Islam and vice versa.

Miles and Brown have also aired similar concerns about the name, albeit from a different perspective.[39] Whilst Halliday argues that Islamophobia is inappropriate because of the foci, Miles and Brown suggest that 'Islamophobia'

---

[36]   Clayton (2002).

[37]   Halliday (1996), Chapters 4 and 6: 109 and 160–65 respectively.

[38]   Halliday (2002), 128 and 206 respectively.

[39]   Robert Miles and Malcolm Brown, *Racism*, second edition (London: Routledge, 2003).

might only be appropriate where a specific and identifiable hatred of the theology of Islam is in evidence. Whilst seemingly arguing the same as Halliday albeit from an alternative perspective, Miles and Brown argue that there is no need for any separation of identifying, defining or conceptualising 'anti-Muslimism' as this can be incorporated and framed within existing theories of racism or xenophobia, in similarity of anti-immigrant phenomena.[40] For both Halliday and Miles and Brown, it is the linguistic meaning of the name that neither adequately defines nor allows understanding of what the phenomenon is, thus rendering it misleading and inappropriate. Whilst both arguments are in some ways contradictory, they do identify a legitimate weakness in naming this phenomenon 'Islamophobia'. What one must ask therefore is whether 'Islamophobia' can name all forms of anti-Muslim, anti-Islamic phenomena including those which specifically target the religious and theological tenets of Islam? Alternatively, could it be that Islamophobia is a form of racism that is expressed against markers of 'Muslim-ness' rather more than the religion of Islam and that as a phenomenon, does not require differential naming? Or finally, could it just be that the name used to identify the phenomenon – 'Islamophobia' – is as equally weak and inadequate as many of the theories, definitions and conceptualisations that are currently in operation?

Aside from these, a further consideration is also pressing. In naming such a phenomenon as a 'phobia', so anti-Muslim anti-Islamic phenomena is also to some degree 'pathologised', a process that diminishes the more active and aggressive elements and activities that underpin it. Through this process, those that perpetrate 'Islamophobic' acts or ideas, are implicitly – if not immediately – exculpated by way of such phenomena being seen to be a 'disease' or 'illness'. Islamophobia therefore becomes something that is entirely naturalised through the implication that as it is biological or pathological, so Islamophobia, and most importantly its perpetrators, can be 'cured', possibly explaining the simplistic propagation of positive images to have been naïvely employed in attempts to 'cure' the 'disease'. Whilst identifying in this way allows some escape and respite for its perpetrators, it also veers understanding into the biologically conceived frames that some traditional forms of racism have been rooted in and subsequently caused so much contestation about whether racism is biologically founded or not. In this context therefore, the 'founded' or 'unfounded' dichotomy becomes secondary what with it being perceived as something that exists quite naturally beyond the control of its perpetrators. When named as 'Islamophobia', the phenomenon fails to become the fault of the perpetrator but a condition of them, neither founded nor unfounded but biological and natural.

As 'Islamophobia' therefore would not appear to be the appropriate name for this particular phenomenon, so it must be necessary to consider the alternatives, the first of which is Halliday's 'anti-Muslimism'. Whilst arguing its greater appropriateness what with it naming the target of the phenomena more accurately, the EUMC report does highlight how both Muslims and Islam, or at least the

---

[40]   Ibid., 166.

material entities of them, became targeted.[41] Evidence elsewhere also exists that suggests that in targeting Muslims, some do so through Islam itself.[42] Consequently, if that which was targeted towards Muslims was named 'anti-Muslimism', so the concurrent phenomena that targeted either the religious or theological aspects of Islam or Muslims via the same focus, would need to be named 'anti-Islamism'. Unfortunately, this terminology might equally fail to offer the necessary clarity required, where further confusion may ensue what with the term 'Islamism' having contemporarily a quite distinct and separate meaning in the current climate: Islamism being increasingly equitable with political and revivalist movements within Islam, both aggressive and non-aggressive. Neither term therefore, either 'anti-Muslimism' or 'anti-Islamism', would appear to be able to adequately name that type of phenomena that targets neither Islam directly, Muslims via Islam, nor even some overlap, however slight, might exist. So whilst Halliday is correct in stressing a greater emphasis upon 'Muslims' rather than 'Islam', his own terminology and those derivative of it would appear to have as equally inappropriate and unworkable dimensions to them, especially when 'Islamophobia' has already achieved public discursive permeation. If multiple terminologies were to ensue, the result could be even greater confusion thus compounding the problem rather more so than alleviating it.

Similarly with Clayton's suggestion of 'anti-Muslim racism', so it might be that this too is as equally problematic when necessarily naming 'anti-Islamic' racism, if such might be appropriate. Whilst Clayton acknowledges the same reasons as Halliday for putting forward an alternative name, the appellation of 'racism' could also be problematic. Whilst some theories of racism will be considered later, Clayton's 'racism' would appear to be rooted in the conceptualisation of race and racism prevalent across mainland Europe as opposed to that which exists in the British context. Across Europe, 'race' is far less rooted in notions of 'colour' as is the case in the UK, and so the concept of 'racism' in Europe is far less rigidly defined and much more transient, identified by more than just markers of skin colour. Consequently, whilst this naming of Islamophobia may be useful and possibly more relevant in a European context, it may not have the same relevance or functionality elsewhere. Indeed as with Halliday's suggestion, not only might problems about clarity and understanding continue to exist but in employing 'anti-Muslim racism' as a working neologism, a situation could ensue where newer and even more misleading understandings and meanings about Islamophobia may emerge. In Britain in particular this could be especially problematic what with 'race' being a legal concept that 'Muslims', because of their multi-ethnicity are not incorporated within, an anomaly in the legal system that those such as the House of Lords Select Committee on Religious Offences were seeking to close.

---

[41]   Allen and Nielsen (2002), 36.

[42]   Chris Allen, 'Justifying Islamophobia: a Post-9/11 Consideration of the European Union and British Contexts', *American Journal of Islamic Social Sciences*, vol. 21 no. 3 (Summer 2004): 1–25.

Nonetheless, whilst it is essential to note that 'anti-Muslim racism' as an appropriate and workable name might be inappropriate, this same inappropriateness should not become confused with the correlative value that exists between Islamophobia and racism, of course which are two entirely different things.

Whilst having explored and identified the weaknesses and the inappropriate nature of employing 'Islamophobia' as an appropriate name for that 'certain identifiable phenomenon', from those alternative terminologies that have been posited elsewhere neither a 'ready-made' nor obviously suitable substitutive name would appear to be in current circulation. None of those posited would appear to offer anything more in the way of better naming, improve understanding or providing meaning, or through which a greater assistance can be located as regards aiding the process of better definition or conceptualisation. Whilst acknowledging its failings however, one advantage 'Islamophobia' has over its alternatives is that it has acquired a reasonable level of discursive permeation in social and public usage, something that any posited alternative – albeit suitable or otherwise – would need to simultaneously achieve and replace, raising the potential for a situation where even greater contestation is in evidence, this time from competing and conflicting terminologies and names being employed for the same phenomena but understood and being used either politically or ideologically to bring about further contestation or confusion. This is not to suggest that 'Islamophobia' can only ever be that which is employed to name anti-Muslim, anti-Islamic phenomena, itself a rather too long and overblown name, but instead to unfortunately acknowledge that at the present time, neither a more suitable, more appropriate, nor more accurate alternative is forthcoming. Because of this, it would seem that 'Islamophobia', for all its weaknesses and inadequacies might be the best, if not only, option at this present juncture. From hereon therefore, 'Islamophobia' will be employed with these qualifications and considerations in mind.

If it is therefore acknowledged that a certain identifiable phenomenon – Islamophobia – exists, albeit an existance lacking clarity then there remains contestation about what it is. And that the neologism employed may indeed contribute to this lack of clarity and contested nature. The final solution to attempting to bring about an end to this contestation therefore, or at least lessen it, must be to offer a newer and more adequate and appropriate theoretical definition and conceptualisation of what Islamophobia is. Again, the question that requires answering is: what is Islamophobia?

Chapter 9
Islamophobia: Comparisons and Correlations

Establishing a new definition and conceptualisation of Islamophobia therefore cannot merely be to construct an equally simplistic and substitutive set of criteria that purport to identify whether or not a given discourse, act or event is Islamophobic. Instead, such is required that informs and gives meaning, furthering and developing the limited theoretical foundations upon which existing discourses and understandings are founded. If defined too broadly, then such phenomena escape censure because of the meaningless nature of the assertion that Islamophobia exists. Broad definitions and meaningless conceptualisations therefore become over-inflated and remove any concretised or empirical grounding, and if the definition is without grounding, then discourses that would otherwise be regarded as socially unacceptable can begin to attain social legitimacy and political agency. Through political agency, such phenomena can become implicitly shrouded beneath the cover of nationalism and national belonging for instance, in preference of explicit or overt manifestations of racism or Islamophobia, even though the resultant consequence or impact may well be largely equitable. Likewise, if overly simple definitions and conceptualisations are put forward, overly simple – and overly inadequate – solutions to the problem ensue, culminating in a situation that has already been sufficiently explored. In addition, both the definition and purported solution obscure the multi-dimensionality, specificity and complexity of the phenomenon, thus undermining, hindering and even negating the problem and enhancing the contestation.

These issues therefore need to be taken into account, as do the criticisms and failings identified earlier. Any means to better defining and conceptualising Islamophobia must therefore be able to identify and accommodate 'Muslims' in such ways that they are neither essentialised nor reduced, nor made out to be a homogenous collective identified by indiscriminate or inappropriate markers or appellations. This would mean being able to accommodate the inherent diversity of 'Muslims', whether in their practice, race, ethnic heritage, or indeed any other marker of difference that might occur, whilst also accommodating those 'Muslims' that have been earmarked 'problematic'. In addition, no apportioning of blame or attributing certain Muslims with any lesser status of legitimacy must occur. The religion of Islam and its theological tenets would also require similar accreditation, overcoming how Sayyid suggested Islam became essentialised through the lens of Orientalism theory. Similarly, Islam cannot be deployed as a common denominator beneath which all Muslims can be conveniently unified. Consequently, what is being suggested here is that any conceptualisation must accommodate the reality and diversity of Muslims and Islam, and not merely reduce all to an imposed or self-grandiose 'true' or 'authentic' Islam that would appear far from existing.

To achieve this, two essentials demands must be met: the first is to identify exactly what needs to be defined and conceptualised; secondly, that a solid theoretical basis is established. For the first, and from the analysis already undertaken, this must be the 'certain identifiable phenomenon' that the EUMC Report identified and most definitely not the products that it suggested were consequential of such. It is therefore quite possible that it will be the first time that this 'certain identifiable phenomenon' has been specifically addressed as distinct and separate from its products and consequences. In separating the 'certain identifiable phenomenon' from the products and consequences, such a theoretical foundation would necessarily be required to be broken down into a number of constituent components. In doing so, a greater transferable relevance to other, less rigidly identifiable and quantifiable social and political strata in addition to the media might ensue. As highlighted beforehand, any criterion that merely identifies products of Islamophobia in newspaper coverage may not necessarily be useful in identifying the products of any similar and inter-related phenomena in the realms of education, employment and so on, let alone the phenomenon itself. Thus the need for transferability is essential in order that the products and resultant consequences, all of which may be vastly different across the vastly different social and political strata, may well be better accommodated and understood. This would therefore begin to provide a route to achieving the second of the essential demands and begin to develop a theoretical foundation upon which a better conceptualisation and definition of Islamophobia might ensue. In attempting this, it is envisaged that further research would be elsewhere undertaken, both theoretically and empirically – particularly into the monitoring of the discourse, events and consequences also – in order that the necessary evidence required to substantiate the existence of Islamophobia in today's society is made that much easier. It is hoped that this might be possible if the positing of a re-defined and re-conceptualised Islamophobia is successful.

From investigating the emergence and development of theories and ideas about Islamophobia throughout its relatively short history, it is apparent that whilst Islamophobia has been compared, albeit superficially, alongside similar comparative and correlative phenomena, this process has never been rigorously undertaken. Yet if indeed it had, then it is possible that some additional insight might have emerged about it, what with the theories, definitions and concepts of similar phenomena, racism for instance, having been developed over a longer period of time. Certain obvious phenomena can be easily highlighted, especially with both racism and anti-Semitism having been mentioned previously, but if these same similar and correlative phenomena are to provide any necessary insight, then it is not only the broad and extremely generalised phenomena that must be explored, but also the processes and functions that simultaneously feed into them, such processes as stereotypification, representation and semiology for instance, each of which can be gleaned from the analyses undertaken so far. It is essential to note however that any such analysis that is to be undertaken as regards the similar and collaborative phenomena and constitutive theories are not merely to locate or provide substitutive or overly simplistic theories gleaned from such a process, but to explore better ways of understanding, defining and conceptualising Islamophobia. The objective therefore is to locate and employ correlative theoretical resonance through the consideration and exposition of selected discourses and theories, rather than provide a full exposition of the field of research relating to similar and inter-related phenomena or to supplant theories of similar phenomena as theories of Islamophobia.

To qualify this, it is necessary to explain why some correlative theoretical phenomena and their respective models of understanding have been excluded from this analytical process, one of the most apparent being that of Orientalism and its more contemporary derivative, neo-Orientalism. Based primarily upon Sayyid's critique of Orientalist discourse and theory and his highlighting of how Islam was negated and reduced to something of an abstract anomaly, the consequence of which was 'erasure',[1] so the theories and discourse of Orientalism may already mirror much of that which has been contemporarily attributed and projected onto the discourses and theories of Islamophobia. Having used the criticisms posited against Orientalism previously to expound arguments against the Runnymede model therefore, so it might be a worthless process and one that provides little more insight or understanding. This is not to repudiate the influential legacy or legitimacy of the concept or theories of Orientalism, nor to deny what might be a shared heritage or aetiological lineage where contemporary Islamophobia may have evolved out of Orientalism, but instead to argue that in terms of comparative and correlative analysis, the theories and discourses associated with Orientalism may, at this particular juncture at least, be inappropriate.

Regarding 'neo-Orientalism', it is unclear whether an adequate working definition exists that would allow such an undertaking. From those that do exist, there would appear to be some difference between the proximities connected to neo-Orientalism as opposed to those relating to Islamophobia, with the latter being much more 'within' or 'internal' as opposed to neo-Orientalist discourse being much more 'without' and 'external'.[2] As Donnan and Stokes, Milton-Edwards, and Richardson amongst others suggest, neo-Orientalism is largely concerned with internationalist dimensions, shaped and determined by the 'clash' thesis thus negating the particularities and specificities that contextualise Islamophobia at the very localised and individual setting.[3] It is possible therefore that neo-Orientalism may have some resonance with contemporary Islamophobia, but may also be

---

[1]   Sayyid (1997), 10.

[2]   Robert J.C. Young, *Postcolonialism* (Oxford: Oxford University Press, 2003). See also: Chris Allen, 'Undoing Proximity: the Impact of the Local-Global Nexus on Perceptions of Muslims in Britain', *The Globalisation and Localisation of Religion: EASR Congress 2003*, 11 May 2003 (University of Bergen, Norway).

[3]   Hastings Donnan and Martin Stokes, 'Interpreting Interpretations of Islam', in Donnan (2002), 1–19; Beverley Milton-Edwards, 'Researching the Radical: the Quest for a New Perspective', Donnan (2002), 32–50; and Richardson (2004).

somewhat different in its context, setting, function and operation. As regards neo-Orientalism therefore, it is possible that further critical analysis and engagement is required with it as a working concept before any comparative or correlative analysis be made with Islamophobia.

In considering and undertaking these comparative and correlative analyses therefore, it is important to set out what is intended to be achieved. Firstly, it is important to broadly consider various different theories and discourses associated in order to identify points of intersection or resonance with Islamophobia. Secondly, it will be necessary to evaluate to what extent these intersections and resonances can offer as regards additional understanding or meaning about Islamophobia.

Stereotypification: 'unanalysed, unquestioned and indiscriminately festering in society'

Stereotypes have been recurrent in much of the writing about Islamophobia. One particular medium is that of the media and much of the analysis given over to the British press in previous chapters would appear to fit into the broader definitions and theories concerned with stereotypification. Asking whether or not stereotypes of Muslims and Islam exist would therefore appear to be the wrong question. Instead, it should be to ask what insight, if indeed any, such recognition might allow. For those such as Jeremy Henzell-Thomas, the former Chair of FAIR, not only are stereotypes problematically recurrent, but so too is their ability to infer and give meaning to Muslims and Islam. In a damning condemnation of Islamophobia, Henzell-Thomas speaks of Muslim stereotypes in the contemporary media reflecting those employed by the Serbs prior to their undertaking of ethnic cleansing, suggesting that stereotypes' danger lies in the way they remain largely unanalysed, unquestioned and indiscriminately festering in society.[4] Less controversially, both the Runnymede and EUMC Reports also refer to the influence of stereotypes in perpetuating negatively evaluated ideas and meanings about both Muslims and Islam. None of these sources however expand upon what a 'stereotype' is.

To aid understanding, Allport offers an authoritative definition: 'an exaggerated belief associated with a category, its function is to justify (rationalise) our relation

---

[4]   Jeremy Henzell-Thomas, 'The Language of Islamophobia', *Exploring Islamophobia Conference*, 29 September 2001 (University of Westminster: London). It is believed that this paper has been presented a number of times elsewhere and transcripts are widely available on the internet, for example: Jeremy Henzell-Thomas, 'The language of Islamophobia', *Masud.co.uk*, 28 September 2001 (22 September 2004) http://www.masud.co.uk/ISLAM/misc/phobia.htm. See also: Jeremy Henzell-Thomas, *The Challenge of Pluralism and the Middle Way of Islam* (Richmond: Association of Muslim Social Scientists UK, 2002).

to that category'.[5] Pickering develops and expands upon this, where for him stereotypes represent broad cultural processes, practices and understandings that create meaning through carrying with them very specific and definite ideological views and values, not necessarily categorising in the process but most definitely establishing meaning and understanding about a given subject – the subject of the stereotype – in wider society.[6] Consequently, stereotypes create a sense of order through the negation of broader or expansive understandings, foreclosing many of the issues relating to the difference and diversity of a subject matter before these same issues can be subsequently put forward, made known or engaged with. As Pickering elaborates, 'stereotypes construct difference as deviant for the sake of normative gain' through both negative *and* positive processes.[7] Stereotypes can therefore be as equally positive as indeed negative, presenting and re-presenting meanings as natural, absolute and largely invariable. In other words, stereotypes function by essentialising and reducing their subject matter to a series of absolute and normative meanings – irrespective of accuracy or appropriateness – that are readily and immediately recognisable and digestible. Thus stereotypes create boundaries and 'fix' that which is opposite, alien and Other upon its subjects as normative and absolute. Importantly and as Allport noted, that which is made known is also exaggerated and rationalised. It is no surprise therefore that stereotypes and stereotypification have been recurrent themes, if not always explicitly expressed, in writing about how Muslims and Islam are contemporarily understood.

Also worthy of note as regards stereotypes is that along with the creation of difference, so that same difference typically has a power relationship inherent within it, where the ingroup (that which establishes and gives meaning to the stereotypes) is superior to the outgroup (the subject group for whom the stereotypes are attributed). With this also emerges an 'us' and 'them' differential that immediately creates – either real or imagined – an evaluative hierarchy, where those that are stereotyped become fixed in marginal positions on the mainstream of society or outside society's normatively accepted characteristics: the 'stereotyped' only ever being seen to be subordinate to those doing the 'stereotyping'.[8] By extension therefore, what with the propensity of contemporary stereotypes about Muslims and Islam and their meaning in society, so it must be concluded that the position of and situation faced by Muslims would be one of subordination, where Muslims and Islam are the 'outgroup' to the 'ingroup' of 'normal' society. It is therefore that which is made known about Muslims and Islam – 'meaning' – through the recurrence of stereotypes, irrespective of positive or negative evaluations, that subsequently attribute and fix difference and Otherness upon Muslims and Islam.

---

[5] Gordon W. Allport, *The Nature of Prejudice* (Cambridge, MA: Addison Wesley, 1954), 191.

[6] Michael Pickering, *Stereotyping: the Politics of Representation* (Basingstoke: Palgrave, 2001).

[7] Ibid., 7.

[8] Ibid.

However, whilst it would be very easy to locate a broad range of stereotypes in a media context, as indeed it might also be in some political discourses as well, there would appear to be too much similarity between what is being suggested here regarding stereotypes and that which was previously considered in terms of the 'closed and open views', at least in terms of function and possibly even form. Stereotypes themselves therefore would appear to fail to provide any significant additional understanding into better defining or conceptualising that 'certain identifiable phenomenon' than existing models. As such, the value of undertaking a more extensive investigation into stereotypes must be questioned. Nonetheless, the actual process of stereotypification would appear to reinforce some of the preliminary observations made about the EUMC Report's Islamophobia: that in recognising the stereotypes – products – one must necessarily and simultaneously acknowledge that underpinning them are a series of meanings that feed into and reinforce the ideas, perceptions and established meanings and knowledge that already exists and is made known in society. This 'meaning' is founded upon and rooted within relations of domination and subordination, largely dictated by an asymmetric 'ingroup-outgroup' dichotomy, where through these same asymmetric relationships, that meaning becomes attributed and fixed, in terms of difference and Otherness to the outgroup in terms of them being different and Other to the normative values and mores of the ingroup. It might be therefore that this 'meaning' be most appropriately referred to in terms of it being 'ideological'.

Referencing this specifically to Islamophobia, two observations would appear to have some direct relevance. Firstly, it would appear to be the process (stereotypification) rather than the product (stereotype) that provides the conduit through which meaning and knowledge about certain groups and individuals enters into the mainstream of societal thought and understanding, in turn becoming a part of that which is normative. In this way, the meanings fixed to them subsequently and indiscriminately overlook and obscure particularities and complexities, and the difference that inherently exists within those communities, groups and individuals that constitute the outgroup. In essence, the process not only provides but also simplifies meaning, homogenising those fixed and characterised as the outgroup to a limited set of concepts and ideas that can and frequently do contradict each other.

Secondly, the process of stereotypification acknowledges the existence of products and their purpose but does not necessarily acknowledge that they have any greater value or function: they are products that provide a means to identify and nothing more. Identifying stereotypes in the media therefore, does not necessarily mean that these same stereotypes can or indeed will translate or be readily identifiable, recognisable or influential in other socio-economic or socio-political spheres. Some products may therefore be quite unique and relevant to one only particular sphere whilst other products may have a transferable value, being relevant and valid in different social, economic and political contexts. This is not to suggest that the meaning that underpins them cannot be translated to other settings and contexts but just the product and nothing more. So whilst stereotypes as products would appear to be similar to the existing models and their associated products, resultantly offering little in terms of better defining or conceptualising Islamophobia, theoretically at least, they would appear to offer some justification for separating process from product and explaining how the relationship between process and product functions.

Representation: 'to say something meaningful about, or to represent, the world meaningfully, to other people'

From the previous consideration, it would appear that the processes rather than the products would appear to demand greater scrutiny and investigation if that 'certain identifiable phenomenon' is to be better defined and conceptualised. In considering these processes, which might be described processes of 'representation', the writing and research of Stuart Hall into the representation of 'black' communities and individuals might be extremely pertinent. However, as has been problematic elsewhere, most of his investigations into representation are rooted almost exclusively in the media, a sphere of operation one might argue the study of Islamophobia be diversified away from. In acknowledging this though, it is the intention here to consider the broader theoretical issues discussed by Hall and the wider field of study within which he operates, rather more than merely offering a further analysis of the media, albeit in a different contextual frame. In his authoritative study on the processes and consequences of representation, *Representation: Cultural Representations and Signifying Practices*,[9] Hall establishes a number of arguments that have a distinct resonance to those set out here. For Hall, the way in which meaning is disseminated, received and subsequently understood is through the concept of 'representation', defining this in terms of how society and voices within society use 'language to say something meaningful about, or to represent, the world meaningfully, to other people'.[10] In this way, representation is concerned with the communicative process that provides meaning to both inform and make known.

From this premise, Hall suggests three modes of representation as existing: the reflective, intentional and constructionist, through which individuals, groups and communities can all be given meaning to.[11] A reflective representation would reflect the meanings that exists in the real world of people, objects and events, maybe possibly a fair or accurate representation for want of a better understanding. An intentional representation would reflect the intended meaning of the representation's creator or author rather than anything else, neither being necessarily true or correct nor indeed inaccurate or false, but necessarily true to the meaning that was intended. Finally, a constructionist representation would be where meaning was constructed – deliberately conceived and put forward – through

---

[9] Hall (1997).

[10] Ibid., 13.

[11] Ibid., 15.

the use of potentially inaccurate and inappropriate terminologies, appellations to terminologies, inferences and so on, being neither reflective nor intentional, but constructed in order that a very specific knowledge or meaning is disseminated.

Yet suggesting the meaning that terminologies either may or may not make known is exactly where the problem arises as regards a constructionist approach: are constructed representations thus determined by the author, who may either intentionally or inadvertently construct a representation that provides negatively evaluated meaning; are constructed representations constructed and given meaning to by the recipient of the representation largely irrespective of the intentions, reflections and so on of the author who may have genuinely attempted to provide a reflective representation; or can meaning be gleaned more combinatively or collaboratively where both can result in negatively evaluated meaning, either of which are largely independent and irrespective of intention and reality because of that which is already known or is in circulation in society? Ultimately, the constructs of the author may not necessarily translate to the recipient or the constructed meaning of the recipient may not be that of the author. Consequently, other factors including discursive practices that incorporate repetition, hyperbole and metaphor to name but a few must also be considered as indeed must the levels of ignorance about the subject matter and also the lack of clarity and accuracy associated with that which is already made known or being given meaning to in society. It is here therefore that problems – either real or potential – exist as regards issues of representation because meaning may already be in circulation that attributes and fixes certain communities, groups, individuals and concepts with certain meanings and understandings even though they may not necessarily have constituted any part of the author's reflective, intentional or constructed representations. Whilst Hall does not necessarily expand upon this, it is an extremely important consideration.

Irrespective of the mode of representation therefore, it would appear that the way in which such representations and that which is made known via such representations, are much more dependent upon the way in which they are received and digested by the recipients, potentially being quite different from that which was either reflected, intended or constructed. From Hall's perspective, and in an attempt to elaborate upon the premise relating to Islamophobia, two important points need further consideration. Firstly, all sorts of individuals, communities, events and acts are correlated within society that embody a broad range of existing concepts that are largely independent of any further isolated or more exclusive representations that either contravene or attempt to negate or counter any positive or negative evaluations inherent within these. So for Muslims and Islam, across society a clear concept and knowledge of both clearly already exists. Unlike previous conceptualisations of Islamophobia that have described Islam and Muslims in society through unrepresentative and homogenised terms, the reality here would be quite to the contrary, where societal concepts of 'Islam' and 'Muslims' would be much more complex and would comprise a myriad range of ways to cluster, organise, arrange and classify these concepts and their associated meanings into established and shared meanings and conceptual maps.[12]

Secondly, these same shared meanings and conceptual maps find a way of being translated into common language where concepts and ideas are correlated with certain language, words, terminologies and visual images. In this way, whilst intentions and reflective modes may well be true and accurate, the employment of a particular word, phrase, terminology or image could trigger the recognition of some of these shared meanings thus insisting that the representation be markedly different to that which was intended. Some might suggest that such an acknowledgement could absolve all those purporting any Islamophobia by suggesting the perpetrators deny any intention in favour of suggesting that it was indeed the recipient who picked up on such ideas and meanings what with the inadvertent use of a negatively evaluated phrase, word, term or so on. For these same phrases, words, terminologies or images, Hall theoretically roots this in semiology, naming them as 'signs', where the signs provide – or signal – meaning about the subject matter and not necessarily the mode of representation or what that mode was suggested as putting forward. Hall argues therefore that it is the meanings and knowledge in society that informs the representations rather more so than the representations themselves that informs society.

To develop this regarding Islamophobia might be to revisit the EUMC Report's 'visual identifiers'.[13] As it stated, the stimulant behind the vast majority of attacks and incidents were identifiers that informed or provided meanings about Muslims or Islam:

> It seems that behind the vast majority of attacks and infringements upon specific communities and individuals was the fact that they were identified as Muslims, whether they in fact were or not, by something that could be recognisably associated with Islam; this we call the visual identifiers. Whilst these were not necessarily in themselves the reason for any attacks, it would seem that they were the single most predominant factor in determining who or what became the victim or retaliation ... the visual identifiers provided a stimulant that offered an outlet for the venting of anger or some other denigratory sentiment.[14]

The 'visual identifiers' would therefore appear to be remarkably similar to the 'signs', in both function and understanding. What emerges from the EUMC Report therefore is that whilst signs are in evidence in the press and media, embodying both meaning and knowledge, so signs that embody and associate seemingly identical sets of meaning also exist in other sectors as well, highlighted in the report across different social, economic and political settings. So whilst issues of representation have been identifiable in the media, as put forward through the

---

[12]   Hall (1997).
[13]   Allen and Nielsen (2002), 34–6.
[14]   Ibid., 34.

overriding foci of previous analyses of Islamophobia, there would also appear to be a somewhat parallelism of signs, and by consequence meaning also, that exist in other spheres of society as well. What this suggests is that for the first time, theoretical justifications would appear to substantiate that in those societal strata and spheres that have yet been afforded the same levels of research and consideration that the media has, where the tendency has been to anecdotalise Islamophobia, equitably functional signs and meanings would also appear to be in evidence and circulation: signs and meanings that purport to that 'certain identifiable phenomenon'.

However, the signs would appear to be somewhat different and possibly even unlinked, suggesting more a transference of meaning through the existence of different signs rather than through any process of replication. What must be therefore required and further investigated is the link between these two apparently concurrent series of signs in an attempt to highlight how the visual identifier of the turban or *hijab* for example would appear to potentially embody the same, or at least similar meanings as say the employment of the appellation 'fundamentalist' or 'extremist' does in the media. What is required therefore is to consider how meaning becomes embodied within signs, before asking how that same meaning might be explained in terms of Islamophobia. To do this, it will be necessary to consider in more detail some theories of semiology.

Semiology: 'in the very heart of society's fabric'

Representation and the notion of visual identifiers would therefore appear to have some correlative resonance. Both signs and visual identifiers would appear to be as Hall suggests functional products through which meaning enters into, and indeed remains in the very heart of society's fabric.[15] In this process, three separate functions appear to be in operation. Firstly, there is the process, or what might be more appropriately termed the 'phenomenon', that informs, shapes, perpetuates and sustains that meaning which exists and circulates in society. Secondly, the products, termed here as the signs, would seem to be the medium through which meaning is given form and subsequently made known. And finally, either a reaction to or consequence of the combinative function of the phenomenon and product would appear to sometimes occur, although not always readily identifiable. Interestingly, this three-fold theorisation reflects the preliminary positing of the EUMC Report's conceptualisation of Islamophobia made earlier in this book, where three distinct components were identifiable. As the report stated, the *hijab* was the primary sign or product following 9/11, embodying meaning that identified those wearing *hijab* as Muslim and being of the same religion as the perpetrators of 9/11, thus feeding into and drawing upon that pool of meaning and knowledge pre-existent to 9/11 about Islam and Muslims – meanings that included interpreting Islam and Muslims

---

[15]   Hall (1997), 29.

as anti-Western and anti-feminist, incompatible and asymmetrically opposed to the ideas and values of the West, fixed as being distinctly Other and different – that was in turn also being supplemented and inflated by the meanings emerging from the volatile post-9/11 climate, thus resulting in Muslim women becoming the primary targets for retaliatory attack and abuse.[16]

A brief overview of semiology, in particular the writing of Ferdinand de Saussure, provides some theoretical insight into this process.[17] For him, the sign has two distinctions: firstly, the meaning underpinning it, and secondly, the form it takes. In semiology, the meaning is that which is *signified*, whilst the form that it takes is the *signifier*. The *hijab* therefore would be the *signifier*, in that it gave meaning to and made known Muslim women – and Muslims per se – in certain frames of reference. Thus the signifiers – identifier, product or sign depending upon the terminology preferred – were organised and interpreted, through that meaning that they made known, by both the perpetrators of such retaliatory attacks and also those who did not undertake retaliatory attacks. So when either 'Muslim' or 'Islam' is made known through a signifier, so a process of signification ensues that organises and classifies into distinct societal categories that have homogenising characteristics and qualities. A similar process would appear to occur when other less readily identifiable social identifiers and strata are employed also, including those visual and linguistic signs where neither 'Islam' nor 'Muslim' is directly identifiable. Signs would therefore appear to be able to become manifested in a myriad of forms that can be either isolated or collaborative from a whole series of interlinked and sometimes incompatible combinative and cumulative representations, whether visual, verbal, audio, textual or linguistic. Thus similarities can be seen between the textual signifier of 'fundamentalist' in the media and the visual signifier of the *hijab* or *niqab* in the more social setting.

Theories of semiology thus suggest, if not conclusively prove, that all who either possess, are aware of, or indeed gain access to either any or all of these concomitant and interlinked signs and their respective meanings could therefore understand and subsequently attribute as a result, the same perceptions, capabilities and qualities irrespective of difference or diversity that would signify without any seeming discriminate judgment being made and irrespective of whether such were negative and derogatory or positive and enhancing. Consequently, when the signifiers of both 'Islam' and 'Muslims' are made known through Hall's identification of shared conceptual maps and shared systems of meaning, social realities and accuracies, whether religious, cultural, social or anything else, become largely irrelevant. There would also appear to be a substantive and significant

---

[16] Allen and Nielsen (2002), 35.

[17] For more information into the history and theories of semiology see: Johansen and Larsen (2002); Dan Fleming, *Formations* (Manchester: Manchester University Press, 2000); Nick Stevenson, *Understanding Media Cultures: Social Theory and Mass Communication* (London: Sage, 2002); and Chris Barker, *Television, Globalization and Cultural Identities* (Buckingham: Open University Press, 1999).

representational and symbolic value in the social imagining and giving meaning to of 'Muslims' and 'Islam' in the contemporary setting, where the meaning signified by the contemporary signs would not only appear to have a contemporary relevance, but also a more retrospective or historical meaning also. So whilst the *hijab*, in the context of the EUMC Report, would appear to have little retrospective value, the report also acknowledges through the observation of the Austrian NFP that 'resentments, fears and constructions of the enemy, which have formed to historic burdens and a lack of information, now come to the surface. The terrorist attacks seem to confirm old prejudices'.[18] Consequently, that which is signified is not merely contemporary but can also be quite historical also.

Signification therefore operates on two levels: the level of denotation where consensus of meaning exists, and connotation where meaning connects to broader historical, socio-economic, cultural, religious and other meanings.[19] Thus the *hijab* was given meaning to via the religion of Islam and understandings of Muslim women, both of which had various discourses and meanings already attributed to them, albeit real or constructed. When the *hijab* was thus acknowledged as a signifier for both Islam and Muslim women therefore, so it made known and reinforced and reinvigorated those pre-existent meanings already associated with both of these entities at the same time as embodying and being further enhanced by the contemporary and fast emerging meanings, discourses and so on of the time. So whilst Muslims may contemporarily be given meaning through violence, terrorism and atrocity, particularly in the context of 9/11, such events and associated meanings would simultaneously link into and be contextualised by the atavistic meanings of Islam and Muslims that have been common currency historically. Not only does this undermine the repudiation of the power of history theory but it adds credence to Halliday's observation that history acts as a frame of reference for the present day. It is understanding how this meaning both exists and operates that allows a broader sphere of reference to be approached as regards how and what Islamophobia might be, beyond simplistic and inappropriate constraints that either do not exist, exist unexplained, do not translate, or at worst, appear incompatible and unworkable.

The signification process therefore is both pragmatic and influential but not necessarily explanatory. The signs (products) must be therefore necessarily separate from the meaning that they give rise to (the phenomenon), both of which are quite separate and different from the potentially ensuing consequences if indeed there are any. Whilst semiology provides an insight into the function of signs and the provision or dissemination of meaning, as well inferring support for a threefold understanding of Islamophobia – based upon meaning, product and consequence – semiology in its own right would appear not to be able to provide a complete foundation upon which Islamophobia might be better defined and conceptualised. Whilst highlighting signs and function, semiology neither

---

[18]   Allen and Nielsen (2002), 41.
[19]   Hall (1997), 39.

necessarily explains nor provides any additional insight into what the meanings of Islamophobia might be, preliminarily suggested here in terms of being that 'certain identifiable phenomenon', that underpin both the signs and the consequential effects of such. Consequently, the problem would appear to be how this particular 'phenomenon' – the signified – might be defined and conceptualised rather more than the signifiers.

From considering theories of stereotypification, representation and semiology, some conclusions can be drawn about that 'certain identifiable phenomenon'. Firstly, a multitude of products would appear to exist that inform and give meaning to that which is understood as being either 'Muslim' and 'Islam', irrespective of whether these might be true or untrue, accurate or inaccurate, discriminate or indiscriminate. Secondly, these products can be either separate or interlinked, taking on myriad and protean forms that incorporate the visual, verbal, linguistic, textual, representational and associative, functioning at times without necessarily even being directly focused upon Muslims or Islam or overtly identifying them. Thirdly, the way in which these products inform and give meaning is through the shared languages and conceptual maps that exist across different social strata, shaped not only by current affairs, events and relationships but also by historical junctures, myths and legacies that can and do seek to reinforce, reinvigorate or re-awaken older, both passive and active, meanings and understandings. Fourthly, these shared languages and societal conceptual maps appear to be contextualised by the historical and geographical constraints within which they are produced and understood, at times taking on a range of different national, linguistic and so on dimensions that are sometimes unique but also concurrent and concomitant with other historical and/or geographical constraints and settings. And finally, there would appear to be sufficient evidence and theoretical reasoning to suggest that three different components of Islamophobia exist: the process of meaning and informing knowledge and understanding; the products or processes through which meaning is perpetuated and sustained by being subsequently recognised, interpreted and eventually understood; plus also forms of exclusionary practice and violent incursion that may or may not be consequential of the preceding components. How then might this be more adequately and appropriately defined and understood?

Racism: 'theoretically shifting from a focus on product to process'

Across the various analyses of Islamophobia undertaken here, one significant phenomenon has been recurrently identified as being particularly concomitant and correlative. Yet despite its recurrent nature, little if indeed any significant correlative consideration has been undertaken in order to identify how the two may well be either complimentarily informing and theoretically correlative, or indeed interconnected with the possibility of Islamophobia being incorporated as a dimension of this much broader phenomenon. This recurrent phenomenon is therefore racism. Indeed as noted here, numerous sources have referred to racism as overlapping and being similar to Islamophobia, whilst elsewhere, traditional markers, forms and consequences of racism have been employed to attempt to substantiate an Islamophobia, something that has detrimentally contributed to the anecdotal nature of the phenomenon. Elsewhere RAREN 3 identified that in some contexts such phenomena might be better termed 'anti-Muslim racism', whilst the EUMC report acknowledged that, 'expressions of Islamophobia have certainly in some instances simply been a "cover" for general racism'.[20] Nonetheless, theories relating to racism, in terms of Islamophobia at least remain not only under-explored but somewhat unexplored, justifying the pursuance of such an investigation here.

To begin, it is worth considering the dual concepts of 'race' and 'racism', both as separate as well as interlinked and interconnected conceptual entities, and from which two interesting factors emerge. The first, and contrary to the British context where race is popularly conceived and determined by skin colour, racism can occur in situations where neither the reality nor concept of race actually exists; the second, in distancing itself from the specifically British context, racist phenomena can be culturally as well as somatically founded.[21] A situation thus occurs where racism can operate and function in such ways that 'racism without race' can sometimes, but not necessarily always, ensue. It is maybe possible therefore – although as yet unsubstantiated – for Islamophobia to operate and function in this way. Despite this sounding potentially quite radical and against the norms of that which might be understood as regards race and racism, the concept of racism without race is not new, where throughout history numerous similar prejudicial, discriminatory and ideological phenomena can be located that fail to have any pseudo-biological justification at its core. As Clarke explains, the notion of 'race' was largely a construct of the eighteenth and nineteenth centuries, so any similar phenomena that pre-existed this time would have been framed in terms of Eurocentrism or xenophobia, or even unacknowledged, unnamed or undefined,[22] one possible example being those anti-Jewish, anti-Judaic phenomena that predated the coining of 'anti-Semitism' in the late nineteenth century. Consequently, it is quite inappropriate to suggest or even locate certain phenomena as being present only with the emergence of suitable or unsuitable names and terminologies for them. As such, whilst notions of 'race' are known and are shaped in particular ways in the contemporary setting, 'racisms' have been evident across the entire spectrum of human history, identifiable through a vast array of different markers, characteristics and processes. It is therefore sometimes only the terminologies that are new and not the phenomena.[23]

---

[20]   Allen and Nielsen (2002), 49.

[21]   Barker (1981).

[22]   Simon Clarke, *Social Theory, Psychoanalysis and Racism* (London: Palgrave, 2003).

[23]   See Etienne Balibar and Immanuel Wallerstein, *New Ethnicities and Urban Cultures: Ambiguous Identities* (London: Verso, 1991); Mike Silverman and Nira Yuval-Davis, 'Jews. Arabs and the Theorisation of Racism in Britain and France', *Thinking Identities: Ethnicity,*

As regards the British context, those such as Brah et al. suggest that 'racism without race' already exists in the contemporary setting, recognisable through sectarianism in Scotland and Northern Ireland for instance.[24] Being rooted in either the religious practice or heritage of the individual, community or group in question, it is contextualised in frames of understanding that simultaneously connote – consciously or otherwise – an Irish lineage that embodies religious, ethnic and racial assumptions that interlink both racial and non-racial dimensions. For them, the assumption that race is solely denoted by skin colour has been the smokescreen that has allowed sectarian arguments to be perpetuated and sustained with little redress. To overcome this, Brah et al. put forward what they believe to be a simple way to redress the problem and begin the process of better informing. For them, 'theoretically shifting from a focus on product to process' not only challenges the phenomenon but also initiates a process of recognition and understanding that such phenomena so desperately require.[25] As regards the contested nature of Islamophobia, so this same approach might offer some reward in achieving better definition and conceptualisation, as well as recognition and validation in the public – incorporating the social, economic and political – space.

From this premise, there may be some validity in approaching Islamophobia as an expression of racism: the problem though is what 'type' of racism might it be? As referred to in the opening chapter, the Parekh Report described contemporary anti-Muslim racism as, 'one of the most serious forms of cultural hostility in modern Europe'.[26] Here Parekh referred to a very specific type of racism, one that was first theoretically set out by Barker in terms of 'new racism'.[27] As referred to previously, Barker identified a shift having occurred in racist processes and identifiers where associated phenomena was beginning to be highlighted by and expressed in terms of culturally focused markers, rather than biological – pseudo or otherwise – or somatic equivalent. For Barker, 'new racism' emerged specifically from British political discourse in the late 1970s, identifiable in Conservative Party political ideology following their 1974 election defeat. What became paramount was the disproportionate focus on the issue of immigration and the allegation that continued immigration would eventually destroy the cultural homogeneity of the British nation, its indigenous population's identity. More simply, immigrants were being put forward as a threat to the existence of 'British-ness'. As Miles and Brown described it some time after, Barker's particular understanding 'formulated a notion of "Other" as naturally different in cultural terms, with a natural "home" outside

---

Racism and Culture, eds Avtar Brah et al. (Basingstoke: Macmillan, 1999), 25–48; and Avtar Brah et al., 'Thinking Identities: Ethnicity, Racism and Culture', Brah et al. (1999), 1–21.

[24]   Brah et al. (1999).
[25]   Ibid., 4.
[26]   Parekh (2000), 60.
[27]   Barker (1981).

Britain',[28] alluding again to this concept of 'racism without race' and having a resonance with the way in which Muslims and Islam are contemporarily seen.

Having dispensed with biological determinants, 'cultural racism' became largely rooted in frames of inclusion and exclusion, specifying who and what may legitimately belong to a particular national, or other, community as well as determining what that community's norms were, simultaneously proposing and advancing quasi-justifications for the segregation, exclusion and banishment of those whose origin, parentage, religion, culture or so on assign them elsewhere. Through this process which re-asserts the Other, an imagined 'Self' thus ensues that appreciates Otherness but to the extent where it is considered better for Others and 'their cultures' to remain separate so that they preserve themselves and their traditions. As Barker established, the consequences of new racism are: that 'our' political and cultural systems are seen to be superior through its difference to the ways of the Other, readily incorporating normative 'ways of life' that include language, beliefs, values, customs and religions; that there is such a strong attachment to 'our' way of life that creates boundaries between 'them' and 'us', founded upon difference rather than inferiority; that other cultures are in some ways pathologically interpreted and understood in that they cause 'problems' for 'us' through the notion of a genuine fear and/or threat; and that all of this culminates as 'common sense', justified and perfectly natural and in no way racist whatsoever.[29]

From each of these, a clear correlation can be drawn that purports to Islamophobia across a variety of social spheres. For example in the first consequence, there has been much geo-political debate about establishing 'Western style democracy' in the Middle East, more specifically 'Islamic' countries, as a means to end the conflict and violence attributed to that area. Likewise, whilst the BNP's *I.S.L.A.M.* document argues that 'no-one dared tell the truth about Islam and the way that it threatens our democracy, traditional freedoms and identity'[30] from the viewpoint of the second consequence of cultural racism, another BNP document establishes another of Barker's identified consequences, giving 'the lie to those who falsely claim that we are "racists" or "haters". We sympathise and identify with every people in the world who want to secure or preserve a homeland for themselves, their traditions and their posterity'.[31] And as the third and fourth consequences can be identified in the heightened sense of fear and suspicion prevalent towards Muslims since 9/11,[32] it could be argued that as Parekh and others have suggested, contemporary Islamophobia may well be a manifestation of new racism.[33]

---

28   Miles and Brown (2003), 62.

29   Ibid.

30   Allen (2004), 13.

31   Ibid., 15.

32   YOUGOV, *Attitudes towards British Muslims*, Islam Awareness Week (4 November 2002).

33   In addition to the Parekh Report others such as Halliday have also expressed a similar conceptualisation for 'Islamophobia'. A useful exploration of notions of culturally

As with most considerations of Islamophobia however, some problems arise and contestation occurs in doing so. Firstly, the very concept of cultural racism has been questioned by some key voices. Those such as Paul Gilroy have argued that whilst culturally based phenomena may have been identifiable around the time of Barker's writing, since that time racist and similarly associated phenomena have continued to change and evolve – as indeed might be the case throughout the entirety of history – taking on new identifiers and signs in order to further normalise and invisibilise those previously identified and culturally defined markers of difference. Conclusively, Gilroy argues that 'the era of that New Racism is emphatically over'.[34] Whether this is as emphatic as Gilroy suggests is of course debatable, but what it does suggest is the possibility that the notion of a 'cultural' racism is not too significantly different from more traditional forms and expressions of racism, maybe even reinforcing and reasserting the concept of the existence of 'racisms without races'.

What appears to be rather more problematic in conceptualising contemporary Islamophobia as cultural racism however is that one would be inadvertently 'culturalising' Muslims and Islam. In this way, what might only be a local colouring of say a specifically British Islam – coloured by the high percentage population and influence of Muslims of South Asian heritage – may become widely regarded as both determinative and fundamental to the expression and manifestation of that faith even though such may not necessarily be regarded as either important or legitimate in other national, geographical or cultural settings.[35] Culturalisation therefore not only strengthens homogenous perceptions that attribute characteristics without differentiation, but the newly culturalised markers can also inappropriately essentialise Muslims where 'Islam' and 'Muslims' continue to be entities that are defined, shaped and determined by outsider perceptions of that which may be inaccurate or inappropriately understood. Solely interpreting Islamophobia in terms of cultural racism therefore could be seen to be imposing an essentialised and culturally determined 'Muslim' against which all Muslims would necessarily need to adhere, characterising and reducing at the same time as relinquishing and denying the process of self-identification, the inherency of diversity, and the embodiment of difference. Suggesting 'Islam' as a culture would

---

manifested forms of racism that relates specifically to Muslims can be found in Werbner (1997). Here Werbner observes that 'it is not, after all, primarily *Asian* collective sacred icons and cultures which are violently targeted by racists in Britain, but the discrete national and religious icons of sub-groupings within the broader South Asian collectivity. As we have seen, the most violent racism at present is directed against British Muslims', 227. Whilst she refrains from using the terminology of new racism per se, she explores and considers a broad range of rhetoric and ideas that fit into Barker's theoretical framework.

[34] Paul Gilroy, *Between Camps: Nations, Cultures and the Allure of Race* (London: Penguin, 2000), 38.

[35] C.W. Watson, *Multiculturalism* (Buckingham: Open University Press, 2000).

also be as equally inappropriate, again being reductionist about the diversity of the faith and its expressions.

One other argument against Islamophobia as cultural racism is from the suggestion that if cultural racism is also 'new', then it must be in some way different and differentiable from pre-existent or historically manifested phenomena, a point which goes against earlier considerations of the shaping influence of history on the way that Muslims and Islam are given meaning to contemporarily. If the historical legacies and power of meaning are not to be repudiated, as indeed argued previously, then understanding or defining 'that certain identifiable phenomenon' as 'new' might be somewhat unjustified and again, quite misleading at a very basic level of definition and conceptualisation. Consequently, whilst cultural as new racisms may have some overlap and resonance with Islamophobia, there would appear to be some issues or at least inferences that would appear to similarly reinforce, or at least have the potential to reinforce, the flaws and weaknesses that have been identified and subsequently necessitated as requiring eradication in earlier conceptualisations and theories of Islamophobia.

From this consideration therefore, both the very fabric of that which constitutes Islamophobia and the requirements of both defining and conceptualising it that are deemed necessary, would appear to have some subtle differences and specifics that differentiate Islamophobia from being entirely accommodated within conceptualisations and theories of similar phenomena that have preceded this particular consideration. As such, there would appear to be something almost unique about this contemporary phenomenon. Alluding and referring to an asymmetrically opposed and constantly protean amalgam of nationalities (Arab, Pakistani and of course the identification of the 'self' within these nationalities, incorporating notions of 'British-ness' and compatibility), religion (Islam), culture (at times inappropriately, where cultural markers are widely substituted and accepted as equitable with religious markers) and militarism (recurrent references to violence, militarism and terrorism), such allusions and references appear, from what has gone before, to be both frequently produced and made known through a multitude of products that incorporate a vast array of different discursive and other social structures. Beyond Islam and Muslims, it is fair to state that no other religion or religious adherents are contemporarily identified or given meaning to through such a similar amalgam of ideas, not being restricted to any one somatic, biological, cultural or indeed any other set of characteristics or markers. The only factor therefore that logically and theoretically brings together and interlocks this contested, variously manifested and framed series of phenomena that cut across and manifest themselves across vast swathes of different social strata, can be the recognition and subsequent identification of a specifically 'Muslim' or 'Islamic' element somewhere within either its process, described here in terms of the meaning underpinning the phenomenon.

If Islamophobia therefore exists, it must be necessary for that 'certain identifiable phenomenon' to have an acknowledged 'Muslim' or 'Islamic' element, albeit one that might be either explicit or implicit, overtly expressed or covertly implied, even just merely nuanced where 'Muslim' or 'Islamic' might be understood or framed in such ways that 'Muslim' or 'Islamic' might be made known through meanings that are 'theological', 'social', 'cultural', 'racial' and so on, never necessarily even specifically naming or mentioning either 'Muslims' or 'Islam' but providing enough nuanced meaning to clearly suggests such. It must therefore be this 'Islamic' or 'Muslim' element that solely codifies what may and may not legitimately be defined and conceptualised as being Islamophobia, irrespective of the subsequent overlap or interaction with other similar phenomena. Whilst Islamophobia would appear to be able to operate concurrently and collaboratively with other similarly related phenomena, to the extent where it may be rooted or initiated through racialised signifiers, so too must it be able to exist, operate and function independently also, where Islamophobia can be identified in those settings and contexts where only the sole identification of signifiers of Islam and Muslims are apparent. Islamophobia therefore cannot be defined and conceptualised solely in terms of one of these similar phenomena nor can it be entirely incorporated into an existing framework of theoretical definition or conceptualisation. Instead, these frameworks of theory must be deployed in order to finally establish, better define and conceptualise an independent and distinct Islamophobia. In the following chapter, Islamophobia will begin to be defined and conceptualised in this way.

Chapter 10

Islamophobia: A New Ideology
for a Media Generation

As highlighted in the deployment of the neologism and concept of Islamophobia, so racism can be deployed in equally inflationary ways, where little or no context or apparent grounding exists. Unlike Islamophobia though, extensive research and evidence has been produced that firstly sought to define and conceptualise racism, and secondly to provide credence and theoretical evidence for its existence. Whilst acknowledging that a wide range of different, and sometimes competing definitions and conceptualisations exist, it is not the intention here to provide a full exposition of these nor to weigh up the individual merits of competing claims and theories. Instead, it remains the intention to continue exploring correlative theories and models from which a better understanding of Islamophobia might emerge. In this chapter therefore, by exploring Robert Miles' theoretical model of racism, so it is the intention that a more adequate theoretical foundation upon which an overdue yet vitally imperative and new conceptualisation and definition of Islamophobia be established.

Racism[1] was begun in 1989 before being subsequently revised and developed with Malcolm Brown in 2003.[2] Miles was concerned with constructing a theoretical model, incorporating an adequate conceptualisation and definition of racism, from which further investigation and research into the consequences and exclusionary practices of racism might be undertaken. Acknowledging the shortcomings and problematic nature of existing theories of racism, Miles concluded that any research into this or any other similar phenomena, necessarily needed to be grounded in empirical evidence and be 'non-inflationary', similar to the concerns aired previously about Islamophobia. In addition, it was paramount that both evidence and theoretical models were neither anecdotal nor superficially simplistic.[3] Without theoretical and empirical grounding and thus substantiating the reality of racism, racism could be easily dismissed and justifiably ignored in the political and moral realms. If grounded evidence was not therefore put forward, then a lack of societal consensus would emerge, both of the reality and problematic nature, presence and influence of racism in society. Until such was achieved, a situation would ensue that would render it socially acceptable, possibly even justifying and perpetuating it. These are indeed issues and concerns that this book has repeatedly referred to

---

[1]   Robert Miles, *Racism* (London: Routledge, 1989).

[2]   Miles and Brown (2003).

[3]   Ibid.

regarding Islamophobia. Miles therefore suggested that the phenomenon of racism – the process of giving meaning and understanding about different 'races' – was the product of ideological and discursive labouring,[4] subsequently contextualised and better framed within the research of Michel Wieriorka.[5] From here it was suggested that racist phenomena consisted of:

1. a political programme or ideology that becomes largely interdependent with the notion and ideology of nationalism as well as providing knowledge and meaning about other both new and existing relations of power and meaning;
2. a set of prejudices, opinions and attitudes that may be held by either individuals, groups, communities or society, or indeed a combination of these;
3. a set of exclusionary practices as a result of prejudice and discrimination in employment, housing and other socio-economic spheres as well as subjection to violence as a tool of exclusion.

And from this premise, so distinct similarities emerge regarding that 'certain identifiable phenomenon's' threefold components: the process or phenomenon; the signs, visual identifiers and/or products; and the resultant and consequential factors and processes that are as yet empirically unsubstantiated. Each of these components will therefore be further explored in an Islamophobic context.

Exclusionary Practices as a Consequence of Islamophobia: 'no longer the preserve of the extreme minority'

If Miles and Brown's theories are correct, as indeed the observations of this research, then anti-Muslim, anti-Islamic phenomena must be grounded and rooted in empirical evidence that proves a consequential impact or effect in different socio-economic and socio-political strata. This, as established previously, is yet to be adequately achieved where the evidence remains anecdotal and founded upon over-inflationary accusations and hyperbole. Thus the substantiating of 'a set of exclusionary practices including such exclusion as in discrimination in employment, housing and other socio-economic spheres as well as subjection to violence as a tool of exclusion' is contemporarily a matter of extreme urgency. If such fails to be substantiated, as Miles and Brown note, the ongoing 'lack of evidence' will contribute significantly to the ongoing social dismissal and negation of Islamophobia. Methodologically also, there is very little evidence that meets the necessary requirements to substantiate that a distinct 'Islam' or 'Muslim' aspect

---

[4]   Ibid., 36.

[5]   Michel Wieviorka, *The Arena of Racism*, translated by Chris Turner (London: Sage, 1995).

has to be apparent, irrespective of how shrouded, covert or nuanced that might be, especially as so little of this stands up to rigorous investigation. At present, little evidence beyond the anecdotes and inflationary assertions criticised and dismissed previously, including that data which substitutes all Muslims per se as 'Pakistani' or 'Bangladeshi', therefore currently exists.

To rectify this, a better understanding of what needs to be proven is required. Consequently, rather than merely dismissing the existing research and models as far from evidential and conclusive, from Miles and Brown's research an understanding might be employed to prove and subsequently initiate the process of shaping and convincing the social consensus towards the reality and problematic nature of Islamophobia, thus allowing for its study and research to distance itself from the phoney and patronising 'Islamophobia problematic' that Hall unequivocally purports. The processes expanded upon here will therefore begin to redress this imbalance, providing an invigorated response that will attempt to go beyond understanding Islamophobia as being 'bad' merely because 'it is' and go some way to proving, through subsequent research, that the consequences of such phenomena in the reality of today's socio-economic and socio-political spheres do indeed manifest themselves in such ways that they negatively and detrimentally impact the everyday lives and experiences of Muslims and their communities. These negative and detrimental consequences will be referred to as 'exclusionary practices'.

What then are 'exclusionary practices'? Firstly, if the threefold theoretical model is valid, then exclusionary practices must be separate from both the ideology and the visual, verbal, linguistic and other products through which such becomes manifested. As an ideological phenomena, it must be possible to analytically distinguish these from any socially, economically or politically manifested practice or process that in some way discriminates, prejudices, restricts or negates the participation or inclusion of Muslims either individually or collectively. If this is so, then this must be clearly and empirically demonstrated and not merely anecdotally inferred or assumed. In this way, what must be demonstrated to substantiate anti-Muslim exclusionary practices is therefore not just to prove that pupils of South Asian heritage are at the lower end of the educational achievement spectrum, even though this may well be correct,[6] but to prove that they are there as a consequence of either their own Muslim-ness or the recognition of their Muslim-ness by others, or alternatively that *all Muslims* per se are in a similar position, both of which must be differentiated from competing claims based upon markers of heritage, ethnicity, race and so on. If achieved, such practices would then be proven to be consequential of Islamophobia rather than consequential of the religious adherence, either practising or otherwise, of one or more ethnic groups. Interestingly, whilst Anwar and Bakhsh highlight the situation as having arisen 'partly due to racial and religious discrimination',[7] they only highlight the

---

6   Muhammad Anwar and Qadar Bakhsh, *British Muslims and State Policies* (Coventry: Centre for Research in Ethnic Relations, 2003), 18–22.

7   Ibid., 71.

potential of one or possibly the other but without categorically proving the latter. Whether the reality of these exclusionary practices is motivated either partially or wholly by anti-Muslim, anti-Islamic, or racist phenomena remains unclear and thus negates the evidence.

Miles and Brown identify two forms of exclusionary practice that can be identified and proven from the premise established here. The first relates to circumstances where exclusionary practices arise from and subsequently embody an Islamophobic discourse but which may not be explicitly justified by it. The second relates to circumstances where explicitly racist discourses are modified in such ways that the explicit content is eliminated and replaced by discourses that carry the original meanings and functions. In both circumstances, Islamophobia discourses would be relatively silent but nonetheless embodied in the continuity and perpetuation of the exclusionary practice or in the necessary deployment of new language or terminologies to support such. Conceptually therefore, Islamophobic exclusionary practices (institutional' Islamophobia?) neither necessarily nor specifically refer to the exclusionary practice itself but to the fact that a once present discourse has either justified or initiated an exclusionary practice to the detriment, discrimination or exclusion of Muslims, either individually or collectively. The practice in itself therefore fails to be 'Islamophobic' whereas the underlying cause or motivation might.

Consequently, exclusionary practices can therefore only exist where a process of determination can be identified and subsequently proven. In doing so, one cannot retrospectively assume that a particular discourse or ideology has duly been causal or influential in any process of exclusion or discrimination, but must instead determine and prove the presence and direct influence of such an ideological or discursive labouring. Thus one must assess not the products or manifestations of such labouring and simplistically put these forward as either evidence for or against, but instead demonstrate that prior to any policy or practice being implemented or indeed any process of discrimination being undertaken, a distinctly Islamophobic ideology or discourse was present that catalytically initiated and socially, economically or politically realised the subsequent and emergent agenda, policy or practice. Whilst this may be controversial in that it renders much of that put forward as being Islamophobia as invalid – much of which has already been proven to be invalid through methodological or empirical weaknesses – it firmly establishes a foundation and methodological criteria upon which further critical investigation be undertaken and from which grounded and empirical conclusions might ensue. If subsequent research therefore operates within this framework, with both the evidence and data meeting the necessary criteria, then the existence of Islamophobic exclusionary practices will begin to be substantiated, thus initiating the slow and laborious process of influencing and shaping the social consensus of the realities and dangers of Islamophobia.

Reassessing Anwar and Bakhsh's data regarding Muslim educational attainment within this framework, the issue of determination can be relatively easily explored. Whilst it would appear that Muslim children are attaining lower academic standards than other groupings – that is if markers of 'Pakistani' and 'Bangladeshi' heritage are equitable with markers of 'Muslim' – there is however little indication to suggest that this is consequential of any Islamophobic ideological labouring or discourse. This is not to suggest that such does not exist, either in the educational sphere or elsewhere, but that this particular evidence fails to prove that the low educational attainment of pupils of 'Pakistani' or 'Bangladeshi' heritage is in any way consequential of their 'Muslim-ness'. Nowhere in the research or its data therefore does it either prove or substantiate the existence of an Islamophobia from which such low educational attainment was either a direct result or consequence of. This is not an outright dismissal of such claims, better research may well prove different, but merely to suggest that as regards this particular evidence, it has neither proved Islamophobia nor that these were in any way consequential of such.

To put forward an exclusionary practice as being 'Islamophobic' therefore, one must be able to demonstrate that such a practice was initiated because of the existence of an Islamophobic discourse, or that one was modified to accommodate alternative discourses, albeit with the same meanings. This type of research cannot be undertaken or readily concluded here although it may be possible for similar explorations to be considered, for example following the Satanic Verses affair, to try and identify whether any changes in practices occurred as a consequence of these that subsequently excluded or discriminated against Muslims, individually or collectively. This is mere speculation but is offered here as a suggested start point from which investigation into 'Islamophobic' exclusionary practices or 'institutional Islamophobia' might begin. What with the policy and legislative changes regarding security to have occurred since 9/11 and the perceived or real threat from terrorism in conjunction with the shifts in attitudes towards Muslims since these events, it would suggest that at least some Islamophobic resonance, if not a direct consequential process would have at least some bearing on what has ensued. Detailed research and analysis, along with the tracing and subsequent recognition of how such practices came about, mapping the necessary changes in discourse about Muslims, could be a building block from which to at least begin the next step of investigating Islamophobia.

Making the Links: 'Islam being to Muslims what race was to black males'

It could be that the situation contemporarily for Muslims reflects the one facing black communities in the late 1970s as identified by those such as Hall et al.[8] In the social context of the time, 'race' came to signify the crisis in society: more precisely, the 'race' of those perceived to be the 'problem' – young black males – and what that 'race' – a natural propensity for criminal activity – came to represent. For Hall et al., the race of young black males provided the 'arena in which complex fears, tensions and anxieties ... [could] be most conveniently and explicitly projected

---

[8]   Hall (1978).

and ... worked through'.[9] Whilst political and social commentators insisted that problems were not a crisis of race, the race of young black men was used to provide the lens through which the crisis could be given meaning and understood: race became 'thematised'. Racism therefore was no longer the preserve of the extreme minority that had repeatedly and regularly propagated such ideas but had instead made the transition into being a mainstream issue. In doing so, the issue and the focus upon which such was given meaning and understood became both naturalised and normalised, resulting in the view that *all* young black males became synonymous with criminal activity, in particular mugging. Through the contextual discourse, which included new terminology in the form of 'mugging', mugging and criminal activity became an everyday perception and experience of the general population. 'Race' and the meaning associated to it therefore became the mobilising force that changed societal perceptions, changed law enforcement procedures, including the dramatic rise in stop and search practices targeting young black men, and created resentment, disillusionment and mistrust between communities along polarised lines of 'black' and 'white'.[10]

This example highlights how a discourse about 'race' was transformed by additional meaning being attributed to it, meaning that subsequently became both socially and politically normative. From this transformation can be mapped a direct and consequential set of exclusionary practices, procedures and perceptions. This type of investigation is that which is now required in order to substantiate 'Islamophobic exclusionary practices', something that may not necessarily be too problematic what with the likelihood of similar transformations having occurred contemporarily. Post-9/11, there has been much debate about the need to safeguard 'our people' and 'our nation' from the threat of 'terror', 'terrorists' and so on. Whilst much of the time this discourse has not included such explicit appellations as 'Muslim' or 'Islamic' (although at times it clearly has), what with pre-existent discourses and meanings in circulation, it is possible that such associations and attributions of 'Muslim' and 'Islamic' with 'terror' and 'terrorists' may have been made anyway, so ingrained and embedded might such meanings have become. Since 9/11 therefore, a 'problem' with Islam and Muslims has become apparent at both the local and global levels, so as 'race' became the lens through which the crisis was understood in the 1970s, so 'Islam' has become the lens through which contemporary crises have become understood: Islam being to Muslims what race was to black males.

In this way, Islamophobia as a catalyst for social exclusion and discrimination will begin to be identified and justifiably substantiated through grounded and empirical evidence. To achieve this, it is imperative that the determinative influence of Islamophobia is demonstrated: without it, such claims will continue to be refuted and be merely anecdotal. It is equally imperative to remember however that not all exclusionary practices that result in disadvantage for Muslims and

---

[9]   Ibid., 333.
[10]   Ibid.

their communities can be assumed either wholly or in part to be based upon an Islamophobic premise: it is not the practices themselves that are necessarily anti-Muslim or anti-Islamic but more so the discourse or ideology deployed to initiate such. Young Muslim males may therefore be seen to be disadvantaged educationally, but whether this is consequential of a specific 'Islamophobic' discourse or ideology would appear from existing research at least to be inconclusive. It could be that young Pakistani and Bangladeshi males who have been proven to achieve lower educational attainment levels than those from other ethnic and racial groups are in fact failing to achieve for reasons that are in no way connected to the religious identity, either internally or externally imposed. Indeed, numerous other factors including poverty, class and so on could all be vitally and legitimately important in locating the cause of such exclusionary practices with religion being no more than coincidental.

This newly posited theoretical and conceptual basis should therefore allow for greater scrutiny across all forms of discrimination and exclusion. Rather than merely situating practices in the vagaries of any discrimination, disadvantage or exclusion being alleged and inconclusively proven as consequential of a perceived 'phobic dread', research undertaken within this framework will be founded upon a premise that will allow serious empirical and grounded evidence to be provided that should withstand the necessary analytical scrutiny that has been proven necessary through the correlative study of racism. It is with this that a better conceptualisation of that meaning and understanding that underpins and informs those discourses that is now required.

Islamophobia as Ideology: 'systems of thought, belief and even just systems of symbols'

To substantiate an exclusionary practice therefore, there must be clear evidence that identifies it as a consequence of Islamophobia. To achieve this, one must know what is meant by Islamophobia and what this entails. Unfortunately, this as yet has failed to be adequately achieved. However, it has been noted throughout that a number of visual, verbal, textual and other products are in evidence through which certain meanings about Muslims and Islam are disseminated. Whilst these are sometimes vastly different and multifarious, there does appear to be a largely similar albeit protean process underpinning them: the EUMC's 'certain identifiable phenomenon'. If Islamophobia is that 'certain identifiable phenomenon', it must also be that Islamophobia is that meaning disseminated about Muslims and Islam. As Miles and Brown note regarding race and racism, this meaning and process of informing, the ideology or ideological content is the signification of visual or other products as the criterion through which individuals and groups are identified and subsequently understood and interpreted, that in the process attains societal validity and justification.[11]

Already this idea has been explored, where visual identifiers have functioned as products through which Muslims and Islam are identified, signified and attributed meaning and understanding. Drawing upon both the historical and contemporary, Muslims' and Islam's signification is 'problematised', constituting a protean and shifting amalgam of historical atavisms, mediatised stereotypes, embedded misunderstandings, mistruths and mistrusts, supplemented and empowered by social constructions and myths that emerge from contemporary events, interactions and associations, as well as representations and interpretations culminating in a situation where Muslims and Islam are inherently different to 'us'. What becomes subsequently normative is the establishment and acceptance of Muslims and Islam as inherently and oppositely different, a process that reifies the perceiving and conceiving of all Muslims unidimensionally. This process, a correlation of the ideological component of racism that Miles and Brown describe, therefore attributes and homogenises Muslims and Islam as an undifferentiated 'outgroup', simultaneously acquiring authority and legitimacy through the unchallenged belief that the 'ingroup' is both superior and authoritative and by consequence, legitimately able to counter any competing or alternative claims, arguments or understandings that emerges from the outgroup. Hence the description of this process as ideological, a term further explored in more detail shortly.

The outgroup becomes simultaneously attributed with attributes and characteristics – signifiers – that by default disseminate meaning that is either negatively evaluated or may be seen to be inducing negative consequences for the ingroup. Such signifiers could be biological, racial, cultural, religious or theological in their essence or representation, or could indeed be a combinative plurality, the type of which would appear to be highlighted in the plethora of examples in the EUMC Report. One particular example being that of how the *hijab* disseminated meanings about Muslim women as inferior, oppressed and of being second class citizens whilst simultaneously disseminating meaning about Islam and its alleged associations with terrorism, anti-Westernism and so on, both inferring knowledge and meaning whilst negating somewhat entirely any spiritual or theological value to the *hijab*.[12] In this one example, cultural, religious and theological signifiers are in operation, each of which are refracted and subsequently understood through the contemporary problematising lens that is the Muslim and Islamic crisis.

Muslims and Islam therefore become identified through their signification and the meaning that this disseminates. The determinative manner and nature of this ideological signification therefore means that all those who possess concomitant characteristics and can be subsequently identified via them, despite them being ever changing, thus become attributed with concomitant meanings – understandings, perceptions, capabilities and qualities – that are typically negatively evaluated

---

[11]   Miles and Brown (2003).
[12]   Allen and Nielsen (2002), 35.

but through which Muslims and Islam are societally defined. The physical, material, religious, cultural, racial and theological signifiers through which one might identify Muslims and Islam thus become the same markers through which meaning about them is disseminated. Unlike 'races' that are identified on the basis of somatic, phonotypical and visual features and the biological constructs that such racist phenomena seek to justify, as regards any anti-Muslim, anti-Islamic equivalent those same constructs must be rather more socially or culturally constructed, framed and contextualised by a historical legacy that recurs, re-emerges, reinvigorates and refines that which is given meaning for contemporary consumption, relevant for the here and now. It is this ideological component of today's Islamophobia that requires better conceptualisation and definition.

To do so, it is necessary to consider what is meant by 'ideology' and 'ideological'. Unlike more historically rooted definitions and understandings, to better understand ideology in terms of contemporary Islamophobia, Thompson's 'neutral conception' theory of ideology would appear to be preferential.[13] Here ideology is conceived both singularly and variously in terms systems: systems of thought, belief and so on, or even just systems of signifiers or symbols – symbolic symbols – any or all of which pertain to influence or impact upon social action, interaction and response as well as shaping and determining that understanding and meaning and the associated attitudes that significantly allude to a previously referred to concept, the social consensus. For Thompson, what makes such a conception most relevant for the contemporary setting is that it was conceived for today's 'mediatised societies' in order to differentiate and distance itself from the more traditional and value-loaded baggage that post-Industrial Revolution class-based ideological theoretical foundations were founded upon. For Thompson, a neutral conception allows for the theories of those such as Marx, Weber, Durkheim and Mannheim to be necessarily acknowledged and referenced, but not to necessarily overshadow or dictate the contemporary determination or usage of such.[14]

Neutral conceptions are therefore designed entirely for the contemporary and refer to newer relationships of interaction, power and meaning, most importantly those that relate to 'the thought of the *other*, the thought of someone other than oneself ...', operable through the intersection of symbolic forms with relations of power and the interaction between ingroup and outgroup. From here, a number of important dimensions emerge. Firstly, a neutral conception stresses the social operation and function of symbolic forms, thus avoiding the tendency to understand ideologies solely in terms of forms of power and meaning 'institutionalised' in the modern state; in relations of power founded upon the sole determinative of class domination; or in the processes of exclusionary practices and discriminations. In the contemporary setting, whilst the infrastructure of the nation state and political institutions and organisations remain vitally important, institutions such as the media can be as equally if not more influential and causal as regards the maintaining

---

[13]   John Thompson, *Ideology and Modern Culture* (Cambridge: Polity Press, 1990), 5.
[14]   Ibid.

of social constructions and the relations of domination that are resultant of such. For Thompson therefore, any conception of an ideology needs to be able to be readily accommodating. Ideologies therefore are not restricted solely to class based struggles and the explicit and direct relationships of power and domination, but so too other equal and possibly even more important sites. Included in these are those that are a part of the everyday experience of the contemporary setting: the classroom, the office, the factory and so on, and as mentioned previously, the media. Neutral conceptions also allow for the avoidance of simplifications that equate ideologies as being rooted in pure illusion, thus inverting or inherently distorting that which is real, thus highlighting how the 'real' can be as legitimately ideological as indeed can the illusory, as has been highlighted as a weakness in the previous theoretical expositions that suggested otherwise.

For Thompson then, it is a range of symbolic forms that offer and provide ideological meaning: but what exactly is meant by 'symbolic forms'? In this context, if a symbolic form is that which contemporarily makes known 'Muslims' and 'Islam', then it must be that such forms encompass a broad range of utterances, images and texts, all of which might be relayed, produced or constructed by individuals, groups or institutions that must be disseminated to, as well as recognised and decoded by others, irrespective of whether real, accurate, erroneous or illusory. Symbolic forms might therefore be linguistic, either spoken or inscribed, non-linguistic or quasi-linguistic in nature.[15] What is important though is that unlike previous conceptualisations of Islamophobia and the notion that such had to be 'unfounded', here a categorical acknowledgement is being made to confirm that irrespective of that which is real or unreal, whether attributed and characterised individually, communally or both, such symbolic forms and the ideological meaning that is disseminated about Muslims and Islam can emerge from and indeed be incorporated within that which is real as much as that which is unreal. From this premise, Islamophobia no longer has to be seen as a purely false doctrine, perpetuated solely on the basis of misunderstandings and inaccuracies.

It is therefore neither essential nor necessary for the symbolic forms through which Islamophobia operates, thus determining the relationship between the ingroup and outgroup to be either incorrect or inaccurate, illusory or erroneous. So whilst some symbolic forms may operate in ways that misrepresent or obscure certain realities, a neutral conception would overcome this and free understanding of how to counter and challenge this from being bogged down with merely relaying and propagating a doctrine of truth and positivism, going beyond the need to repeatedly refer to and indiscriminately stress the 'true' or 'real' Islam, the 'open views', or indeed the 'Islamophilia' that is as equally inappropriate, essentialising and reducing as any 'Islamophobia'. Instead, what this new conceptualisation of Islamophobia becomes concerned with is not demonstrating if, why or how such forms are indeed false or inaccurate, or indeed laying claim to what might be

---

[15]   Whilst referring to anti-Muslim, anti-Islamic ideology in this particular context, these have been adapted from Thompson's theories of ideology in a modern cultural setting.

true or accurate, but rather more in demonstrating and highlighting how these forms establish and sustain ideas, meaning, relations, and most importantly, the power between the different and competing groups. Truth and reality are therefore no longer entirely valid or relevant regarding Islamophobia when understood ideologically.

Symbolic forms – largely interchangeable and substitutable with the signifiers, products, signs and visual identifiers referred to previously – are not therefore necessarily ideological in themselves, as indeed was observed about how the products could neither be wholly 'Islamophobic'. Instead, it is the meaning, that which is disseminated in order to serve or sustain particular relations and processes of meaning and understanding, that is ideological. In this way, the *hijab* – as a symbolic form – is that which is ideologically anti-Muslim and anti-Islamic because of the meaning that is attributed to it and subsequently disseminated by it, and not because it is a piece of material that some Muslim women choose to wear. It is the meaning (ideology) and not the symbolic form therefore that operates as such thus explaining how the *hijab* as visual identifier became the motivation for reprisal responses. Whilst this sounds obvious, it is essential that such a distinction is made in order that confusion does not ensue.

Ideology as Meaning: 'the stigmatisation, marginalisation and intolerance'

Islamophobia is not then any specific action, practice, discrimination or prejudice, but more accurately the meaning disseminated that subsequently shapes, determines and initiates actions, practices, discriminations and prejudices. And by the very nature of ideologies, so Islamophobia must be consequently highly changeable, continually reinterpreting, reinventing, reinvigorating and re-negotiating a range of meanings to maintain a contemporary relevance whilst simultaneously acknowledging the necessary transitory nature of both the ideologies and their associated discourses in order that exclusionary practices can and indeed do emerge. Symbolic forms are therefore socio-historic specific, but specific to the extent where meaning from other socio-historic contexts can be acknowledged that in turn aids the process of receiving, understanding, interpreting and evaluating by the socio-historically specific society that is also the contemporary one for whom those contemporary forms are relevant to. The process of reception must therefore also be necessarily creative and changing, constantly re-interpreting and re-evaluating those symbolic forms that are actively constituted and reconstituted in order to 'make sense' of both the forms and the socio-historical context in which they operate. As Clarke puts it, through the perpetuation and provision of meaning, ideology 'creates a form of order, who we are, or perhaps more precisely who we are not, by the stigmatisation, marginalisation and intolerance associated with this'.[16] Symbolic forms and the meaning made known through them create

---

[16]   Clarke (2003), 15.

and sustain the relationships of power and interaction between the ingroup and outgroup: the self and the Other.

As ideologies are produced and subsequently re-produced in such ways, a context of inequality naturally emerges that establishes hierarchical relationships. Because of this, relationships of domination and subordination become evident although not just along the lines of differentiation that traditional models of ideology suggest, namely class.[17] Consequently, symbolic forms and the ideological content they disseminate must be asymmetrical in their nature, a fact that may have been in evidence across different socio-historical junctures. Since the initial expansion of Islam, it could be suggested that either 'Muslims' or 'Islam' have been given meaning through numerous highly protean symbolic forms that have been primarily negatively evaluated, incorporating markers of race, biology, religion, theology, culture, politics and so on that have always been problematic and presented in frames that purport a threat, whether in terms of Christianity historically or in terms of the West contemporarily. Irrespective of the intensity or dormancy of such ideological content, one might conclude that despite there being little evidence of a continuum existing, a sense of interconnectedness would appear to be present that, if nothing more, at least seeks to provide contexts within which newer and more contemporary ideological content and symbolic forms be framed and understood. Dialectically, it could be argued that this interconnected ideological process has contributed to the process of establishing and making known today's ingroup, the 'self'.

Throughout this interconnectedness, a process of disseminating meaning as a means of understanding and conceptualising 'Muslims' and 'Islam' thus emerges that whilst remaining highly changeable and dependent upon the contextual settings, requires certain observed and known regularities, accuracies and truths to be employed in order to either construct or justify particular programmes of action, systems of thought, or any similar series of focused responses or attitudinal changes. These regularities, accuracies and truths – irrespective of their legitimacy or validity – thus become the factors and meanings used to constitute a solution to the problematic nature of both 'Muslims' and 'Islam', again reinforcing the suggestion that viewing and positioning Islamophobia as an entirely false doctrine negates and overlooks some of the broader and less explicit forms of ideological content. As this ideological content assists making sense of the world, so too does it make sense of the world's 'problems' also, 'problems' that in the contemporary setting are primarily focused upon 'Muslims' or 'Islam'. Such ideology therefore constitutes a significant part of describing and explaining how the world is contemporarily perceived to be, underpinning and justifying the way in which the 'self' – here 'the West' – responds across a variety of levels, both locally and globally, to Muslims and Islam, their perceived problematic presence, and the alleged threat believed to be present. Quite worryingly, and as noted previously,

---

[17]   A reference here to the class defined lines of differentiation that both underpinned and subsequently emerged from Marxism and associated and emergent theoretical interpretations.

these responses also become both naturally and normatively self-assuring and perpetuating. Islamophobia therefore does not necessarily have a 'start point' or a particular source of dissemination or construction, instead being both disseminated and constructed, as well as finding resonance, across a vast array of different sources. In putting this forward, this sits in stark opposition to those who have identified the media as being the disseminative source of such ideas. Whilst the preceding analyses confirm that ideological content is disseminated through some parts of the media, albeit with little regularity, unanimity or organisation, it cannot be concluded that the media is the only source for such: nor indeed was it the 'start point' from which such ideology initially began or emerged.

Meaning and the processes of 'making sense' are therefore neither explicit nor direct, nor even necessarily untrue or inaccurate, and most importantly, neither static nor unchanging. Yet through making sense of the world, Islamophobia can successfully, albeit in ways that are sometimes grossly mistaken and dangerously irresponsible, provide a strategy for political action and even the creation and subsequent implementation of exclusionary practices, a strategy that finds resonance with 'new racism'. As Barker observed, this particular form of ideological content was resultant of the significant shift in Conservative Party politics in the late 1970s, both discursively and practically, to the increased immigration from the Commonwealth to Britain and the 'threat' this posed to 'our way of life'. A similar contemporary 'threat' is identified by the BNP who sought to make sense of the growing numbers of British Muslims and the presence of Islam in Britain through similar means.[18] Consequently ideology, would appear to be able to locate both social and political resonance and responses within that which is being disseminated by invigorating, uniting and subsequently responding to, within frames of meaning and understanding that seek to 'make sense' of those or that which are either problematised or alleged to be posing a threat.

Such ideological content can therefore take on a relatively coherent theory based upon solid foundations and justifications where the mere suggestion that such is unfounded or unwarranted might not necessarily be accepted or acknowledged let alone seeking to change or influence those perceptions, ideas and meanings that are already disseminated and in circulation. Thus the rise in fear towards, and the mistrust of Muslims following 9/11, might therefore be – ideologically at least – entirely logical, rational and justifiable by those who feel increasingly fearful or at risk even though the reasons and meaning for such – the ideological content being disseminated – might be inappropriate, inaccurate and without empirical justification. Nonetheless, it is understood to be natural and normal and therefore also logical, rational and justifiable. So whilst existing conceptualisations have focused upon the issues relating to ignorance, misrepresentations and misunderstandings primarily in the media, it is as equally likely in terms of Islamophobia that similar will also occur across all walks of everyday life what with such meaning being already 'out there' and in circulation, shaping and determining perceptions and

---

[18]   Allen (2005).

understanding both consciously and unconsciously. Islamophobic ideological content therefore is already known and, to a certain degree, already accepted as natural and normal within the social consensus, necessarily qualifying that for those identified within the ingroup, *all* its constituent members cannot be homogenised as one, and so different shades of opinion, perspective and interpretation must be acknowledged and accounted for accordingly.

Islamophobia as ideology is therefore highly fluid and shifting, creatively interpreting and re-interpreting, shaping and re-shaping that which is already known in the social consensus, relevant for the 'here and now' as opposed to either the future or the past, balancing those reworked and reinterpreted historical ideologies of Muslims and Islam, whilst being shaped and contextualised by the wholly new symbolic forms, meanings and contexts within which today's ideology operates, emphasised and reified in the contemporary period by both local and global influences and given voice to and disseminated through today's globalised and mediatised environment. With ideological content being contemporarily dynamic and fluid, continuities and interconnections with different historical and geographical contexts remain, thus refuting suggestions that ideologies are either entirely 'new' or entirely 'historical'. For any symbolic form to be given meaning, so 'Muslims' or 'Islam' or indeed both need to be identified and this is achieved through a constantly changing series of both independent and overlapping identifiers, attributes, categories, characteristics and qualities – the symbolic forms – that cut across such differentiable markers as race, ethnicity, theology, class, gender and so on. Resultantly, whilst Islamophobia as ideology may operate and function largely in isolation from other similar ideological content, it must be remembered that such content can also be interdependent and overlapping with other similar ideologies, in particular racism.

In giving meaning to that which is understood to be natural and normative of 'Muslims', 'Islam' or both, it is possible that such be either founded upon gross inaccuracies, misunderstandings and misrepresentations, typically all of which are derogatory and negatively evaluated, whilst equally simultaneously or independently also being made known and disseminated through those symbolic forms that are accurate, correctly understood and true representations of 'Muslims' or 'Islam', grounded in reality and actuality. Irrespective of questions of accuracy, legitimacy or so on, *all* symbolic forms must embody a sense of the Other, diametrically opposing those symbolic forms identified as natural to the 'self', thus establishing an asymmetrical relationship of meaning and power between the 'self' and the Other constructed along lines of naturalness and un-naturalness. In addition, the ideological content may also be the catalyst from which exclusionary practices evolve and subsequently differentiate, prejudice and discriminate, albeit at this stage still being far from having been categorically or empirically proven. Ideology therefore, its content and processes, must be analytically differentiable from exclusionary practices as indeed must both the ideology and exclusionary practices be from the symbolic forms through which the meaning is disseminated.

Modes of Operation: 'temporal, transient, protean, disposable'

If Islamophobia is therefore ideological, then it must operate ideologically. For Thompson then, 'modes of operation' must be in evidence. But as he unequivocally stresses, the modes of operation are not equitable with the symbolic forms of which both are in some ways interchangeable. So as ideology gives meaning, so the modes of operation are concerned with the way in which that same meaning is sustained and perpetuated. Yet as the symbolic forms can be temporal, transient, protean, disposable and contextually specific to socio-economic, political, geographical and historical settings but not necessarily universal, constant or permanent, so the modes of operation function differently. So for example as Yemelianova suggests, whilst the symbolic form 'fundamentalist' might have a certain meaning and understanding in the British context, so '*Wahhabi*' as a symbolic form has much the same meaning in the Russian context despite both being non-interchangeable to the opposite socio-geographical contexts within which they operate. Whilst the symbolic form therefore is different but socio-geographically specific to each, irrespective of the specificity or context within which the symbolic form is manifested, the connotative process or mode through which it operates – the mode through which the same meaning is sustained and perpetuated – remains remarkably the same.

This section will therefore seek to consider these modes of operation and how they function in order to sustain and perpetuate meaning. Being based upon a series of broad operative modes, each of which is made up of a series of derivative strategies, the five modes that Thompson puts forward are: legitimation, dissimulation, unification, fragmentation and reification. To expand upon these, a number of examples will be drawn from both the media, thus maintaining a consistency with the critical analysis undertaken previously, as well as from other sources in order to show how the modes are not restricted or constrained to one particular disseminative medium. Before doing so however, Thompson insists upon a number of qualifications concerning the limitations and constraints of his model, each of which are as equally relevant to that being established here.[19] Firstly, whilst the modes encompass a broad spectrum of ideological content, they cannot be seen to be the only modes through which meaning is sustained or perpetuated, being neither entirely independent nor combinative in their function. Secondly, the modes and respective strategies are neither concretised nor unchanging, being indicative rather more than conclusive, where new modes and strategies may at some stage evolve and multiply whilst others may subsequently disappear or be replaced. The final qualification is that whilst various modes and strategies are being explored, neither the modes nor strategies are ideological. Only when the modes and strategies sustain or perpetuate certain ideological meaning – whether intentionally or otherwise – can they be understood to have an ideological function. At all other times, this may not necessarily be the case.

---

[19]   Thompson (1990), 60–61.

Legitimation: 'the way ideology makes sense'

As with the new racist discourses that seek to justify the BNP's Islamophobic views,[20] legitimation operates in exactly the same way. Legitimation is how ideological content becomes reasonably perceived to be legitimate and justified through sustaining meaning that ensures that certain individuals, groups or communities remain the Other or outgroup. In doing so, such perceptions acquire a sense of natural or normative order or function, seen beforehand in the way ideology 'makes sense' of the world. Thus legitimation not only finds resonance in the normative values within the social consensus but it also helps cement certain meanings, further reinforcing and legitimising that which is already known and in circulation about any given subject. Such a process can also naturally hinder or restrict the shifting of ideas and understandings about issues and subjects, so unlike racist ideologies that have over the past three decades shifted towards a societal position of intolerance and unacceptability, being seen to be illegitimate and unjustified, so the same has failed to occur regarding Islamophobia. Indeed it could be argued to the contrary. The process of legitimation therefore reinforces and codifies the ideological content behind symbolic forms in such ways that it is sustained as that which is socially relevant and socially normative.

An example is the BNP's *I.S.L.A.M.: The Truth About Islam*, where legitimation is sought by sourcing 'Asian' groups to perpetuate meaning about Muslims and Islam to suggest that it is not the BNP that is being unfairly anti-Muslim, but 'those who know' who are saying the same things and by default, attributing the same claims with greater credibility and substance, and ultimately, greater legitimacy.[21] In making this differentiation, legitimation operates via establishing the concerns and views of other 'Asians' – those that are 'in the know' because they have a shared history with Muslims and Islam – as natural, normal and significantly more informed than their own and thus acquiring greater legitimacy and weight. It is therefore not the mode of operation that is ideological, but the meaning disseminated that is. Consequently, it is not the reasoning of the BNP or Asian groups that are ideological per se, but instead the meaning that Muslims and Islam represent 'Intolerance, Slaughter, Looting, Arson and Molestation of Women' that is: an extremely subtle differentiation.

Legitimation's first strategy is 'rationalisation' where 'a symbolic form constructs a chain of reasoning which seeks to defend or justify a set of social relations or institutions, and thereby persuade an audience that it is worthy of support'.[22] From the prior example, rationalisation occurs in the way in which the BNP substantiates its views by the rationalisation that someone better informed than they can substantiate 'I.S.L.A.M.'. Not only does this rationalise Muslims as a necessary outgroup but also that a threat to the ingroup was present also,

---

[20]   Allen (2005).

[21]   BNP (2001).

[22]   Thompson (1990), 60–61.

rationalising the threat and subsequently the need for mistrust and fear. Another example of this can be identified in Oriana Fallaci's, *The Rage and the Pride*.[23] Whilst being a somewhat incoherent text, one rationalised argument running through it is that as the 'Sons of Allah' enacted 9/11, so *all* Muslims as 'Sons' have the same capabilities and desires to enact the same. Tracing her argument from the building of mosques, through spiritual leadership to the incidence and manifestation of terrorist atrocities against the West, Fallaci reinforces her argument by inferring that Islam should not be in 'our' lands what with it being indeterminably Other. A chain of reasoning therefore emerges that rationalises and self-legitimates by arguing that if Muslims and Islam had not, and indeed were not, allowed in 'our' lands, 'we' would be safe and thus free from 'their' terror. The sustaining and perpetuating of Islamophobic meaning is therefore disseminated through a semi-rational argument, albeit contentious and quite unwarranted.

Aside from Fallaci, a potentially important aspect of legitimation might be to investigate how exclusionary practices could become consequential of it. Taking the premise that certain practices or arguments are employed to rationalise or justify other practices and responses, a link between Islamophobia and exclusionary practice might therefore exist. This might become more apparent through Thompson's second strategy, 'universalisation', where certain arrangements, either institutional or otherwise, are devised, implemented and acted upon in order to serve the interests of individuals or sub-groups from within the ingroup whilst being put forward as being legitimate and necessary in serving the interests of all in preference of the few who actually benefit. As mentioned beforehand, a particularly relevant investigation as regards universalisation might be in the changes made to security following 9/11. If universalisation could be identified in the discourse used to legitimate such legislation as necessary, homogenously earmarking 'Muslims' as a threat to the security of the ingroup, then it might be possible to highlight how exclusionary practices become directly consequential of an ideological premise. Universalisation would therefore appear to have a distinct resonance regarding the sustaining of Islamophobia, and may be a useful start-point from where further research into exclusionary practices is undertaken.

The final strategy of legitimation is 'narrativisation', which is where meaning becomes embedded in contemporary symbolic forms that recount or reiterate the past and its atavistic meanings. Narrativisation therefore treats the contemporary as part of a timeless and cherished tradition, meaning-wise at least, where that which is disseminated about Muslims and Islam is such that it recounts a cherished, almost nostalgic tradition, past or legacy where today's Muslims and Islam become known and understood in such ways that they are familiar to and normative of historical familiarities and norms. History therefore becomes a taken for granted, known premise where time and the influences of the socio-historical setting are seen to be largely irrelevant. The familiarity attached to meanings about Muslims and Islam from the past therefore continues to recur, recount and

---

[23] Fallaci (2001).

reinterpret the contemporary in order to maintain legacies of meaning, historical stories and atavistic myths that embody ideological content from where Muslims and Islam were historically Other.

The evidence for this is widespread and has been unwittingly referenced throughout this book, where the recurrence and recounting of the contemporary potency of historical images, caricatures, stereotypes and stories have been repeatedly highlighted. From Bush's rhetoric of America's response to 9/11 being a 'crusade' to numerous other instances of discourse and speech that suggests that Islam remains rooted in the dark ages, all sustain and perpetuate meaning through strategies of narrativisation. In independence, narrativisation is also a complete and unequivocal argument against repudiating the power of history, a point repeatedly suggested throughout. Strategies of narrativisation therefore embed in symbolic forms how Muslims and Islam have always been outgroups and how their contemporary role, relation and interaction with the ingroup is merely one juncture in an ongoing process.

Dissimulation: 'a way which deflects from or glosses over'

The second mode of operation is 'dissimulation', which Thompson defines as the process through which meaning is 'established and sustained by being concealed, denied or obscured, or by being represented in a way which deflects from or glosses over existing relations or processes'.[24] Here Thompson is putting forward a mode of operation that is relatively overlooked yet vitally important in exploring Islamophobia. For him, whilst the reality of any given situation might be that ideological content is being disseminated through symbolic forms, counter processes may also be in operation to diminish and obscure recognition by means of strategies of deflection or obfuscation. Whilst it has been suggested that Muslims' criticisms against the West have been rejected out of hand, in this instance what Thompson is suggesting is that more conscious, even deliberate processes may occur that not only reject the criticisms but also obscure the reality that such criticisms are even being voiced. Regarding Islamophobia, such criticisms and activities therefore become 'smoke-screened' or skewed in order that ideological content is sustained unchallenged and without question. Reality, as indeed does the process of refutation, therefore becomes distorted. This is not to suggest conspiratorial theories where society deliberately operates against Muslims and Islam, but to suggest that the dissemination of anti-Muslim, anti-Islamic content can in itself be self-countering and embedded within refutations, deflections and ulterior representations. Ideological content therefore does not always have to be explicitly anti-Muslim or anti-Islamic, especially when processes or strategies can be deployed that detract from either actual, or indeed perceived, realities.

---

[24]   Thompson (1990), 62.

The first strategy of dissimulation is 'displacement', where symbolic forms are employed to identify and disseminate meaning to a subject in order that the connotations of that symbolic form – whether negative or positive, appropriate or inappropriate – become indiscriminately projected onto all those that might be associated or identified by means of that same subject, all of which can be an individual, group, community or inanimate object or concept, irrespective of appropriation or accuracy. Reflecting upon Muslims and Islam as Other, where the outgroup becomes attributed with the characteristics and traits that the ingroup either are not, or possibly more appropriately do not want, such a strategy is again clearly evident. A good example is highlighted by those few Muslim fringe figures that embody all that is stereotypically anti-Western and stereotypically Other about Muslims in the social consensus, who are then represented in such ways that they become representative of all Muslims without differentiation, irrespective of legitimacy or accuracy. All Muslims without differentiation therefore become equitable with those fringe figures and their typically radical voices and opinions – identified by way of those such as Omar Bakri Mohammed and Abu Hamza – symbolised as such and with the same characteristics, voices and opinions whilst at the same time displacing attention from the vast majority onto an inappropriate minority. Displacement therefore can be a rather dangerous and indiscriminate strategy through which quite inaccurate and misleading meaning can be disseminated. Displacement also gives some insight into the dilemma faced previously as regards how the disproportionate coverage of those on the fringes of the Muslim 'mainstream' in the British press can be better contextualised and understood.

Another function of displacement having contemporary resonance is where inappropriate appellations – 'fundamentalist', 'extremist', 'fanatic', 'militant' and so on – are repeatedly and regularly employed as symbolic forms. In this way, whilst the appellations themselves were either originally coined to describe or define something quite clearly non-Muslim or applicable to only a very small number of Muslims, through the strategy of displacement such appellations become indiscriminately attributed where contemporary usage immediately conjures a connotative resonance with all Muslims as well as the tenets of Islam, thus displacing the fact that such applies to extremely small numbers only. Consequently, the appellations, themselves symbolic forms, become displaced onto the homogenous whole rather than a constituent part, thus obfuscating the actual diversity that exists across Muslims and their respective communities. Through displacement, major realities can be very easily and indiscriminately displaced by somewhat minor and quite discriminate realities.

Dissimulation's second strategy is that of 'euphemisation' where, through a range of inferences, dialogues, actions or events, an outgroup is attributed with negatively evaluated meaning via symbolic forms, that whilst they may in actuality be largely negative, derogatory or detrimental to the outgroup, are identified by symbolic forms that elicit a seemingly wholly positive evaluation. Thompson highlights this by describing how the violent suppression of a protest by a minority group might be symbolically represented in such ways that 'violent suppression' becomes 'the restoration of order'. As regards Islamophobic ideological content, it is likely that this particular strategy would require a very specific instance or setting within which to operate. Nonetheless a number of key symbolic forms that elicit positive evaluations of non-Muslims whilst simultaneously eliciting opposite evaluations of Muslims can be identified particularly in reinforcing 'Islam against the West' misconceptions.

A useful example of this can be found in a leader article from the *Daily Telegraph*. 'In this War of Civilisations, the West Will Prevail',[25] euphemisation can be clearly identified in the way in which the first US strikes against Afghanistan are positively evaluated, describing the strikes as 'a tested Western response to Islamic aggression': 'tested' representing balance and fairness and 'aggression' representing something far less uncontrolled. Similarly, the West is a 'civilisation', whilst 'Islam' is 'the peoples of the desert and empty spaces', with the leader concluding that the desert people cannot exist on the same level as a civilisation: the choice and attribution of positively imbued euphemisms – textual symbolic forms – overwhelmingly evaluating the non-Muslim world oppositely to the Muslim world. Similar strategies were also identifiable in the way in which the *Telegraph* re-evaluated evidence of an anti-Muslim backlash following 9/11 as being evidence of Islamophilia, based upon the somewhat invalid premise that the vast majority of Muslims did not become victims of indiscriminate violence or hostile acts, rather than Islamophobia through the growth of attacks against Muslims. As it concluded, that Britain is 'tolerant of Islam is a tribute to them in general'.[26] Overlooking the number and reality of Islamophobia therefore, that it was not greater or more prevalent is consequently euphemised as a positive sign, one of Islamophilia rather than Islamophobia.

The last strategy of dissimulation 'trope', can be seen in the figurative use of language that encompass such similar linguistic strategies as metaphor, metonymy and synecdoche, clearly connecting with displacement where text and language include such symbolic forms as 'fundamentalist' and so on. Metonymy is particularly relevant what with such appellations being so negatively evaluated despite them also being the known metonyms of Islamophobic ideological content. Another aspect of this is the way in which either the whole or part of certain terminologies or concepts are conflated in order to reciprocally represent either the part or the whole, in much the same way that terms such as 'Muslims' and 'Islam' have themselves taken on synedochical meanings and understandings, where small, minority, fringe or rogue elements of a greater whole are indiscriminately conflated to sustain widespread and undifferentiated meaning, resulting in gross misunderstandings and misrepresentations. Such strategies are highlighted in the EUMC Report where it was noted that stereotypical misrepresentations and misunderstandings were being increasingly normative in that they became

---

25   8 October 2001.
26   'Islamophilia', *The Daily Telegraph*, 12 October 2001.

somewhat synonymously accepted as 'realities' of Muslims irrespective of how inaccurate or untrue they might be.[27]

Unification: 'irrespective of the differences and divisions that may separate them'

'Unification' is where meaning is sustained 'by constructing, at the symbolic level, a form of unity which embraces individuals in a collective identity, irrespective of the differences and divisions that may separate them',[28] a mode that identifies with the recognition earlier regarding how 'Islam as monolithic' rather than being a compartmentalised category instead seemingly permeates all understandings and meanings about Muslims and Islam. Unification also embodies distinct similarities to the processes of reductionism and essentialism. Islamophobia as ideology operating through these modes and strategies would therefore appear to not only improve conceptualisation and understanding in that it overcomes those issues and problems highlighted concerning existing models and what they are unable to accommodate, but it also provides access to, accommodation of, and understanding about that which previous models were either unable to and even reinforced rather than combated. In terms of unification therefore, it might be suggested that this is how the Runnymede model operated, reducing – or unifying – everything about Muslims to the merest common denominator, simultaneously its symbolic form also, namely Islam and nothing more.

Unification therefore elaborates the way in which 'Islam' as a marker of identity assumes, quite inappropriately and inaccurately, how all Muslims can be accommodated and subsequently essentialised by it. Through its reductionist unifying function, the personal, human and 'real' becomes lost, or at least hidden through unification, especially when strategies as dissimulation are also in operation. Through unification therefore, inherent and actual diversity and difference becomes unidimensionalised and homogenised where meanings about 'Islam' and 'Muslims' undergo a process of 'standardisation', unification's first strategy. Negatively evaluated Islamophobia can, as was highlighted not in the Runnymede model itself but in the exposition of it, be disseminated as much in overtly positive and inappropriate evaluations as indeed it can from overly negative and equally inappropriate evaluations. Anti-Muslim, anti-Islamic meaning therefore does not always have to appear to be unjust or unfounded, as it can be as easily and readily disseminated and propagated through positive means that simultaneously and reciprocally function to reduce or essentialise. Both unification and standardisation therefore operate quite irrespective of whether such forms are either positively or negatively evaluated, substantiating the fact that the symbolic forms are irrelevant to the meaning disseminated. Within either evaluation, Muslims and Islam become

---

[27]   Allen and Nielsen (2002), 48.
[28]   Thompson (1990), 64.

unified by the need, or more appropriately the imposed need, for conformity to those acceptable or unacceptable characteristics that such evaluations demand.

Unification therefore highlights how ideological modes of operation and strategies differ, quite significantly, from any given typology or series of products in that the modes and strategies explain how meaning is sustained and perpetuated, embodying the necessary fluidity, overlap, interconnectedness and so on that any necessarily complex system must be able to accommodate, rather than merely identifying a small number of rigid forms through which some equally rigid and at times questionable forms may be identified. Unification, as indeed do the other modes, therefore highlights a multi-layeredness to Islamophobia, both in the way that meaning and dissemination are understood and in the processes through which it operates. And this is extremely important, because no longer is the focus or need for conceptualising Islamophobia reliant upon the symbolic forms – the identifiers, actions, events or qualities – but instead on that underpinning them, that which the strategies and modes sustain and perpetuate about who and what 'Muslims' and 'Islam' are. Such strategies therefore exist irrespective of whether or not all Muslims conform to the imposed and essentialised requirements that some have put forward, largely because individual qualities, traits and qualities remain independent and unknown to the meaning that is already established, being sustained and continually perpetuated within the social consensus.

This recognition brings about the second strategy of unification, where a 'symbolisation of unity' establishes a collective identity for the outgroup that allows identification across any number of differences or pluralities. Thus from the EUMC Report:

> behind the vast majority of attacks and infringements upon specific communities and individuals was the fact that they were identified as Muslims, whether they in fact were or not, by something that could be recognisably associated with Islam; ... the relevance of the visual identifiers of Muslims and Islam cannot be underestimated ... it would seem that there is a very real possibility that those visual identifiers that are mentioned here will be the tools for identification, upon which Islamophobia and anti-Muslim sentiments will continue to be founded for the foreseeable future.[29]

Whilst the report clearly explains the visual identifiers in both the real and social settings, it is the theoretical premise of the symbolisation of unity that allows a greater understanding of how they operate: providing recognisable symbolic forms as a means of identification and stimulation that simultaneously disseminate ideological content about Muslims and Islam. It is therefore neither the identifiers nor the identification of such that are ideological, but that which is disseminated and received. Whilst the symbols of unity therefore can be widely different and diverse, all would appear to have the same function, transforming particularities into

---

[29]   Allen and Nielsen (2002), 35–7.

universalities subsequently unifying them into normatively attributed and, visually or otherwise, identifiable as being that which is 'Muslim', 'Islam' or both.

Fragmentation: 'earmarked as evil and either potentially or actually harmful and threatening'

'Fragmentation', in what might be misunderstood as being contradictory to unification, asserts that not only by unifying the outgroup can ideological content be disseminated but also through fragmenting and differentiating it as well. This is achieved by fragmenting the outgroup into definite and constituent parts that are subsequently earmarked as being evil and either potentially or actually harmful and threatening to the position and safety of the ingroup.[30] Such processes are however quite irrespective of whether such threats are genuine or not. From the analysis of practice, this mode of operation would appear to have some resonance where a recurrent feature of press coverage was not only the repetitive deployment of such terms as fundamentalist, extremist and so on, but also the use of such descriptors as 'moderates' and 'mainstream', fragmenting Muslims into 'friendly' or 'good' and 'enemy' or 'bad'. Unsurprisingly, the 'moderates' became the acceptable face, seen to be practicing their religion in ways that were deemed acceptable to outsiders to the faith. In doing so however, the 'moderates' became essentialised and normative, a process that simultaneously fragmented those Muslims not being identified as such into a classification and identification that represented them as being in contention with or posing a threat to the ingroup. Fragmenting and subsequently differentiating the homogenous whole therefore allows negatively evaluated meanings to be disseminated in the same way that similar meanings are perpetuated and sustained, albeit reciprocally, through the process of unification.

'Differentiation' therefore is a strategy of fragmentation, where the diversity of characteristics and markers between different Muslims are over-emphasised and conflated to disunite and differentiate between them. Rooted again in essentialist processes, differentiation can be seen in the way that symbolic forms such as 'moderate' or 'mainstream' are as equally value-loaded as such terms as 'fundamentalists'. And as with earlier conceptualisations, if certain Muslims or their communities fail to adhere to the essentialised norms of those deemed 'moderate' or 'mainstream', then those same individuals and communities become further marginalised, more Other and eventually eradicated. Not only does this differentiate Muslims behind homogenous markers of identification but it also unifies different individuals and groups into being essentially 'good' and essentially 'bad', highlighting how two seemingly contradictory modes of operation can function simultaneously at any given time. Whilst 'open' and 'good' views were concluded as being inadequate and unacceptable as a means of identifying and combating Islamophobia, this particular example substantiates such conclusions,

---

[30] Thompson (1990), 65.

highlighting how ideological processes that fragment and differentiate between 'good' or 'bad' – and by default, 'open' or 'closed' – can disseminate exactly the same meanings, neither of which are necessarily positive nor conducive to presenting a more balanced understanding. Differentiating between 'good' and 'bad', and by consequence also 'good' *or* 'bad', can therefore disseminate much the same ideological content as indeed might any operable process of homogenisation or unification primarily because differentiating between 'good' and 'bad', 'moderate' and 'extremist' is itself a process of homogenous sub-stratification. Fragmentation and differentiation are therefore both as equally unifying thus highlighting the problem of 'mainstream' Muslim voices being used in the press possibly as much as employing 'extreme' Muslim voices too. Fragmentation can also be seen in the way the Runnymede model dichotomised between 'good' and 'bad', 'mainstream' and 'marginal'.

Another related strategy is the 'expurgation of the Other'. Having already considered how processes of 'Othering' function, this strategy operates through 'the construction of an enemy, either within or without, which is portrayed as evil, harmful or threatening and which individuals are called upon collectively to resist or expurgate'.[31] Already, it has been noted that Muslims and Islam in the contemporary socio-historical are understood to be the enemy of 'us' – typically the 'enemy within' – prone to violence and atrocity thus presenting a threat to 'us' and 'our' security. At the very highest and homogenous level therefore, the expurgation of the Other is already operable. Through the concurrent and sometimes seemingly contradictory modes of operation therefore, so all Muslims become attributed with meaning that insists that the Other that needs to be expurgated is seen to be 'Muslim' and 'Islam' per se, those unified collectivities referred to previously. However, as Thompson's definition of such suggests, and when considered in line with other processes of differentiation and fragmentation, so too can these same strategies be employed to identify specific individuals, groups and communities within the larger, equally homogenous whole. In being seen to present such a threat, whether real or otherwise, so other modes and strategies, including those such as legitimation and rationalisation, come into operation reinforcing and substantiating fragmentation.

Strategies of expurgation can be most vividly seen when individuals become the personification of ideological content. In the contemporary setting, those such as bin Laden have become symbolically personified as such, presenting the greatest perceived threat to the safety and wellbeing of the ingroup, that ingroup being a vast swathe of different peoples, countries, religions, continents and civilisations, encompassing a vast array of social, moral, economic and political processes all allegedly at threat from this one person and his ilk. In achieving this, the construction of bin Laden as the epitome of evil that expurgates the Other, has been a recurrent feature across a range of different socio-political contexts, shaped, defined and constructed in the most extreme forms of hyperbolic and euphemistic

---

[31]   Thompson (1990), 65.

ideological content. Such strategies of expurgation have also occurred at the local level, with Abu Hamza, Omar Bakri Mohammed, Anjem Choudary – the list goes on – at the British level being similarly dealt with. And as set out in earlier chapters, those such as Saddam Hussein, the Ayatollah Khomeini and more recently, Usama Bin Laden have held similar positions, constructed through similar if not entirely identical strategies. As highlighted, 'the images of the black cloaked Khomeini reinforced the Western media's practice of personifying him as the epitome of evil, anti-Americanism and anti-values',[32] a comment that could easily be attributed to bin Laden also.

Reification: 'drawing upon and reinvigorating meanings from historical settings'

The final suggested mode of operation is 'reification', where meaning is represented in terms of a transitory, almost continuous process that is largely permanent and mostly natural, largely existing independent of time constraints. Thus meaning becomes disseminated through what Thompson names a 'quasi-natural' process, eclipsing the social and historical nature of different events, actions and so on. This mode therefore draws upon and reinvigorates meaning from historical settings that maintain a resonance within the contemporary or are embedded in the defining characteristics or psyche of the ingroup. In this way, transitory events become deployed to reinforce and reify rather more so than replace contemporary ideological content. Current ideologies – and their particular contexts and settings – therefore remain separate and different from historical ones whilst deploying reference points of connotative meaning in order to further frame and contextualise. One way of understanding this better is through the strategies of reification, the first of which is 'naturalisation', interestingly identified as a 'view' in the Runnymede model. However unlike 'views', naturalisation here becomes defined as a social or historical creation, act or event that is either understood or perceived to be natural or the inevitable outcome of the natural characteristics of the outgroup. As regards Muslims and Islam, terrorism is therefore seen to be quite natural for Muslims because not only are they seen to be naturally violent, barbaric and incompatible with non-Muslims but so too is the Qur'an believed to endorse such: highlighting how Islam attains validity, albeit inaccurately, as the common denominator of all meaning. Everything that subsequently emerges in any given social or historical setting therefore becomes understood as the inevitable outcome of the natural characteristics of that common denominator. It is the ideological content disseminated about Islam and subsequently given meaning to by its recipients therefore that is then employed to make sense of the world and where all that is Other becomes natural and normal.

---

[32] Chris Allen, *Islamophobia: Western Perceptions of Islam in the Contemporary World* (Dissertation: University of Wolverhampton, 2001).

Reification's second strategy is 'eternalisation', where:

> social-historical phenomena are deprived of their historical character by being
> portrayed as permanent, unchanging and ever-recurring. Customs, traditions and
> institutions which seem to stretch indefinitely into the past, so that any trace of
> their origin is lost and any question of their end is unimaginable, acquire a rigidity
> which cannot be easily disrupted. They become embedded in social life and their
> apparently ahistorical character is re-affirmed by symbolic forms which, in their
> construction as well as their sheer repetition, eternalise the contingent.[33]

The recurrence and repetition of atavistic images and historical stereotypes
therefore unequivocally continue to frame and contextualise today's symbolic
forms. The strategy works bi-directionally, history re-affirming and informing the
present, and the present re-affirming and informing the past that both subsequently
reify the Otherness of Islam and Muslims. The meaning embedded in narratives,
both historical and contemporary, therefore establishes Muslims and Islam – their
role, relation and interaction as well as their Otherness – as part of a historical
evolution that remains timeless: eternalised. Most worryingly though is that if
this is so, not only is it impossible to pinpoint where such ideological content
began but it must also be the case that this same ideology may not necessarily
have an end point either, whether now or in the future. With no start point and
no end therefore, bringing about an end to eternalisation becomes unimaginable.
Eternalisation therefore must finally destroy the suggestion that history's power
be repudiated. Contemporary Islamophobia therefore cannot be new and unique
to the current or recent setting because history and the eternalised nature of its
stories, myths and narratives continue to substantiate and shape contemporary
meaning about Muslims and Islam. This is not to suggest that both are identical,
but instead to suggest that whilst today's is relevant and valid for the here and now,
so this has been and indeed continues to be, indeterminably shaped, influenced and
informed by those eternalised, naturalised and ultimately reified meanings to have
gone before.

Thompson offers one final strategy of reification and that is 'nominalisation'
or 'passivisation', strategies that focus attention on certain themes, ideas and
events at the expense of others, where certain actors and events take precedence
and dominate, strategically deleting others in the process, both contemporarily
and historically. Interestingly, it was noted in the textual analysis earlier that the
establishment of an essentialised Muslim in the Runnymede Report induced a
process of passivisation. As regards ideology though, it is quite typical for Islam
and Muslims to be negatively evaluated through the recurrence of stories and
references to the Crusades although highly un-typical for similar processes to
reference more positively evaluated historical junctures, for example when Islam
ruled Spain. The incidence of negative to positive is therefore significantly more

---

[33]   Thompson (1990), 66.

prevalent but this cannot be understood to mean that merely stressing or replacing the 'positives' would necessarily combat the 'negatives', something that has been shown previously to undermine theoretical complexity. Instead, what is being put forward here is that nominalisation most definitely occurs, that by consequence deletes events and actors to reify the meaning being disseminated. Such content therefore is not concerned with mere negative images, stories and so on as previous conceptualisations of Islamophobia have been, but instead a strategy that nominalises or makes passive certain events, individuals and groups that in turn feed into and assist other strategic processes including those such as dissimulation that require obfuscation to function.

Chapter 11
Towards a New Definition of Islamophobia

Having concluded upon the existence of a 'certain identifiable phenomenon' and that at this present juncture, 'Islamophobia' is the best, if not only, terminology with which such a phenomenon can be reasonably identified, it is necessary therefore, in an attempt to lessen the problems associated with it being a contested concept, to put forward a new definition and conceptualisation. To do so however will not be to repeat the mistakes of the past, and so it will be worthless merely constructing a new set of criteria through which it might be purported that any given discourse, act or event be identified as Islamophobic or otherwise. To do so would simply continue to obscure the asymmetric multi-dimensions, specificities, complexities and embeddedness of the phenomenon. Any conclusion must therefore begin to give credence and meaning to that 'certain identifiable phenomenon'.

To achieve this and overcome the previously highlighted inadequacies, inconsistencies and inappropriations, a number of pre-requisites have been established, including the need to be able to identify and accommodate diversity and difference without essentialising or reducing, whether self or externally imposed, including those seen to be 'problematic', upon whom blame was/is apportioned, and those attributed with lesser status, for whatever reason. It was also highlighted that Islam must be able to acquire a similar accreditation, overcoming the negation of the reality and diversity of the faith and its expressions, neither employing it as a homogenous common denominator, a substitute for the actions and motivations of Muslims, nor where any claims to the true authenticity of Islam can be made, either by Muslim or non. To achieve this, two essentials needed to be met: first, to identify exactly what needed defining and conceptualising; and secondly, that a solid theoretical foundation underpinned it.

As regards the first, what is established about that 'certain identifiable phenomenon' is that it employs a multitude of products through which meaning about 'Muslims' and 'Islam' is disseminated and through which both are identified, irrespective of whether such products and their disseminative meanings are true or untrue, accurate or inaccurate, discriminate or indiscriminate. Such products can be either separate or interlinked, acquiring myriad forms that incorporate the visual, verbal, linguistic, textual, representational and associative, functioning at times without necessarily even being expressly focused upon Muslims or Islam, or even identifying them directly but instead providing meaning through the shared languages and conceptual maps that already exist in the public and private spaces across the different social strata: shaped not only by contemporary interactions and events but also by historical and atavistic myths and legacies, whether real or imaginary, that reinforce, reinvigorate and re-awaken both passive and active meanings. These same shared languages and conceptual maps, whilst having similar transferable and transitory disseminative meanings, are contextualised by the social, political, economical, geographical and theological constraints within which they either were or are produced, sometimes taking on a range of different national, linguistic, religious and other dimensions and connotations that are at times unique, and at others concurrent and concomitant.

Secondly, in order that a solid theoretical foundation is established, the different analyses undertaken here – incorporating content, theoretical and practical analyses of the Runnymede Report and model as well as comparative and correlative analyses of similar theories and phenomena – suggest that three different components of Islamophobia exist. The first is that Islamophobia is an ideology, one that provides meaning about Muslims and Islam in the contemporary setting in similar ways to that which it has historically, although not necessarily as a continuum except in its nature as ideological. That is, that Islam and Muslims are conceived through various systems: thought, belief and symbols, all of which pertain, influence or impact upon social action, interaction, response and so on, shaping and determining understanding, meaning and attitudes in the social consensus: the shared languages and conceptual maps. Being a neutrally conceptualised ideology, so new relationships of interaction, power and meaning that relate to the thought of the Other, the relations of power, and the interaction between ingroup and outgroup exist. Islamophobia thus avoids the tendency to be understood solely in terms of power struggles institutionalised in the modern state, primarily through class and exclusionary practices only. Whilst such remain vitally important, in the contemporary setting, those such as the media can be as equally if not more influential and so Islamophobia cannot be restricted to explicit and direct relationships of power and domination but instead, and possibly even more importantly, to the less explicit and everyday relationships of power that we contemporarily encounter in the classroom, office, factory and so on, and as before, the media whilst not negating those more historically understood relationships, for example those constructed around class. Of equal importance is that Islamophobia does not equate solely in terms of pure illusion. Instead, Islamophobia can be identified in that which is real as indeed it can in that which is clearly not, a line that is increasingly difficult to identify in today's 'mediatised' world.

If Islamophobia is therefore ideological, then it must operate and function as such, where ideological content – meaning about Muslims and Islam – must be disseminated to the public and private spaces through a vast range of different actions, utterances, images and texts, that must also subsequently be recognised and digested as meaningful by its recipients: both dissemination and reception being as equally important and necessary. To achieve this, the second component of Islamophobia is the 'modes of operation' through which meaning is sustained and perpetuated. It is imperative to stress though, that modes of operation are not equitable with the symbolic forms through which Muslims and Islam are either identified or recognised. The modes of operation relevant to Islamophobia therefore include: legitimating, dissimulation, unification, fragmentation and reification, each of which is made up of a range of strategies that contribute to the sustaining and perpetuating of such meaning including: rationalisation, universalisation and narrativisation; displacement, euphemisation and trope; standardisation and the symbolisation of unity; differentiation and the expurgation of the Other; naturalisation, eternalisation and passivisation respectively. These are not the only modes and strategies nor are they concretised or unchanging, thus suggesting that new modes and strategies may at some stage appear whilst others may similarly disappear, be replaced or substituted. Neither the modes nor strategies are in themselves ideological in that they only sustain ideological meaning, whether intentional or otherwise.

The final component of Islamophobia is exclusionary practices: practices that disadvantage, prejudice or discriminate against Muslims and Islam in social, economic and political spheres. Exclusionary practices must also include the subjection to violence as a tool of exclusion. However, as yet, such exclusionary practices remain far from being empirically proven, a situation that desperately requires additional research be undertaken; firstly to identify and subsequently substantiate their existence; and secondly to necessarily shift the evidence for such away from the anecdotal and over-inflationary. It is recommended that this be the next stage for developing research into Islamophobia and its consequences. Despite empirical evidence being at present wanting, it would seem theoretically fair to presume that Islamophobic exclusionary practices do exist.

If this establishes the necessary theoretical foundation required, what then the 'symbolic forms' that were previously so integral to understanding and conceptualising Islamophobia? Symbolic forms encompass a broad range of utterances, images and texts encompassing the linguistic, either spoken or inscribed, non-linguistic or quasi-linguistic in nature. Such forms therefore have to be relayed, produced or constructed before being disseminated, in order that they are eventually recognised and decoded in the process of reception by others as meaningful, whether real, accurate, erroneous or illusory. Again it is important to stress that unlike previous conceptualisations, ideological content is not only to be found in symbolic forms that are 'unfounded', but also in those deemed to be 'founded', incorporating that which is real and that which is not. Islamophobia therefore is not a purely false doctrine, dependent solely upon misunderstandings and inaccuracies. Consequently, it is neither essential nor necessary for symbolic forms to be incorrect or inaccurate, illusory or erroneous for them to be employed ideologically. It is therefore quite irrelevant and unnecessary to demonstrate if, why or how certain symbolic forms are false or inaccurate, or even to make claims about what might be true or accurate, because both are to little or no avail.

Despite being so integral to previous conceptualisations therefore, symbolic forms find no place in this new ideological conceptualisation. As considered previously, symbolic forms are also socially, politically, geographically, economically, historically and theologically specific, specific that is to the contextual setting within which they are produced, constructed, recognised and decoded, where the ideological content they disseminate and the processes involved in their subsequent reception creatively and constantly re-interpreting and re-evaluating the symbolic forms in order to 'make sense' for that specific contextual setting. In explanation, whilst a range of recurrent and repetitively employed symbolic forms can be identified, quite irrespective of the symbolic form being employed – for example 'fundamentalist', 'extremist', 'fanatic', 'radical' or as has recently entered popular discourse, 'Islamist' – the *meaning* underlying the symbolic form and the *modes* and *strategies* employed through which this is sustained and perpetuated remains largely the same. What is therefore happening is that the same meaning is being sustained across different symbolic forms, something that occurs quite irrespective of the symbolic form, thus constituting the form quite arbitrary. Placing too great an emphasis on the symbolic form therefore can only detract from understanding what Islamophobia is, thus causing further confusion and greater contestation.

Islamophobia: 'a new definition'

Having offered a conceptualisation of Islamophobia, in returning to the primary research question therefore: what then is Islamophobia? How might Islamophobia be defined?

Islamophobia is an ideology, similar in theory, function and purpose to racism and other similar phenomena, that sustains and perpetuates negatively evaluated meaning about Muslims and Islam in the contemporary setting in similar ways to that which it has historically, although not necessarily as a continuum, subsequently pertaining, influencing and impacting upon social action, interaction, response and so on, shaping and determining understanding, perceptions and attitudes in the social consensus – the shared languages and conceptual maps – that inform and construct thinking about Muslims and Islam as Other. Neither restricted to explicit nor direct relationships of power and domination but instead, and possibly even more importantly, in the less explicit and everyday relationships of power that we contemporarily encounter, identified both in that which is real and that which is clearly not, both of which can be extremely difficult to differentiate between. As a consequence of this, exclusionary practices – practices that disadvantage, prejudice or discriminate against Muslims and Islam in social, economic and political spheres ensue, including the subjection to violence – are in evidence. For such to be Islamophobia however, an acknowledged 'Muslim' or 'Islamic' element – either explicit or implicit, overtly expressed or covertly hidden, or merely even nuanced through meanings that are 'theological', 'social', 'cultural', 'racial' and so on, that at times never even necessarily name or identify 'Muslims' or 'Islam' – must be present.

PART 6
Conclusion

Chapter 12
Tentative Steps into the
Twenty-First Century

This book has therefore been concerned with Islamophobia as a contested concept in the public space: more precisely, the definitions and conceptualisations of Islamophobia that contribute to it being a contested concept.

At the outset, it was noted that as both a term and a concept, Islamophobia had begun to acquire a social, political and discursive prevalence. With this discursive prevalence however, so too some apparent confusion and a lack of clarity, with competing voices lay claim and counter-claim to Islamophobia which resulted in some contestation. In an attempt to try and contextualise this, a historiography was mapped, exploring Islamophobia's origins as well as its key developments and influences across a number of different events, actors and sources at both the local and global levels. From here it was apparent that a contested Islamophobia was rooted in the way in which it had failed to be either properly defined or conceptualised. The question that was necessitated by this historiography therefore was to ask: what is Islamophobia? In addition, other questions also emerged, about the appropriateness of the neologism; about whether new ways to understand and define the phenomenon were required; and even whether Islamophobia existed. These questions therefore became those upon which this research was subsequently undertaken.

The Runnymede Report and its model of Islamophobia was clearly the seminal source from which the most common and widespread definitions and conceptualisations about Islamophobia had evolved. So much so that it could be argued that it had provided and established *the* definition and conceptualisation of Islamophobia, particularly when its influence on determining so much of the discourse to have emerged since was considered. Possibly because of its authoritative status and subsequent acceptance, little critical analysis or engagement had however been applied to it. Seeking to redress this, a series of critical analyses that considered the report and model's content were initiated where its theory, conceptualisation and definition and finally, its validity in practice and function, contextualising this within the report and model's development from conception through consultation, to publication, response and impact were all scrutinised. In doing so, a number of significant issues were identified that questioned not only the legitimacy of the report and its model, but also its highly determinative influence. Consequently, the whole notion of Islamophobia was questioned, concluding the report and model's authority somewhat refutable: inappropriate, misguided and largely unworkable in practice; theoretically and conceptually weak; and lacking the necessary depth of thought and comprehension required if greater clarity and less contestation were to ensue. Most worrying was that the report and its model were self-reinforcing and self-perpetuating of that which it deemed to be Islamophobia. The Runnymede model of Islamophobia – *the* model of Islamophobia – was shown to be conceptually, theoretically and practically invalid, essentialising Muslims whilst simultaneously subjecting Islam to processes of reductionism.

The latter part of the book therefore sought to re-evaluate the question 'what is Islamophobia?' from a range of different perspectives. As a result, adequate justification was located to conclude that Islamophobia as a 'certain identifiable phenomenon' did indeed exist but was difficult to substantiate empirically, what with most of the evidence and subsequent justification for it being primarily theoretical. Nonetheless, it was concluded that this was enough to establish that Islamophobia was a real phenomenon. As regards naming that phenomenon, reluctantly it was decided that 'Islamophobia', at the present juncture at least, remained the best if not only option that could be realistically employed. Having addressed these questions, so it was necessary to begin the process of answering what Islamophobia was. To do this, comparative and correlative evaluations were undertaken of similar and inter-related processes and phenomena that had been either recurrent or referenced in the earlier chapter's analyses. From here, primarily through the theories of racism put forward by Robert Miles, the shift towards understanding Islamophobia as an ideology emerged.

Seeking a contemporarily relevant and functional framework with which to develop this, John Thompson's neutral conception of ideology was employed. In being able to adequately and legitimately frame and contextualise the preceding arguments and observations, so Islamophobia was codified in terms of being an ideology: in function, conceptualisation and definition. In this way, a threefold conceptualisation of Islamophobia was established: the first component being an ideology that informs and shapes meaning about Islam and Muslims; the second, a series of different modes of operation, comprising different and changing strategies through which ideological meaning is perpetuated and sustained; and the final, albeit unsubstantiated empirically at the present stage, a series of exclusionary practices. From this conceptualisation so too was a new definition posited:

"Islamophobia is an ideology, similar in theory, function and purpose to racism and other similar phenomena, that sustains and perpetuates negatively evaluated meaning about Muslims and Islam in the contemporary setting in similar ways to that which it has historically, although not necessarily as a continuum, subsequently pertaining, influencing and impacting upon social action, interaction, response and so on, shaping and determining understanding, perceptions and attitudes in the social consensus – the shared languages and conceptual maps – that inform and construct thinking about Muslims and Islam as Other. Neither restricted to explicit nor direct relationships of power and domination but instead, and possibly even more importantly, in the less explicit and everyday relationships of power that we contemporarily encounter, identified both in that which is real and that which is clearly not, both of which can be extremely difficult to differentiate between. As a consequence of this, exclusionary practices – practices that disadvantage, prejudice or discriminate against Muslims and Islam in social, economic and political spheres ensue, including the subjection to violence – are in evidence. For such to be Islamophobia however, an acknowledged 'Muslim' or 'Islamic' element – either explicit or implicit, overtly expressed or covertly hidden, or merely even nuanced through meanings that are 'theological', 'social', 'cultural', 'racial' and so on, that at times never even necessarily name or identify 'Muslims' or 'Islam' – must be present."

Having finally answered 'what is Islamophobia?' by positing a suitable definition and conceptualisation, so a final question is necessary: that is, to what extent might this research impact upon Islamophobia as a contested concept in the public space?

Whilst this new definition and conceptualisation is theoretically, conceptually and practically long overdue, the mere positing of such will neither necessarily, nor immediately insist that those authoritative models be either relegated or replaced by such in the public space. What with the credibility and authority they have acquired – quite inappropriately this book justifiably argues and concludes – any process of substitution or replacement will be extremely difficult. Nonetheless, what might be at least begun is the slow and possibly laborious process of Islamophobia being theoretically and conceptually re-evaluated, re-interpreted, re-contextualised and even just re-questioned: processes that as regards Islamophobia have somehow been overlooked for over a decade or more. In this way, this new conceptualisation and definition may be successful therefore in merely acting as a catalyst in raising some now vital and necessary questions.

Through Islamophobia as ideology, no longer are processes of essentialism, reductionism, exclusion, exacerbation, apportionment and intentionality amongst others integral pre-requisites to either understanding, explaining or defining that which already affects the lives and everyday experiences of many Muslims. No longer does the theory, definition or conceptualisation of Islamophobia place demands upon anybody – whether Muslim or non – necessarily shifting understanding and acknowledgement away from over simplifications, unnecessary dichotomies and widely different and interpretative symbolic forms, all of which are somewhat arbitrary and subjective. As has been highlighted throughout, simplified problems demand simplified solutions: but these solutions are rarely, if indeed ever adequate enough to solve those problems what are typically far more complex and far more challenging Having posited a new conceptualisation and definition of Islamophobia therefore, no longer is it either necessary or indeed possible to merely argue that Islamophobia is a problem just 'because it is'. From here, Islamophobia is no longer an over-simplified and easily compartmentalised phenomenon.

And from this new premise, Islamophobia is no longer restricted to understanding and defining it in terms of highly questionable and sometimes unreasonable unfounded hostilities and widely interpretable misconceptions, both of which remain relevant and important but not as pre-requisites for definition or identification. Instead Islamophobia must now be conceptualised in terms of it being about the way in which Muslims and Islam are thought about, spoken about and written about; perceived, conceived and subsequently referred to; included and also ultimately excluded: Islamophobia cam now be concerned with every means of thought, deed and action that relates to or references Muslims or Islam, whether true or untrue, fact or fiction, real or imaginary. Islamophobia can also no longer be – as indeed Muslims and Islam are no longer – something that exists marginalised on the fringes of society because of a lack of understanding. Whether contextualised socially, politically or economically, Islamophobia is that which contemporarily informs and provides meaning about Muslims and Islam, whether through operation, dissemination, reception or perpetuation. Islamophobia therefore does not necessarily always manifest itself in high levels acts of violence and retaliation – indeed rarely is this the reality – but more so in the thinking and meaning that are inherent within the less explicit and everyday relationships of power that we contemporarily encounter: in the classroom, office, factory and so on, and as before, the media but not restricted solely to this. 'Islam', 'Islamic' and 'Muslim' are no longer in the contemporary climate therefore banal, harmless signs, that are either simple 'givens', or words that can be neutrally employed without some ideological content being disseminated: their mere employment immediately conjures and informs in a myriad of ways through meaning that is shaped ideologically. Islamophobia therefore is most definitely not a 'phobia', but instead a name for that which perpetuates and sustains those meanings which are relevant and acknowledged in the shared languages and conceptual maps of today's setting.

Many of the words and concepts we use in our everyday lives therefore, we assume we 'know': that is, 'know' what they mean and what they are, where they come from, and what meaning underpins our use of them. In this context, we assume we know 'Islam' and 'Muslims'. Similarly but less obviously, the same applies also to Islamophobia. This confusion and lack of realisation, possibly because of the distracting nature of the name, has unfortunately caused contestation to the detriment of what we assume we know not only about Islam and Muslims, but also Islamophobia as a concept. Through this research therefore, hopefully something more will have been established about what is meant by and about the concept of Islamophobia: something more that will inform and shape the way in which we employ and utilise these words and concepts in order that they are more meaningful and more relevant. Maybe then this will begin, but by no means conclude, the contesting of Islamophobia as a contested concept in the public space.

Bibliography

Abbas, Tahir, *Muslim Britain: Communities Under Pressure* (London: Zed Books, 2005).

Abedin, Syed Z. and Ziauddin Sardar, *Muslim minorities in the West* (London: Grey Seal, 1995).

Aix, Jose Maria Ortuno, 'Report on Islamophobia in Spain', Cesari (2006).

Allen, Chris and Jorgen Nielsen, *Summary Report on Islamophobia in the EU after 11 September 2001* (Vienna: European Monitoring Centre on Racism and Xenophobia, 2002).

Allen, Chris, 'From race to religion: the new face of discrimination', Abbas (2005).

———, 'A "Normal" Week', INSTED (2007).

———, 'Endemically European or a European Epidemic? Islamophobia in Contemporary Europe', Geaves et al. (2004).

———, 'Justifying Islamophobia: a Post-9/11 Consideration of the European Union and British Contexts' in *American Journal of Islamic Social Sciences*, vol. 21 no. 3 (Summer 2004): 1–25.

———, 'Down with Multiculturalism, Book-burning and Fatwas' *Culture and Religion* (8:2, 125–38, 2007).

———, *Fair Justice: the Bradford Disturbances, the Sentencing and the Impact* (London: FAIR, 2003).

———, *Islamophobia: Contested Concept in the Public Space* (Ph.D diss., University of Birmingham, 2006).

Allport, Gordon W., *The Nature of Prejudice* (Cambridge, MA: Addison Wesley, 1954).

Ansari, Humayan, *Muslims in Britain* (London: Minority Rights Group International, 2003).

Anwar, Muhammad and Qadar Bakhsh, *British Muslims and State Policies* (Coventry: Centre for Research in Ethnic Relations, 2003).

Ashraf, Shahid, 'Beyond Islamophobia', *Multi-Cultural Teaching* (Spring 2001).

Baghajati, Carla Amina, 'Islamophobie: Gedanken zu einem Phänomen', 24 November 2004 (3 October 2005) http://www.derislam.at/islam.php?name=Themen&pa=showpage&pid=60.

Balibar, Etienne and Immanuel Wallerstein, *New Ethnicities and Urban Cultures: Ambiguous Identities* (London: Verso, 1991).

Barker, Chris, *Television, Globalization and Cultural Identities* (Buckingham: Open University Press, 1999).

Barker, Martin, *The New Racism: Conservatives and the Ideology of the Tribe* (London: Junction Books, 1981).

Baylis, J. and S. Smith, *The Globalization of World Politics an Introduction to International Relation* (Oxford: Oxford University Press, 1997).

Bonnefoy, Laurent, 'Public Institutions and Islam: a New Stigmatization?', *International Institute for the Study of Islam in the Modern World* no. 13 (December 2003), 22–3.

Brah, Avtar et al., *Thinking Identities: Ethnicity, Racism and Culture* (Basingstoke: Macmillan, 1999).

Briggs, Rachel, Catherine Fieschi and Hannah Lownsbrough, *Bringing it Home: Community-Based Approaches to Counter-Terrorism* (London: Demos, 2006).

British National Party, *I.S.L.A.M.: The Truth About Islam* (Bexley: BNP, 2001).

Bromley, Michael and Stephen Cushion, 'Media Fundamentalism: the Immediate Response of the UK National Press to September 11th', Zelizer and Allan (2003).

Buckley, Richard, *Iran and the West a Failure to Communicate*: *Understanding Global Issues* (London: Bantam, 1997).

Bulmer, Martin and John Solomos, *Racism* (Oxford: Oxford University Press, 1999).

Caeiro, Alexandre, 'French report', Cesari (2006).

Cesari, Jocelyne, *Securitization and Religious Divides in Europe: Muslims in Western Europe after 9/11 – Why the Term Islamophobia is More a Predicament than an Explanation* (Paris: Challenge, 2006).

Choudhury, Tufyal, *Monitoring Minority Protection in the EU: the Situation of Muslims in the UK* (London: Open Society Institute, 2003).

Clarke, Simon, *Social Theory, Psychoanalysis and Racism* (London: Palgrave, 2003).

Commission for Racial Equality, *Anti-Islamic Reactions in the EU after the Terrorist Acts Against the USA: United Kingdom Second Country Report* (London: CRE, 2001).

Commission on British Muslims and Islamophobia, *Islamophobia: Issues, Challenges and Action* (Stoke on Trent: Trentham Books, 2004).

da Torri, R. Gritti, *Comunicazioni, Media e Nuovi Terrorismi dopo l'11 Settembre* (Rome: Fillenzi).

Daniel, Norman, *Islam and the West: the Making of an Image* (Oxford: Oneworld, 2000).

Davids, M. Fakhry, 'There But for the Grace of God, go You or I', Hamid and Sharif (2002).

Del Olmo Vicen, Nino, 'The Muslim Community in Spain', Gerd Nonneman et al., (Reading: Ithaca, 1995).

Diamantopoulou, Anna, *The Fight Against Anti-Semitism and Islamophobia: a Summary of Three Round Table Meetings* (Vienna: EUMC, 2003).

Dinet, Etienne and Sliman Ben Ibrahim, *L'Orient vu de l'Occident* (Paris: Piazza-Geuthner, 1925).

Djavann, Chahdortt, 'From the Franz of Anja Nattefort', 2003 (3 October 2005) http://www.marburgnews.de//views/forum/posting.php?mode=topicreview&t =2&sid=bebdecf759f0a9670a18fe6f13f8dcde .

Donnan, Hastings and Martin Stokes, 'Interpreting Interpretations of Islam', Donnan (2002).

———, *Interpreting Islam* (London: Sage, 2002).

Esposito, John, *The Islamic Threat: Myth or Reality?* (Oxford: Oxford University Press, 1994).

European Monitoring Centre for Racism and Xenophobia, *Perceptions of Discrimination and Islamophobia: Voices from Members of Muslim Communities in the European Union* (Vienna: EUMC, 2007).

———, *Muslims in the European Union: Discrimination and Islamophobia* (Vienna: EUMC, 2007).

———, *The Impact of 7 July 2005 London Bomb Attacks on Muslim Communities Across the EU* (Vienna: EUMC, 2005).

European Union Agency for Fundamental Rights: *Data in Focus Report: Muslims* (Vienna: FRA, 2009).

Fallaci, Oriana, *The Rage and the Pride* (New York: Rizzoli, 2002).

Fleming, Dan, *Formations* (Manchester: Manchester University Press, 2000).

Fourest, Caroline and Fiammetta Venner, 'Islamophobie?: Islamophobes? Ou Simplement Laiques!' *Pro Choix* (Autumn/Winter 2003).

Garner, Steve, *Racisms* (London: Sage, 2010).

Geaves, Ron, Theodore Gabriel and Yvonne Haddad, *Islam and the West: a Post September 11th Perspective* (Aldershot: Ashgate, 2004).

Gilroy, Paul, *Between Camps: Nations, Cultures and the Allure of Race* (London: Penguin, 2000).

Githens-Mazer, Jonathan and Robert Lambert, *Islamophobia and anti-Muslim Hate Crime: a London Case Study* (Exeter: University of Exeter, 2010).

Griffith, Phoebe and Mark Leonard, *Reclaiming Britishness* (London: Foreign Policy Centre, 2004).

Haddad, Yvonne Y., *Muslims in the West: from Sojourners to Citizens* (Oxford: Oxford University Press, 2002).

Hafez, Kai, *Islam and the Mass Media: Fragmented Images in a Globalizing World* (Cresskill: Hampton Press, 2000).

Halliday, Fred, *Islam and the Myth of Confrontation: Religion and Politics in the Middle East* (London: IB Tauris, 1999).

———, *Two Hours That Shook the World: September 11, 2001 – Causes and Consequences* (London: Saqi, 2002).

Hamid, Abdul Wahid and Jamil Sharif, *The Quest for Sanity: Reflections on September 11 and its Aftermath* (London: Muslim Council of Britain, 2002).

Henzell-Thomas, Jeremy, *The Challenge of Pluralism and the Middle Way of Islam* (Richmond: Association of Muslim Social Scientists UK, 2002).

Hepple, Bob and Tufyal Choudhury, *Tackling Religious Discrimination: Practical Implications for Policy-Makers and Legislators*, Home Office Research Study 221 (London: Home Office, 2001).

House of Lords Select Committee on Religious Offences in England and Wales, *Select Committee on Religious Offences in England and Wales, Volume I – Report*, HL Paper 95–I (London: The Stationary Office, 2003).

————, *Select Committee on Religious Offences in England and Wales, Volume II – Oral Evidence*, HL Paper 95–II (London: The Stationary Office, 2003).

————, *Select Committee on Religious Offences in England and Wales, Volume III – Written Evidence*, HL Paper 95–III (London: The Stationary Office, 2003).

Huntington, Samuel P., *The Clash of Civilisations and the Remaking of World Order* (London: Touchstone, 1997).

Hussain, A., *Western Conflict with Islam: Survey of the Anti-Islamic Tradition* (Leicester: Volcano Books, 1990).

Hussain, Dilwar, 'The Impact of 9/11 on British Muslim identity', Geaves et al. (2004).

INSTED, *The Search for Common Ground: Muslims, Non-Muslims and the Media* (London: GLA, 2007).

Inter Faith Network for the UK, *Local Inter Faith Guide* (London: Inter Faith Network for the UK, 1999), 24.

Islamic Human Rights Commission, *The Hidden Victims of September 11: the Backlash Against Muslims in the UK* (Wembley: Islamic Human Rights Commission, 2002).

James, Jenny, 'When Fear is a Crime' *The Muslim-Christian Debate Website*, March 1997 (14 November 2004) http://debate.org.uk/topics/politics/jenny4.htm.

John, Peter et al., *The BNP: the Roots of its Appeal* (Colchester: Democratic Audit, University of Essex, 2006).

Karakasoglu, Yasemin et al., 'German report', Cesari (2006).

Khan, Khaleda *Preventing Violent Extremism (PVE) and PREVENT: a Response from the Muslim Community* (London: An-Nisa Society 2009).

Kurtz, Leo, *God's in the Global Village – the World's Religion in Sociological Perspectiv*e (London: Pine Forge Press, 1995).

Lane, Richard J., *Jean Baudrillard* (London: Routledge, 2001).

Lewis, Philip, *Islamic Britain: Religion, Politics and Identity among British Muslims* (London: IB Tauris, 1994).

Leyens, Jacques-Philippe et al., *Stereotypes and Social Cognition* (London: Sage, 1994).

London Bible College, *The Westophobia Report: Anti-Western and Anti-Christian Stereotyping in British Muslim Publications* (London: London Bible College, 1999).

Maussen, Marcel, 'Anti-Muslim Sentiments and Mobilization in the Netherlands: Discourse, Policies and Violence', Cesari (2006).

Miles, Robert, 'Racism as a Concept', Bulmer and Solomos (1999).

————, *Racism* (London: Routledge, 1989).

Millward, P., 'Rivalries and Racisms: "Closed" and "Open" Islamophobic Dispositions amongst Football Supporters', *Sociological Research Online* 13:6, www.socresonline.org.uk/13/6/5.html, 2008.

Milton-Edwards, Beverley, 'Researching the Radical: the Quest for a New Perspective', Donnan (2002).

Mirna Liguori, 'Report on Islamophobia', Cesari (2006).

Modood, Tariq, 'The End of a Hegemony: the Concept of "Black" and "British Asians"', Rex (1994).

————, *Not Easy Being British* (Stoke on Trent: Runnymede Trust and Trentham Books, 1992).

Modood, Tariq, Anna Triandafyllidou and Richard Zapata-Barrero, *Multiculturalism, Muslims and Citizenship* (London: Routledge, 2006).

Murden, S., 'Cultural Conflict in International Relations: the West and Islam', Baylis, J. and S. Smith (1997).

National Centre for Social Research, *British Social Attitudes Survey 2010*, 26th Edition (2010) http://tinyurl.com/yeo48hf .

Nima, Riaz, *The Wrath of Allah, Islamic Revolution and Reaction in Iran* (London: Pluto Press Ltd, 1983).

Nonneman, Gerd et al., *Muslim Communities in the New Europe* (Reading: Ithaca, 1995).

Parekh, Bhikhu, 'Europe, Liberalism and the "Muslim question"', Modood et al. (2006).

————, *The Future of Multi-Ethnic Britain: Report of the Commission on the Future of Multi-Ethnic Britain* (London: Profile Books, 2000).

Phizacklea, Annie and Robert Miles, *Labour and Racism* (London: Routledge & Kegan Paul, 1980).

Pickering, Michael, *Stereotyping: the Politics of Representation* (Basingstoke: Palgrave, 2001).

Poole, Elizabeth, 'Framing Islam: an Analysis of Newspaper Coverage of Islam in the British press', Kai Hafez (2000).

————, *Reporting Islam: Media Representations of British Muslims* (London: IB Tauris, 2002).

Rex, John, *Ethnic Mobilisation in a Multi-Cultural Europe* (Aldershot: Ashgate, 1994).

Richardson, John E., *(Mis)representing Islam: the Racism and Rhetoric of British Broadsheet Newspapers* (Amsterdam: John Benjamin, 2004).

Rokeach, Milton, *The Nature of Human Values* (New York: The Free Press, 1973).

————, *The Open and Closed Mind* (New York: Basic Books Inc, 1960).

————, *Understanding Human Values* (New York: The Free Press, 1979).

Runnymede Commission on Anti-Semitism, *A Very Light Sleeper: the Persistence and Dangers of Anti-Semitism* (London: Runnymede Trust, 1994).

Runnymede Trust, 'Who We Are', *The Runnymede Trust Website* (26 February 2003) <http://www.runnymedetrust.org/who.html>.

Runnymede Trust: Commission on British Muslims and Islamophobia, *Islamophobia: a Challenge for Us All: Report of the Runnymede Trust Commission on British Muslims and Islamophobia* (London: Runnymede Trust, 1997).

Ruthven, Malise, 'Islam in the Media', Haddad (2002).

Said, Edward, *Covering Islam: how the Media and the Experts Determine how we see the Rest of the World* (London: Vintage, 1997).

————, *Orientalism* (London: Penguin, 1979).

Sardar, Ziauddin, 'Racism, Identity and Muslims in the West', Abedin and Sardar (1995).

————, 'The Excluded Minority: British Muslim Identity after 11 September', Griffith and Leonard (2004).

Sayyid, Bobby, *A Fundamental Fear: Eurocentrism and the Emergence of Islamism* (London: Zed Books, 1997).

Shaheen, Jack, *Reel Bad Arabs: how Hollywood Vilifies a People* (London: Roundhouse Publishing).

Sheridan, Lorraine and Nadeem Malik, 'Religious Discrimination: Historical and Current Developments in the English Legal System', *Encounters*, 7 (2001).

Sheridan, Lorraine, *Effects of the Events of September 11th 2001 on Discrimination and Implicit Racism in Five Religious and Seven Ethnic Groups: a Brief Overview* (Leicester: University of Leicester, 2002).

Siddiqui, Kalim, *The Muslim Manifesto: a Strategy for Survival* (The Muslim Institute: London, 1990).

Silverman, Mike and Nira Yuval-Davis, 'Jews. Arabs and the Theorisation of Racism in Britain and France', Avtar Brah et al. (1999).

Solomos, John, *Race and Racism in Britain*, third edition (Basingstoke: Palgrave, 2003).

Stevenson, Nick, *Understanding Media Cultures: Social Theory and Mass Communication* (London: Sage, 2002).

Stuart Hall et al., *Policing the Crisis: Mugging, the State and: Law and Order* (London: Macmillan, 1978).

Tanter, Richard, *Rogue Regimes Terrorism and Proliferation* (London: Macmillan, 1999).

Thompson, John, *Ideology and Modern Culture* (Cambridge: Polity Press, 1990).

United Kingdom Parliament, 'Examination of Witnesses', *Select Committee on Religious Offences in England and Wales*, 23 October 2003 (29 October 2004) http://www.parliament.the-stationery-office.co.uk/pa/ld200203/ldselect/ldrelof/95/2102307.htm.

United Nations, *World Conference Against Racism, Racial Discrimination, Xenophobia and Related Intolerance: Declaration and Programme of Action* (New York: United Nations, 2002).

Vertovec, Steven, 'Islamophobia and Muslim Recognition in Britain', Haddad (2002).

Watson, C.W., *Multiculturalism* (Buckingham: Open University Press, 2000).

Weller, Paul et al., *Religious Discrimination in England and Wales*, Home Office Research Study 220 (London: Home Office, 2001).

Werbner, Pnina and Tariq Modood, eds, *Debating Cultural Hybridity: Multi-Cultural Identities and the Politics of Anti-Racism* (London: Zed, 1997).

Whitaker, Brian, 'Islam and the British Press', Hamid and Sharif (2002).

Wieviorka, Michel, *The Arena of Racism*, translated by Chris Turner (London: Sage, 1995).

Yemelianova, Galina M., *Russia and Islam* (Basingstoke: Palgrave, 2002).

Young, Robert J.C., *Postcolonialism* (Oxford: Oxford University Press, 2003).

Zakaria, R., *The Struggle Within Islam the Conflict Between Religion and Politics* (London: Penguin Books, 1988).

Zaki, Y., 'The Politics of Islamophobia', *Re-present* (Winter/Spring 2002), 8–18.

Zelizer, Barbie and Stuart Allan, *Journalism after September 11* (London: Routledge, 2003).

Index